# EXEMPLARY LIFE

## Modelling Sainthood in Christian Syria

Based on over five years of ethnographic fieldwork in Syria, *Exemplary Life* focuses on the life of a Damascus woman, Myrna Nazzour, who serves as an aspirational figure in her community. Myrna is regarded by her followers as an exemplary figure, a living saint, and the messages, apparitions, stigmata, and oil that have marked Myrna since 1982 have corroborated her status as chosen by God.

*Exemplary Life* probes the power of examples, the modelling of sainthood around Myrna's figure, and the broader context for Syrian Christians in the changing landscape of the Middle East. The book highlights the social use of examples such as the ones inhabited by Myrna's devout followers and how they reveal the broader structures of illustration, evidence, and persuasion in social and cultural settings. Andreas Bandak argues that the role of the example should incite us to investigate which trains of thought set local worlds in motion. In doing so, *Exemplary Life* presents a novel frame for examining how religion comes to matter to people and adds a critical dimension to current anthropological engagements with ethics and morality.

(Anthropological Horizons)

ANDREAS BANDAK is an associate professor in the Department of Cross-Cultural and Regional Studies at the University of Copenhagen.

# ANTHROPOLOGICAL HORIZONS

*Editor: Michael Lambek, University of Toronto*

This series, begun in 1991, focuses on theoretically informed ethnographic works addressing issues of mind and body, knowledge and power, equality and inequality, the individual and the collective. Interdisciplinary in its perspective, the series makes a unique contribution in several other academic disciplines: women's studies, history, philosophy, psychology, political science, and sociology.

For a list of the books published in this series see page 251.

# Exemplary Life

*Modelling Sainthood in Christian Syria*

ANDREAS BANDAK

UNIVERSITY OF TORONTO PRESS
Toronto  Buffalo  London

ISBN 978-1-4875-4293-1 (cloth)     ISBN 978-1-4875-4295-5 (EPUB)
ISBN 978-1-4875-4294-8 (paper)     ISBN 978-1-4875-4296-2 (PDF)

Anthropological Horizons

---

**Library and Archives Canada Cataloguing in Publication**

Title: Exemplary life : modelling sainthood in Christian Syria / Andreas
   Bandak.
Names: Bandak, Andreas, author.
Series: Anthropological horizons.
Description: Series statement: Anthropological horizons | Includes
   bibliographical references and index.
Identifiers: Canadiana (print) 20220210020 | Canadiana (ebook) 20220210284 |
   ISBN 9781487542948 (paper) | ISBN 9781487542931 (cloth) |
   ISBN 9781487542955 (EPUB) | ISBN 9781487542962 (PDF)
Subjects: LCSH: Naẓẓūr, Mīrnā, 1964– – Cult – Syria – Damascus. |
   LCSH: Saints – Cult – Syria – Damascus. | LCSH: Christians – Syria –
   Damascus. | LCSH: Soufanieh (Damascus, Syria) – Religious life and customs.
Classification: LCC BT660.D3 B36 2022 | DDC 235/.209569144 – dc23

---

We wish to acknowledge the land on which the University of Toronto Press
operates. This land is the traditional territory of the Wendat, the Anishnaabeg,
the Haudenosaunee, the Métis, and the Mississaugas of the Credit First Nation.

University of Toronto Press acknowledges the financial support of the
Government of Canada, the Canada Council for the Arts, and the Ontario Arts
Council, an agency of the Government of Ontario, for its publishing activities.

Canada Council    Conseil des Arts
for the Arts       du Canada

ONTARIO ARTS COUNCIL
CONSEIL DES ARTS DE L'ONTARIO
an Ontario government agency
un organisme du gouvernement de l'Ontario

Funded by the    Financé par le
Government      gouvernement
of Canada        du Canada

Canadä

*In memory of my father, Christian Bandak (1952–2015), himself an example of how human life is characterized by both ordinary and extraordinary capacities*

# Contents

*Illustrations appear on pages 197–202.*

# Prologue

As I write these sentences in the winter of 2022, sitting in Copenhagen and far from Damascus, Syria has for more than ten years experienced the worst crisis in the country's recent history. Starting in mid-March 2011, the situation has gone from hopes for a better time to desperately worse. The Arab uprising that the world has borne witness to in Tunisia, Libya, Yemen, and Egypt has – in its Syrian unfolding – turned into an enormously complicated affair, which has been labelled everything from a revolution to a civil war and a proxy war. The Syrian tragedy, as al-Haj Saleh (2017) designates it, surely entails elements of all the above but cannot be conceived of without an eye to the state's open violence and persecution of parts of its own population.

I do not go into developments since early 2011 in the main body of this book. My fieldwork was conducted between 2004 and 2010, and it is this period that will be the primary focus. My work centres on the followers of Our Lady of Soufanieh and the modelling of sainthood in contemporary Damascus as a prism through which to understand the precarious situation of Syrian Christians and the conditions of coexistence. In this sense, the work that I present provides a crucial background against which Syrian Christian experiences can be understood on the cusp of the later tragic developments. While pre-2011 is the focus of the book, the epilogue more directly takes on the predicament of Christianity in the Middle East, returning to the question of what the current situation is an example of: inevitable strife between religions, world politics gone awry, or the travails of living with different legacies.

It is my hope that the future will bode well for Syria as a country and that the current tragedy will soon halt its pace and stop continuing to unleash further despair and loss of life. This hope, however, is mixed with fear, as friends, interlocutors, and acquaintances in Syria for way too long have been faced and still are facing an uncertain future. What will come we do not know, but the followers of Our Lady of Soufanieh will surely also place these recent developments in the hands of the Virgin Mary, hoping and praying for her intercession. If she answers them, or how – depending on one's perspective – will be for her followers and the rest of us to see in the time to come.

# Acknowledgments

This book would not have been possible had it not been for the sustained relationships that I have had with a great number of people, to whom I owe much gratitude.

In Syria, I had the chance to get close to Myrna Nazzour, Nicolas Nazzour, and their family. They all heartily accepted the anthropologist. I thank Salwa Farah, in particular, for taking such good care of me, but my thoughts also go to all of the followers of Our Lady of Soufanieh, who contributed to my understanding of the modelling of sainthood and the structure of exemplarity. Particularly helpful for my work in Syria have been Claude Salame, George Khoury, Elian Ahmer, and Karim Rafleh. They have, in various ways, all been great sources of amusement, assistance, and knowledge. Many other names could be listed, but I prefer not to, as Syria is still not a country where it is advisable to put all names out in the open.

The Danish Institute in Damascus and its various directors have all, over the years, been stimulating conversation partners. I thank Jørgen Bæk Simonsen, Jørgen S. Nielsen, Hans Christian Korsholm Nielsen, and Anders Hastrup for their interest and support. I would also like to thank the various employees at the institute for their work and attentiveness towards my family and me. Similarly, grants from the institute have made research and publication much easier.

My work has over the years been generously funded by the Danish Council for Independent Research in the Humanities, funding first my PhD project and later a postdoc project on the social life of prayer. In 2010, I received the Danish Ministry of Science, Technology and Innovation's Elite Research Travel Stipend, which funded my affiliation with the London School of Economics and Politics (LSE) as a visiting research student, as well as covered my travels to the University of

California, San Diego, (UCSD) and participation in several conferences and seminars abroad.

At the Department of Anthropology at the LSE, I was particularly grateful to Matthew Engelke, Tom Boylston, and Alice Forbess, who all were excellent conversation partners and read and commented on chapters of the book. At UCSD, I presented a paper and received great feedback from Jon Bialecki, John Dulin, and Naomi Haynes. Joel Robbins most generously read two of my chapters. Later on, I have had research stays at the University of Toronto, where I have enjoyed exchanges and generous hosting by Simon Coleman and family, but also from Girish Daswani, Pamela Klassen, Valentina Napolitano, and Amira Mittermaier. In particular, I am grateful for the extended conversations I have had with Simon Coleman on this book as well as on the theme of repetition.

I have been so fortunate in having strong interlocutors to sharpen my argument in articles and in this book with their comments and exchanges at various international seminars, workshops, and conferences. Various chapters have been presented at departmental seminars at the University of Toronto, University College London, University of Stockholm, Universidade Federal Fluminense de Rio de Janeiro, and University of Oslo, and I thank the organizers as well as the audiences for productive comments and questions. I appreciate all the different forms of collaboration and exchanges, which have sharpened the pages of this book, and I want to thank Paul Anderson, Walter Armbrust, James Bielo, Ruy Blanes, Glenn Bowman, Rebecca Bryant, Lotte Buch, Matei Candea, Fenella Cannell, Dawn Chatty, Magnus Course, Alice Elliot, Ghassan Hage, Courtney Handman, Chris Hann, David Henig, Angie Heo, Martin Holbraad, Caroline Humphrey, Willy Jansen, Timothy Jenkins, Hillary Kaell, Maria Kastrinou, Charlotte al-Khalili, Ashley Lebner, Johan Lindquist, Webb Keane, Daniel Knight, Sonja Luehrmann, Diego Malara, Magnus Marsden, Maya Mayblin, Evgenia Mesaritou, Nefissa Naguib, Vlad Naumescu, Kristin Norget, Elaine Peña, Paulo Pinto, Simion Pop, Annika Rabo, Adam Reed, Bruno Reinhardt, Christa Salamandra, Monique Scheer, Samuli Schielke, Anthony Shenoda, Patricia Spyer, Leif Stenberg, Charles Stewart, Edith Szanto, Kabir Tambar, Matt Tomlinson, Joseph Youssef, Joe Webster, and Lisa Wedeen.

In Denmark, I have benefitted from conversations with Nils Bubandt, Anne-Line Dalsgaard, Thomas Fibiger, Martin Demant Frederiksen, and Jakob Egeris Thorsen (Aarhus University); Morten Nielsen and Rane Willerslev (The National Museum of Denmark); Thomas Brønd, Lise Galal, Sune Haugbolle, Bjørn Thomassen, Astrid Trolle and Miriam Younes (Roskilde University); Kirsten Hastrup, Heiko Henkel,

Stine Krøijer, Morten Axel Pedersen, Inger Sjørslev, and Henrik Vigh (Department of Anthropology, University of Copenhagen); Trine Brox, Mikkel Bunkenborg, Rasmus Elling, Dan Hirslund, Annika Hvithamar, Jakob Skovgaard-Petersen, Simon Stjernholm, Catharina Raudvere, and Margit Warburg (Department for Cross-Cultural and Regional Studies, University of Copenhagen); and Frida Hastrup, Nina Grønlykke Mollerup, and Tim Flohr Sørensen (Department for History and Ethnology, University of Copenhagen).

I owe special thanks to all my colleagues in the vibrant research milieu around the Centre for Comparative Culture Studies and Section for Minority Studies at the Department for Cross-Cultural and Regional Studies, University of Copenhagen. It is truly a joy to work with such insightful and generous people. I thank all, but in particular I want to mention Thomas Brudholm, Christine Crone, Birgitte Schepelern Johansen, Anders Hastrup, Birgitte Stampe Holst, Regnar Kristensen, Stine Simonsen Puri, Frank Sejersen and Kirsten Thisted for their fellowship and their readings of various parts of my work. As former head of the Centre for Comparative Culture Studies and as my mentor, Esther Fihl endorsed my work on this topic and challenged me to substantiate my ideas.

Further to these good people, I owe an enormous debt of gratitude to Sune Haugbolle, Lars Højer, Jonas Adelin Jørgensen, Daniella Kuzmanovic, Christian Suhr, and Bjørn Thomassen, who over the years have all contributed with insightful readings, well-placed criticisms, and stimulating suggestions that I have tried my best to incorporate. Paul Anderson, Mikkel Bille, David Henig, and Anja Kublitz at different stages of the maturation of this book took upon themselves the daunting task to read the entire manuscript, which was an immense gift from which I received invaluable advice to sharpen the text.

The book found a perfect home with Michael Lambek's Anthropological Horizons Series at the University of Toronto Press, where Jodi Lewchuk did a marvellous job in soliciting reviews and overseeing the process during the protracted COVID-19 situation. Thanks to the reviewers for substantial engagements with the book, which greatly improved the ideas presented herein. I am most grateful for the careful attention my book received, and I hope the book will complement the other great titles in this series. I also would like to thank Carolyn Zapf for assiduous copy editing and Jesper Possing for carefully checking the Arabic transliterations.

Parts of the book have been published previously but here appear in reworked versions. An abridged version of chapter two was published under the title "Repeated Prayers: Saying the Rosary in Contemporary

Syria" in the thematic issue *The Social Life of Prayers*, edited by A. Bandak (2017), *Religion*, 47(1): 92–110. A version of chapter three was published under the title "Saintly Series and Christian Typology: Modelling on Sainthood in Damascus" in A. Bandak and L. Højer (2015), *The Power of Example: Anthropological Explorations in Persuasion, Evocation and Imitation*, special supplement of *The Journal of the Royal Anthropological Institute*, 21(S1): S47–S63. Lastly, a version of chapter five was published under the title "Our Lady of Soufanieh: On Knowledge, Ignorance, and Indifference among Christians of Damascus" in A. Bandak and M. Bille, *The Politics of Worship in the Contemporary Middle East: Sainthood in Fragile States* (2013, Brill).

Lastly, I want to thank my parents, Merete and Christian Bandak, and my parents-in-law, Kirsten and Egon Christensen, for their interest and care throughout my work. Thanks are due to all of our family for following my work and us as a family in our lives, as well as for visits to Damascus back when it was possible to do so. To my wife, Elisabeth: you have truly been one of a kind in participating all along in fieldwork, even if your trade is somewhat different as a trained physiotherapist and researcher in chronic pain. This work would never have been possible without your support and guidance. Thanks for sharing joys and sorrows, and for providing a base of stability and learning for us and our children, Jonathan, Filip, and Marie.

As always, despite advice and conversations, all infelicities naturally remain my own.

# EXEMPLARY LIFE

Modelling Sainthood in Christian Syria

# Modelling Sainthood in Christian Syria

Every form of life is morally didactic, in that it presents an alternative, and perhaps a challenge to our own; and we cannot remain indifferent to the contrast.

– Rodney Needham, *Exemplars*

Soufanieh is the name of a quarter located just outside the old city of Damascus. From Bab Touma, the famous Christian quarter named after Thomas, Christ's disciple of little faith, you can cross a small bridge leading over one of the branches of the Barada River. Here you find shops, food stalls, and a traffic-ridden one-way street leading towards the neighbourhoods of al-Qusour and al-Qassaʿ. If you turn right just after the bridge, you will pass a mosque and walk along the Barada River at Soufanieh Street. Here you can either enter a park or continue the walk by the river with the park on the right-hand side and houses, a school, and a few shops on the left. If your eyes wander, you may notice something peculiar. On the terrace of one of the inconspicuous houses, a large icon of the Virgin Mary can be seen, often with difficulty due to the laundry that hangs in front of the house hiding the icon from view. If you approach the house, you will notice the same icon in postcard format on the right side of the door of the house, behind a glass screen. One of the stones in the wall has been removed, and an icon has been placed behind a golden frame and glass screen. Here it is possible to dwell on the icon with more focus. The Virgin Mary is holding the Baby Jesus in her arms and below the image is written in Arabic: "Our Lady of Soufanieh. Source of Holy Oil." As you stand in front of the door, you may see passersby touch the screen in a devotional gesture; some may also kiss their fingers afterwards. If you take a closer look, you will see a notice board where a schedule in Arabic announces visiting hours. The home is open, the schedule announces, from ten o'clock until one o'clock and then again later from three o'clock until eight o'clock. Daily prayers start at five o'clock in the evening, and a five o'clock mass is held each Saturday. The door may be open, and if not, you can ring the bell. If you do push the plastic button, the bell can be heard from an open window playing a melody. The release of the typical, heavy Damascene door and its lock is done electronically. "Click" it says, as the door opens inwards some ten centimetres. Perhaps you will hear a voice welcoming you in through the open door: "Come in, the door is open." At this point, you could choose to continue your walk or enter the open door and pay Our Lady of Soufanieh a visit. I will leave that decision to you. However, if you continue reading, you will have to enter the door, climb the stairs with me, and hear who Our Lady of Soufanieh is.

During a walk like the one just presented, I first stumbled upon Our Lady of Soufanieh in the autumn of 2005. Today these areas have been afflicted by the Syrian uprising and the regime's hard and violent push-back, but by no means as much as in other Syrian cities, such as Aleppo, Homs, and Hama, or in other parts of Damascus. If we take one step back, we might ruminate over how the situation was for the Christian communities in the time leading up to the events following the 2011 up-rising and thereby reflect on what Syria might become. Back in 2005, I was conducting eleven months of fieldwork in Damascus on space and place-making for the Christians of various minorities in a Muslim ma-jority context, and wanted to take some photos of the old city focusing on the location of churches and mosques (Bandak 2014b). As my wife and I were taking these photos, I suddenly noticed the icon of the Virgin Mary on one of the houses on the other side of the street. What amazed me was the sheer size of the image. It is fairly standard to see statues, icons, and devotional images in people's homes, and altars with icons or statues can also be found of Jesus, Virgin Mary, Saint Francis of As-sisi, Saint George, and Saint Ananias in the classic Christian quarters. However, the size of the icon on this terrace by far surpassed anything that I had seen before. It measured at least one and a half metres by one metre. I took a photo of it, but at that time I did not enter the door, nor did I sound the bell. Only later was I made aware by a pious Christian woman of the annual celebrations of Our Lady of Soufanieh, in which I then partook in late November in the Greek Catholic Patriarchate in the old city. The church was full, and with a friend, I was invited to take a seat in one of the front pews. People of all ages were in the church: elderly women, gentlemen, younger couples, children, and families, as well as pilgrims from France and Germany. Badges were distributed to everybody present, and a service was held with songs and prayers in praise of Our Lady of Soufanieh. During the service, several people presented parts of Our Lady of Soufanieh's story: Virgin Mary had met a local lady, Myrna Nazzour, in apparitions and had later given her messages. On several occasions, Myrna had been the source of oil flowing from her hands and body, and had had stigmata, the bloody marks of Christ upon his crucifixion, several times. My first reaction was surprise. I had been in Damascus for a year, and nobody had told me this story before. Of course, neither had I asked, but it was a phenomenon that I had expected to know of, and I did not. In the days following the annual celebrations, I asked about Our Lady of Soufanieh in my Christian Damascus circles. Nearly all admitted to knowing of the story, but most had not necessarily been a part of the celebrations or, for that matter, frequented Myrna's premises. I immediately found the annual celebrations of Our Lady of Soufanieh so intriguing that I decided it would be the topic of a novel fieldwork with a focus of its own. Consequently, after shorter stays in 2006 and 2008, I returned to do fieldwork on Our Lady of Soufanieh and her followers in early August 2009. For the next six months, I came almost daily to the home of Myrna Nazzour and her husband, Nicolas Nazzour, to learn what Our Lady of Soufanieh was all about. This book is the result.

**The Aim of the Book: Exemplarity and Sainthood**

This book is about examples. It contains a sustained reflection on the role of exemplarity in human life from an anthropological perspective. It examines the use of a particular life of a woman in Damascus, Myrna Nazzour, to instigate a certain life to be emulated. As such, the book probes the power of examples and the modelling of sainthood around Myrna's figure. Myrna is regarded by her followers as an exemplary figure, a living saint, and the messages, apparitions, stigmata, and oil, which have marked Myrna in various ways, have corroborated her status as chosen by God. These phenomena are regarded by the followers as miraculous signs, divine interventions in their local reality in Soufanieh, Damascus, Syria, which attest to the grace of God. Furthermore, they are seen as an invitation to live a life in his nearness. The messages Myrna has received from the Virgin Mary and Christ centre on different aspects of devotional life: prayer, joy, suffering to be borne, participation, and service to fellow man. Most centrally, the messages underscore three tenets as heart matter by being repeatedly mentioned: faith (*imān*), unity (*waḥda*), and love (*maḥabba*). These three tenets are seen as directed not just at a local community in Damascus but at the world as such.

In a Syrian context, but also more widely, Damascus as a locality holds a particular place in what Christians regard as the divine plan of salvation. Christianity, it may be recalled, turned global in the vicinity of Damascus. In the Bible, we read in Acts (9:1–31) that Saint Paul was blinded on his way to Damascus to persecute Christians and that, later, by the intercession of Ananias, he was converted and became the exemplary missionary to the Gentiles. Paul, in other words, fashioned Christianity not just as a parochial and local Jewish faction but as a religion for all, despite differences in terms of ethnicity, gender, wealth, social status, and age. From this perspective, Paul is a divinely ordained precedent that the followers see as prefiguring the life of Myrna in today's Damascus. Myrna and her followers critically want the message of faith, love, and unity to be spread in local families in Damascus, in Syria, beyond in the Middle East, and in the whole world. They themselves want their lives to exemplify God's grace, and they spend a considerable amount of energy attempting to flesh out this message in words and, more importantly, deeds. However, the wider circles of Christians in Damascus do not necessarily go beyond a general knowledge of Myrna and Our Lady of Soufanieh. Indeed, many appear to be satisfied to know *of* the alleged miracles, but they do not feel any great inclination to visit the place if no ailments are suffered, no petitions are to be made, or no personal grievances are to be placed in the hands of the Virgin Mary. The door remains open, but that does not mean everybody will actually step over the threshold, let alone ring the bell. Even if the devotees aim to flesh out examples and model sainthood in their own lives, the force of the example is situated in broader economies of knowing, feeling, and relevance, which have Our Lady of Soufanieh remain a potentially important figure, albeit not one Damascus Christians in any way agree on. Rather, contestation remains a central part of the immediate horizon of reception for Myrna and her followers. Contestation is a central feature in local receptions, as claims to miracles bring about much wider debates regarding evidence, authentification, and authority, which pertain lay Christians but also clergy and the establishment in the churches, who in different ways may see Myrna as a force to be controlled or harnessed.

The force of the example, it seems from the outset, already points us in the direction of fundamental questions that cross the world of scholar, devotee, and ordinary person. What is it examples can do? How are examples used to corroborate more general claims? What does it mean to follow an example? What is a good example? Or, for that matter, what is a bad one? Are examples only mere instantiations? In other words, do examples simply point to features that, with a counterexample, would have looked rather different? Or is the example the most perfect form, the exemplar, the ideal form or model that best renders a given reality? What I want to delve into is the particular role and effect of utilizing examples in a local world to make heard, seen, and felt the divine presence in Damascus as a locality and to model sainthood.

It is my contention that the social use of examples in a local world, such as the one behind the door of Our Lady of Soufanieh, is revealing of broader structures of illustration, evidence, and persuasion in social and cultural settings. It is therefore puzzling that the role of the example has only recently begun to receive anthropological reflection, albeit anthropologists use examples all the time, as do scholars who want to convey other forms of life (see Bandak & Højer 2015). In the anthropological legacy, we find the notion of the exemplar gaining some ground with the work of Rodney Needham (1985) and Caroline Humphrey (1997). Whereas Needham's work on exemplars was of a more personal and speculative kind in his weaving together figures as diverse as Archilochus of Naxos and Emmanuel Swedenburg, and accordingly has rarely been picked up, Humphrey's text "Exemplars and Rules: Aspects of the Discourse of Moralities in Mongolia" has had an uptake in several important works in the recent turn to morality and ethics in anthropology (Zigon 2008; Rogers 2009; Faubion 2011; Laidlaw 2014; Robbins 2015; Keane 2016). Although Humphrey (1997) points to the importance of exemplars for providing moral guidance in her Buddhist Mongolian context, she too hastily and sharply draws a contrast to Western tradition, which on her reading is governed by rules and systematic thought. Humphrey thereby glosses over the role examples have had from Greek thought, through Roman thought, to a Christian thought and history (see Koselleck 2004; Hartog 2011, 2015[2003]; Lowrie & Lüdemann 2015). We shall return to this much wider purchase of examples, exemplars, and exemplarity over the course of this book. I will demonstrate that exemplification is a social process, which in itself is socially formative as a way of crafting worlds, one that both attests to local ways of relating particulars and universals, and establishes connections by selecting particular features and omitting others. To place a thinking with and through examples as a contrast between Eastern and Western thought is untenable, at least in a hard formulation, and we should rather explore what purchase particular lifeworlds have in using examples.

My aim with this book is to explore the world of Our Lady of Soufanieh's followers in order to understand the role of exemplarity in social life. My main argument is that the role of the example should engage us in identifying which trains of thought set local worlds in motion. The study of the use of examples, I argue, is a central way to grasp how reality is conceived and made to matter in local worlds. Ethnographically, my argument is that exemplarity, and the concerns Our Lady of Soufanieh's followers have in corroborating the message of unity, faith, and love, is to be understood as a modelling of sainthood, a modelling that pertains to Myrna and her figure but also to the followers themselves. In this tension, I will demonstrate how a particular Catholic vision of the world can be seen put into practice. Life itself, for the followers of Our Lady of Soufanieh, is to be rendered exemplary, and in this way, more people are to be persuaded of the divine plan of redemption working in and through Damascus. In examining the role and structure of exemplarity as a modelling of sainthood, I critically engage with three different fields of anthropological work, which we will soon turn to.

### Philosophical Locations: *Mithāl, Eximere,* and *Paradeigma*

Before addressing the anthropological locations of this book, it is necessary to briefly introduce the notion of the example. In Arabic, the root of the word "example," *mithāl*, is composed of the three letters *mim, tha,* and *lam* (see Bandak 2015a; Mittermaier 2015). From this root, a whole class of words is constructed, words which point to objects that, in different forms, relate to representation or are a type of representation. According to Hans Wehr (1961) and his *A Dictionary of Modern Written Arabic*, the verbal form *mathala* can mean to resemble, to look like, to bear a likeness, to imitate, to copy, to compare, to liken, to represent, to mean, to signify, to stand for, to appear, to make one's appearance, particularly as an actor, and to set an example. The series of denotations outlined is, in this sense, vast and difficult to delimit. Furthermore, in different forms as nouns, the root can render instantiation, a parable or popular saying, mimesis, a statue, precedent, imitation, acting and actor, representation, and ideal. In Arabic, to give an example is likewise rendered by the same root as *mathalan*, which correlates to the English "for example." In diverse ways, the Arabic root that renders example points to the quality of having something stand for something else.

In a general sense, this feature of the example has been well presented by philosopher Nelson Goodman (1976, 1981): exemplification is all about what is made to stand for something else. For Goodman, exemplification is part of symbolization, something he critically started to unravel in his 1976 *Languages of Art*. Goodman, followed by his close friend Catherine Z. Elgin (1983, 1996, 2017), explores how the processes of exemplification are critical modalities to engage not just knowledge but also ways to attain epistemic access to phenomena. Goodman and Elgin are both enormously perceptive in their explorations of such processes of exemplification, which they see as only seldomly treated philosophically (Goodman 1976: 52). For both, items that instantiate as well as refer to a feature can be understood as exemplifying that feature (Elgin 1996: 171). As such, exemplification may never be complete, but may partially and selectively point to and instantiate what is to be seen in the example. We shall return to Goodman later in this book. At this point, it is rather instructive to trace the notion of the example and its legacies more widely than what has just been described. The term "example" derives from the Latin *eximere*, meaning a cutting out, a singling out from a whole, or an incision (Arendt 1982: 77; Lyons 1989: 9; Gelley 1995: 2). In order for something to stand for something else, that is, to become an example, a cutting out is needed. A related meaning is evident in Greek, where the word "example" is derived from *paradeigma* – that which stands alongside or plays alongside (Lyons 1989; Gelley 1995; Warnick 2008; Agamben 2009[2008]; de Looze 2010). The quality of having something stand for something else is highlighted by the example, here in a relation between part and whole. However, the quality of the example to stand for something else has, from the inception of Greek thought, resulted in two markedly different approaches to the category and status of examples and exemplarity. Plato, on the one hand, thought of *paradeigma* as a model or exemplar. This idea was captured in the quest for ideal forms known from the Socratic dialogues. Aristotle, conversely, thought of *paradeigma* as an instance from which inductive conclusions can be derived. Alexander Gelley (1995: 1) argues: "Whereas the Platonic model displays a vertical directionality, from a primary exemplar down to multiple instantiations, for Aristotle example involves something like a lateral movement." Aristotle, then, would not go from part to whole or from whole to part, but rather would place part and part alongside. On the one hand, the example can be thought of as just one case or instance among many, a flat and discrete example. On the other hand, the example can be seen as the most fully embodied form of a class, an ideal form. The relationship between the *example* as an instance or instantiation and the *exemplar* as the ideal form highlights a certain tension in the way particularity and universality relate.

Theoretically, many have found the example lacking in that it never amounts to a full theorization. Paul de Man, to take but one prominent thinker, vehemently critiqued the example for never arriving at universality and general propositions (1984: 276). The example is not thought to be able to put a case to rest once and for all, as it merely

sums up and stands for singularity. However, this aspect – in contrast
to a philosophy of the example – is what is of particular interest to an
*anthropology* of the example: to remain interested in the particular and
in how local worlds are set in motion. The example – as emphasized
by Brian Massumi (2002: 18) – harbours terrible powers of digression
and deviation. However, the example is also productive in establishing
meaning, contrasts, and comparisons for ethical conduct and reflection.
Examples and exemplification highlight the tension between ideals
and models for practice and actual practice. In this manner, thinking
through examples is a way to work towards trying to catch what, in
Michael Lambek's felicitous phrasing, is called "the leap between the
ostensible and subjunctive, to dress up the old distinction between the
'is' and the 'ought'" (2010a: 6). As philosopher Onora O'Neill (1986: 8)
explains, ostension, as in pointing to real features of lived lives, may be
"fully determinate"; however, the actual drawing of a lesson from such
lives is less determinate, as ostension "is always equivocal and requires
interpretation" (8).

It is in this tensioned force field that the exploration of this book is situated. In other words, is Myrna an exemplar, a model, or is she merely
an example, one among others? And who are to discern and decide on
the matter? The range of meanings of the root of the example, in this
sense, is rather vast. However, there is quite a difference in the way in
which things stand for other things. A statue may, with greater or lesser
likeness, resemble the original. On paper, one can represent somebody
in terms of official role and office, but in practice, that person may be
less persuasive in filling his or her part. An actor can be more or less
convincing in his imitation of a historical figure. Furthermore, acting
may be construed as false, as pretence, when it comes to personal or
devotional life, whereas imitation and emulation of worthy examples
of others is seen to enhance the Christian character being striven for.
As we shall see later, these aspects of exemplification as various forms
of standing for something else are all prevalent among Our Lady of
Soufanieh's followers. For them, the power of the example is tied to the
modelling of sainthood as seen in the life of Myrna and Christian tradition, but also in the lives of the followers who participate in spreading
the message of Soufanieh. In this sense, the book is a contribution to
seeing how a local world is set in motion around particular powerful
examples; accordingly, it probes the role of exemplarity in concrete
practices. This book is an anthropological contribution to the study of
exemplarity and the modelling of sainthood, but it is inspired throughout by various ways in which the example has been understood in adjacent disciplines such as philosophy, history, and rhetoric. The example,

in this book, is grounded ethnographically in Damascus and in the world and practices of the followers of Our Lady of Soufanieh. In this sense, it is a contribution and an ethnographical challenge in form of a reading from the East.

## Anthropological Locations: Models of and for Sainthood

One of the intriguing questions regarding Myrna is whether she is a saint. In the eyes of her followers, Myrna is definitely regarded as a living saint. The general category of sainthood is accepted by many others, but Myrna and her status as such are not – or at least not yet – tied to that category. That many Christians in Damascus do not yet endorse Myrna's status as a saint may very well rest on the protocols of establishing sainthood. A person may have a certain reputation for holiness, but to be categorized as a saint beyond local recognition needs clear corroboration from the church. In Catholic traditions, although a person may have a great following and be widely known during his or her lifetime, the status of formal sainthood can only be assessed and consigned by the church after the death of the saintly prospect (Kieckhefer 1988; Woodward 1990; McBrien 2001). There may be the *potential* for a formal declaration of sainthood, but during the life of a person, an official assessment cannot be given in case he or she should later work to the detriment of the church or the status of saint. The famous Catholic theologian David Tracy (2011) has captured this danger: "On the one hand, the authorities wish to honor and encourage exemplary models. On the other hand, authorities often fear a loss of their own power if they cannot control the emerging autonomous spiritual power of the saint, living or dead. Authorities wish to be the only ones to name and thereby institutionalize as their own these potentially dangerous and autonomous spiritual powers in the community" (98). As Myrna is still very much alive, it would be ill advised to focus on a formal verdict concerning her status, because the Catholic Church deliberately postpones such formal verdict until after the death of the prospective saint. However, in a more subtle way, the Catholic Church has spoken, as it does in cases where a living saintly prospect is in the running for official recognition; it has spoken by not talking against Myrna and by allowing her access to churches and her home to be frequented by local priests. This subtle language reveals that the Catholic Church is not against Myrna. If it were, it would publicly pronounce against the phenomenon, declaring it unworthy of devotion. In the Catholic Church, the local bishop is instrumental in establishing a case for sainthood, as his approval is needed to bring the subject further. Several cases in more recent years have been ruled out due to the lack of recognition by local bishops (Apolito 2005[2001]; Badone 2007). The local bishop in Damascus has so far given his consent to the proceedings in the form of an *imprimatur*[1] for more books about the life of Myrna (Salbato 1992; Zahlawi 2008). On this ground, then, the case for the phenomenon of Our Lady of Soufanieh, and by extension Myrna's possible sainthood, has not been obstructed by the local bishop.

As is evident from the preceding paragraph, the very question of Myrna's status brings us to another central part of this book, namely the issue of sainthood as seen from an anthropological perspective. In the classic anthropological literature on the Middle East, sainthood has been a central theme. Great work has focused on saints and sainthood in different Muslim communities. In that body of work, sainthood can either descend from the Prophet or be bestowed upon the individual by divine favour and ensuing miraculous feats (Geertz 1968: 45). Divine favour, or *baraka* in Arabic, has remained a central concept with which to understand the relationships between ordinary people and the saint (see Westermarck 1926; Crapanzano 1973; Gilsenan 1973, 1982; Cornell 1998; Pinto 2004; Mittermaier 2011). The saint in much of this literature is designated as a friend of God, in terms of his or her proximity to God, and is sought for advice and benevolence in times of hardship, ailments, or personal or communal grievances. Muslim saints have often been seen in the political role of mediating figure in conflicts (Gellner 1969; Marcus 1985; Reeves 1995; Ewing 1997; Zeghal 2009), whereby the living saint or the shrines and graves of the dead saint are objects of pilgrimage as well as centres for devotion (Eickelman 1976; Hammoudi 2006). The work on sainthood among Muslims in various parts of the Middle East, in other words, is well developed and continues to thrive (Gilsenan 2000; Stauth 2004; Stauth & Schielke 2008; Bandak & Bille 2013b). Conversely, little anthropological work exists on Christian communities in the Middle East, and far less on Christian conceptions of sainthood (for notable exceptions, see Bowman 1993, 2012; Jansen 2009; Poujeau 2010; Shenoda 2012; Heo 2013, 2018). This book fills a considerable gap by focusing on an often overlooked group, as it deals with the Christian minority, here Syrian Christians in Damascus.

More than merely placing itself directly in a regional debate, however, the book is located in recent anthropological discussions of Christianity. These anthropological studies have, with great emphasis, centred on the basic question: what difference does Christianity make? (see Cannell 2006). This question has only recently been dealt with anthropologically, and when studied, it has often emphasized the global spread of Pentecostal and Charismatic Christianities in the Global South and beyond (see Meyer 1999; Coleman 2000; Robbins 2004; Engelke 2007). The field of anthropology of Christianity has in various ways forced substantial and subtle ways of exploring what it means to be a Christian (Robbins 2003), or, for that matter, who is a Christian (Garriott & O'Neill 2008). Such questions have allowed for a general rethinking of the role Christianity holds in the lives of people, something that previous generations of anthropologists were less preoccupied with (see also Crapanzano 2000; Harding 2000; Cannell 2005; Robbins 2007; Bialecki, Haynes, & Robbins 2008; Jenkins 2012). A tendency in these studies, however, has been to focus on the more devoted parts of Christian communities and not necessarily on people who only see themselves so at times (Keane 2008; Bandak & Jørgensen 2012). Likewise, less focus has been given to varieties of Christianity, such as Catholicism and Orthodoxy, and when they are examined, the study has been primarily located in the Eastern European world (see, for example, Hann 2007; Mahieu & Naumescu 2008; du Boulay 2009; Hann & Goltz 2010; Luehrmann 2011; Boylston 2018).

In this book, I take up the fertile question of Christianity in a Middle Eastern context, but I also want to explore the role of sainthood and exemplarity, which has not been substantially dealt with in the recent body of work (for exceptions, see Coleman 2009; Mafra 2011). Sainthood, however, has been studied in previous anthropological work on Catholicism, both in Europe and the Latin world (see Boissevain 1965; Christian 1989[1972]; Gudeman 1976; Piñas-Cabral 1986; Mitchell 1997; Cannell 1999). Another branch of anthropological studies that has dealt with Christianity has been the tradition inspired and provoked by the work on pilgrimage initiated by Victor and Edith Turner (1978). Following their work, substantial focus has been allotted to various forms of pilgrimage as well as to Marian devotion (see Eade & Sallnow 1991a; Dubisch 1995; Coleman 2002; Coleman & Eade 2004b; Badone 2007; Jansen & Kühl 2008; Hermkens, Jansen, & Notermans 2009; de la Cruz 2015). Likewise, studies with a more sociological, historical, and theological bent have delved into the role of sainthood (see Brown 1981; Weinstein & Bell 1982; Wilson 1983; Hertz 1983; Orsi 1985, 1996, 2005; Hopgood 2005; Meltzer & Elsner 2009; Clarke & Claydon 2011). In this book, these different trajectories are brought into the frame of an anthropology of Christianity.

On a general level, what I explore through these various traditions is a tension between different senses of exemplarity in the form of human models and modelling. Clifford Geertz (1966) famously captured the human capacity to not just live in the world but also to add to it and change it by his distinction between models *of* and models *for* reality. If we transpose Geertz's idea to the domain of the saints, I will argue that we can locate a tension in the relation between models *of* and models *for* sainthood (see also Bandak & Bille 2013a). By models *of* sainthood, I wish to point out that culturally specific expectations surround the saintly prospect chosen as a subject worthy of special attention. Saints are fitted and modelled on past figures, ultimately Jesus, Mary, or other recognized saints (see Brown 1983; Kieckhefer 1988; Woodward 1990). The model *of* sainthood points to the general viability of concrete people to function as a source of blessing and influence. The model *for* sainthood, however, points to the power of the saintly subject to attract and foster emulation. More than just presenting a model worthy of veneration, this perspective presents a model worthy of imitation. It is precisely between these two forms of models that a tension exists. Does the saint demand imitation? Does the devotee want to emulate the saint at all?

William James (1982[1902]) famously argued that the health of many saints would perhaps have been reconsidered in our times. However, James wisely did not rule out the importance of saints as models in people's lives. Rather, James argued that, in the life of extraordinary individuals, we can find the mirrors, prisms, and windows that allow us to grasp the way in which religious experiences are circulated more widely. However, the saint is not a figure that can be used to sum up religious experience. What the saint can do is articulate with greater force the concerns persisting in a particular time and context (see Starrett 2010). For the followers and surrounding society, the saint may also be unaccommodating and problematic, as James (1982[1902]) wrote regarding the saints in his all-time classic *The Varieties of Religious Experience*:

> We are glad they existed to show us that way, but we are glad there are also other ways of seeing and taking life … We are proud of a human nature so passionately extreme, but we shrink from advising others to follow the example. (339)

In other words, saints may be met with enthusiasm, but not an enthusiasm signifying that people who meet the saint will necessarily want to put the saint's qualities into practice themselves by actual imitation. Whereas philosopher Linda Zagzebski (2017) unravels the importance of exemplars and exemplarism – in the form of heroes, sages, and saints – for moral thought and admiration, an ethnographical elucidation needs to contextualize such admiration and esteem that people may bestow on these figures. Reluctance or just general interest may often be the prevailing attitude, rather than longing to become more pious and change one's life in imitation of the saint. Reluctance, ignorance, and also downright willed indifference may be some of the responses with which the saint is met in the wider society (see also Mayblin 2017). As we shall see in this book, these attitudes are negotiated on the part of both Myrna's followers and the surrounding society, but here this insight points us towards a critical assessment of much recent research on piety and popular religion, which has emerged from two rather different fields as a very strong contribution to the study of religion.

Professor of religion David Morgan has published several original works on the role of images and photos in popular devotion (1998, 2010, 2012). Morgan argues that visual piety is at play whereby stereotypical images allow for the devout to feel and experience the proximity of the saint, the Virgin Mary, or Jesus in their lives. The intimate knowledge of the saint, in this sense, is mediated by visual forms and allows for an exchange of gaze and touch between devotee and saint. Another field in which the piety trope has been introduced is in recent anthropological studies on Muslim communities in the Middle East. A spate of studies has explored the lifeworlds of highly committed Muslims in order to understand the world of the Muslim faithful. Most notable have been the studies of Saba Mahmood (2005) and Charles Hirschkind (2006). Both studies attest to the pious longings of Muslims in Cairo, and both explore the affective dimensions of practices of listening to the Quran and to sermons. These studies capture very well the efforts at making Islam the path in the life of the devout. The zeal is very strongly conveyed by both monographs. However, the inherent danger in both usages of piety as a paradigm to understand the lives of religious subjects – for Mahmood, Hirschkind, and Morgan, respectively – is that we hear when people succeed in their devotion or when the devout meet the saint in and through the image of the saint. We hear little, if anything at all, about when pious attitudes do not yield the hoped for results. As pointed out by Samuli Schielke (2008, 2009, 2010) regarding the piety trope found in the work on devout Muslims, we are presented with a totalizing image of devout Muslims, where conspicuously little is conveyed concerning the problems people have in living the ideals (see also Soares & Osella 2009; Simon 2009).

This book is also situated among a group of highly pious people. The followers of Our Lady of Soufanieh are fervent in their efforts to promote her message, both in their own lives as well as by inviting the wider society to follow their lead. However, this focus on the pious subjects does not rule out the troubles that exist in getting things right (Hastrup 2004). In the totalizing image presented by some of the recent research on piety, we do not hear much about these problems, contestations, and misgivings, and how they affect the group of pious people. We might ask in this regard about the pressure to be exemplary, to fulfil the ideals and expectations of others but also those of oneself. In the chapters to follow, I view these problems and misgivings as a productive counterpart in the modelling of the saint and her followers. In this sense, I follow the lead of Françoise Meltzer and Jaś Elsner (2009) in their assertion that a productive relationship exists between the polemics and apologetics of sainthood. The modelling of sainthood viewed as an active process may be, if not a remedy, then a corrective prism with which to situate pious attempts at getting life right. Sainthood also relates to broader structures of exemplarity, and the way sainthood is tested, debated, and lived comes down to how examples can be set for others. Concomitantly, the role of sainthood needs to be tied to discussions of exemplarity. Such discussions have thrived of late in disciplines adjacent to anthropology but have hitherto only in a very limited sense met an anthropological assessment. However, an ethnographical engagement with powerful examples also allows an anthropological pushback against too neat forms of conceptualization.

**Syrian Locations: Historical and Ethnographic Context of the Study**

This book also contributes to an understanding of Christianity in the contemporary Middle East. This aspect is not merely – as hinted at above – a needed contribution in anthropological terms but also one that adds to the knowledge now developing from historians (see Braude & Lewis 1982; Heyberger 1994; Pacini 1998; Makdisi 2007, 2019; O'Mahoney & Loosley 2010; Robson 2011; Khater 2011). Christians have lived in the Middle East and in Syria since the first church and the time immediately after Christ. However, the role of Christians has changed markedly over the past two millennia. While Christians gradually became a numeric majority in the region in the first centuries, it was in many ways a heterodox assemblage of groups. Christian belief and dogma at that time were vigorously fought over, and the great many church councils are but one reminder of this conflict. As far back as at the Council at Chalcedon in the year 451 CE, it was decided that Christ had both a divine and a human nature, and vehement opposition was found among the Christians in Syria (Burns 2005: 91). As Byzantium was trying to control matters of belief, it was seen as a relief by some Christians when Syria and Damascus were captured by Arab Muslims under the command of Khalid Ibn Walid in the year 635 CE (Degeorge 2004: 31). At that time, the majority of the citizens of Damascus were Christian, and they were left pretty much to themselves after recognizing Islamic supremacy. By paying a particular tax, *jizya*, Christians were given the status of *dhimmi*, people on contract. After the first major wave of Arab conquest, the Umayyad dynasty governed from Damascus during the period 661 to 750 CE. Christians remained a majority well into the tenth century (Courbage & Fargues 1998[1997]: 10–14, 20ff.; Burns 2005: 105, 133), but the situation gradually changed, and Christians became a numeric minority. A particular pact, the Pact of Omar, regulated both the behaviour and public appearance of Christians who, for instance, were not allowed to ride horses or ring bells (see Goddard 2000a: 197; Masters 2001: 22ff.).

The response to the Arab conquest came in the form of the crusades initiated by Pope Urban II in 1095. The various crusades in many ways complicated living conditions for local Christians, as they often ended up being targeted from both sides (Maalouf 2004[1983]: 20, 95, 134). The crusaders often did not consider local Christians to be more than Muslims or heretics, and they were looked down upon or attempts were made to use them as brokers in the conflict. For the Muslim populations, the local Christians ended up being suspect, due to the campaigns led by the crusaders claiming to free the country. As the Ottomans gained power in the sixteenth century, the crusades were finally abolished as a strategy, and Pope Clement V instead instigated missions as the novel approach (Degeorge 2004: 159ff.; see also Goddard 2000b: 116ff.). In the ensuing centuries, European powers grew increasingly interested in the Christian minorities since the various forms of missions and proselytizing failed among Muslims. Instead, Christians from the numerous Orthodox churches were targeted, and several churches split up and formed a Catholic counterpart (Salibi 1988; see also Makdisi 2007). In this vein, the Greek Catholic Church split from the Greek Orthodox Church, and the Syrian Catholic Church split from the Syrian Orthodox Church. Severe cleavages and scars were inflicted because of these divisions.

Over the centuries, one finds various forms of coexistence and domination, which is why it is impossible to claim any single lesson from history. Recently, this insight has been elucidated by historian Ussama Makdisi (2019) in his important work *The Age of Coexistence*. Makdisi scrutinizes the way sectarianism and coexistence as notions rise to prominence in the discourse on the Arab world, particularly in the period from 1860 to 1948. Often these notions are read with very limited knowledge of what complex historical circumstances created the actual living-together conditions of diverse communities in the region. For instance, the pogroms against Christians in Damascus in 1860 were central episodes in the long history of coexistence. The changing power situation in the Near East had the Ottoman Empire trying to alter its policies to accommodate the ascending European powers in France and England (Fawaz 1994; Masters 2001; Mahmood 2016). During the tragic events of 1860, in which several thousand Christians were killed, some Christians, it is important to note, were protected by Muslims, and the areas hit the most were those with a predominantly (wealthy) Christian population, not the mixed areas. The incidents are therefore typically interpreted by historians as animated by social inequalities and not religious difference. However, among my Christian interlocutors, it is not necessarily easy to disentangle the social from the religious, and it is therefore possible to hear the same incident used as an example of a general Muslim animosity but also, in the opposite vein, of Muslim help in a troubled situation.

During the 1800s, the Ottoman Empire saw a period of unprecedented pressure, not just from European powers but also from Russia, which repeatedly attempted to capture land and ensure protection of local Christian communities. This pressure resulted in the creation of independent nations such as Serbia, Romania, and Bulgaria. For instance, the Russo-Ottoman War of 1877–78 resulted in Russia forcing the Ottoman Empire to capitulate and sign an armistice in January 1879 and later to sign other treaties, which made way for the creation of Greater Bulgaria (Chatty 2017: 34). As a direct consequence, Muslim populations residing in these former European provinces of the empire were expelled and started to enter the Ottoman province of Greater Syria. In the later part of the same century, Greek, Assyrian, and Armenian Christians were evicted – at times voluntarily, at other times violently – from Muslim parts of the Ottoman Empire, and many sought refuge in Syria and its major cities such as Aleppo and Damascus. These resettlements, as Dawn Chatty has eruditely shown, have had lasting effects on the Syrian social fabric, enabling traits of tolerance and senses of unity despite differences (2017: 9, 206).

Eventually, the Ottoman Empire collapsed after the First World War, and Syria came into existence for a brief spell, only for France to mandate the area from 1920 (Provence 2005: 2). During this period, the borders with Lebanon were drawn, and the French played a clever divide-and-rule game whereby Christians were given clear advantages. At that time, the seeds for the later pan-Arabism were sown, which, after independence from France in 1946, led to a free Syria and, following a misguided joint venture with Egypt in a united Arab union, to the takeover of the country in 1963 by the Ba'th Party. After a successive coup in 1966, Hafez al-Assad seized power in 1970 and remained at the head of the country until his death in 2000. Hafez al-Assad's reign has been rightly labelled authoritarian, characterized by a highly repressive system (Wedeen 1999; Ziadeh 2012; al-Haj Saleh 2017; Ismail 2018). His son Bashar al-Assad followed him and has governed the country under an authoritarian regime, with a strong secret service, both in the 2000s and beyond (see Salamandra & Stenberg 2015; Wedeen 2019; George 2003; Borneman 2009). In the years before 2011, as we shall see in this book, the regime was not something most Christians worked against; rather, many endorsed its secular ideology because it guaranteed Christians a place in the nation (Bandak 2015b). The regime, which we with today's perspective assess with a clear eye to later developments, here needs to be read through the ethnographical situation prevailing before 2011, where no such prescience or clarity existed.

Christians have historically been faster in migrating from the region as compared to various Muslim counterparts (Courbage & Fargues 1998[1997]: 190–1). Changed demographic patterns have also been seen first among many Christians, who have settled in the cities and focused on education and fewer children (Abu-Lughod 1987: 165; Rabo 2005: 26). This general pattern means that the number of Christians has been declining, even before 2011, and concomitantly, does not fit the official ratio. By 2010, the population in Syria numbered approximately 21.5 million inhabitants.[2] Officially, 74 per cent of the population is considered to be Sunni Muslim, 12 per cent Alawite, 10 per cent Christian, and the remaining consists of Druze, Ishmailis, and tiny Jewish communities. However, the actual percentages have looked different for Christians due to declining birthrates and a higher number emigrating. Ethnically, roughly 90 per cent of the population is Arab, whereas the remaining 10 per cent are Kurds, Circassians, and Armenians (see Rabo 2012). As numbers and statistics in contemporary Syrian society are always a politically sensitive issue, it is not one that people address openly. Christians as a minority in a given power relation will be a recurrent theme throughout the pages of this book.

**Methodological Considerations: Fieldwork and Material**

As I embarked on the fieldwork for this book, I did not expect examples to figure prominently in what I was to explore. However, the role of exemplarity and of persuasion very soon came to occupy my mind, as it was a pressing concern among the followers of Myrna Nazzour. During this work, I have been brought into a sustained dialogue with Our Lady of Soufanieh's followers. They have attempted to model sainthood, their own and Myrna's, and to attest to what they perceive as the workings of the Virgin Mary on this particular spot. I have methodologically –

in the spirit of George Marcus (1995) – aimed at *following* the thing, here the attempts at modelling sainthood and the crafting of specific structures of exemplarity in and around the home of Myrna Nazzour and her family. In this endeavour, I have explored how structures of exemplarity set a particular world in motion. More precisely, I have traced this very movement. The followers of Our Lady of Soufanieh want to invite more people to become closer to Mary – including the anthropologist. I have methodologically found myself moved by the attempts my interlocutors have made in modelling sainthood and asserting the force of the example. My analysis is situated in the play of the movement between intimation and distancing, in what Theodor Adorno (2005[1951]: 90) formulated in *Minima Moralia* as "a distanced nearness." The play between proximity and distance, accordingly, is not to be conceived as a choice between opposites in a fixed antinomy but rather, as Paul Ricoeur (1981) pointed out, a positive, or fertile, pair that attests to the constant productive tension in the humanities between truth and method, between pregnancy and objectivity (see also Bandak 2014a).

All in all, the book rests on twenty months of fieldwork in Damascus. Fieldwork – one month in 2004, eleven months in 2005, and two weeks in both 2006 and 2008 – initially focused on the Christian minorities and their use of social space to create viable ways to live the nation. Subsequently, fieldwork has focused on how Christianity is lived and, concomitantly, on the ways in which both practising and non-practising Christians articulate and live local traditions. In the period of fieldwork conducted from August 2009 through to January 2010, complemented with extended case studies in March, April, and December 2010, I frequented the home of Myrna Nazzour almost daily. I participated in and recorded daily liturgical prayers, weekly novenas or spiritual lessons, and weekly masses.

Besides the structure given by the context of the daily prayers, novenas, and masses in the home, I had conversations with various members of the extended family of Soufanieh – the designation the followers themselves use. This work was to yield material in the form of written entries as well as to develop trust over time. I have had conversations with more than one hundred people in and of the family of Soufanieh. In addition, I have conducted recorded interviews with many key individuals, including Myrna and her husband Nicolas; the three most important pastors, Abuna Elias Zahlawi, Abuna Elias Saloun, and Abuna Boulos Fadel; and several key and lay members of Soufanieh. The interviews have been semi-structured and pursued topics around themes such as miracles and veracity, relations to Myrna and her persona and sainthood, Soufanieh, Christianity in Syria, and the importance of Damascus as a location in this story. These interviews have been supplemented with both formal and informal interviews with people not frequenting Soufanieh. Here, I have interviewed pastors and lay people, and discussed the topic of Soufanieh and unity in families and among broader circles. The extended focus not just on the pious circles has situated the strength but also the weakness of the quest for exemplarity.

Another important source for this study is the messages Myrna has received. All the messages are distributed in booklets; in addition to the shorter version found in the booklet, Abuna Elias Zahlawi has published a three-volume work numbering some staggering 1,500 pages on the miraculous occurrences in the first twenty-five years from 1982 to 2007. Besides the Arab versions, several theologians have written about Our Lady of Soufanieh, from the minor and not that clear essays by Niels Christian Hvidt (2001) to wholesale books by authors such as American Richard Salbato (1992), Theodore Khoury (2005), Antoine Arjakovsky (2010), and Christian Ravaz (2009). These books are all valuable but examine the phenomenon of Our Lady of Soufanieh from theological and positive positions. The books have informed my wider knowledge of the phenomenon; however, I have carried out the research as an anthropologist, not a theologian, and have therefore placed a different emphasis, since the task of the anthropologist is not to verify or falsify particular worlds but to think through their terms and stakes (see Christian 1996: 9; Apolito 2005[2001]: 19–20). The distribution and spreading of the messages of Our Lady of Soufanieh are by no means bound to the classical book and paper forms. Under the rubric of *The Miracle of Damascus*, thirty-one official parts of the Soufanieh story are available on YouTube. Each part is about ten minutes long and gives a thorough presentation of the happenings as seen from an inside perspective. In other words, the many parts summon up a positive picture of divine intervention in Damascus and, furthermore, directly link this intervention to the famous conversion of Saint Paul on the road to Damascus. This story is also presented on a DVD distributed free of charge in Soufanieh, which, in a two-hour video, presents all the key members, recounts their testimonies, and narrates their life stories and moments.

Besides these mediated versions of the story of Soufanieh, the followers of Our Lady of Soufanieh initiated a new strategy in November 2009, the month of the twenty-seventh anniversary of the first apparition. The icon, which on numerous occasions has shed oil, was for the first time since a brief spell at the very beginning taken from the house of Myrna to four main cathedrals in Syria on each of the four Sundays of November. I participated in two of these trips and have extensive coverage in the form of field notes and sound and video recordings. These trips are very important case material, as they function to show how the messages are spread and circulated, not just in the form of Myrna in person but also in the form of the travelling icon. During these trips and the preceding planning of them, I obtained valuable material regarding the importance of spreading the messages as well as concerning evaluations of the trips and their purpose, as I had conversations with most of the fifty or so people involved. The sense of participation in something big was on everybody's lips. Of even greater significance were the very different receptions the icon, Myrna, and the family of Soufanieh were met with on the different occasions. On the first trip to Aleppo, the bishop did not even mention Our Lady of Soufanieh with as much as a word, whereas on the trip to Homs, Tartous, and Khabab, respectively, celebrations were abundant. These trips, as well as the annual celebrations in the home, where testimonies are given by many people, are critical material with which to analyse the workings of the messages upon subjectivities and their way of creating accounts about the efficacy of the divine in specific lives.

I was invited by several members of the family of Soufanieh to make visits or follow them on tours in their everyday life. These visits and tours are important forms of knowledge, as they attest to how the communal life relates to the life of the individual. In other words, by following people across contexts, critical insights have been gained into how individuals relate to a Christian message outside the place believed to be sanctified. These forms of conversation were at times jotted down as the conversations unfolded and, at other times, written down afterwards in extensive field notes.

Instead of solely delimiting my focus to Our Lady of Soufanieh's followers, I have kept my contacts from previous fieldwork and used their reflections on a more mundane level. By taking the research questions into ordinary families, the scope of Our Lady of Soufanieh could be reflected and concomitantly brought back to the followers, which was critical on both accounts in gaining insights into various forms of belief and disbelief among Damascus Christians. My material therefore spans the lives of ordinary Christians, sceptics, believers, and people suspending judgment for later times. The material also reflects my different relations and involvement with people with whom I have been in contact for longer or shorter periods of time. For some, the relationships have lasted seventeen years and, for others, no more than the later spell of time in Damascus. In this book, I use the actual names of the public persons in Soufanieh and Syria, while the names of ordinary people have been changed. For many of the followers of Our Lady of

Soufanieh, this policy may not be what they wanted; however, I have deemed it wiser not to follow them in this regard.

## Exemplary Ethnography: Structure of Argument

In this book, I do not merely write about examples but also take exemplification as the central method to open the door to reflection, both on how local worlds produce structures of exemplarity and how an anthropologist uses examples and exemplars in the crafting of analysis. The unravelling of structures of exemplarity that I here undertake emerges from the ethnography. Ethnographically, we hone in on prayers and icons, sermons, life stories, questions of evidence and signs, pilgrimage, and recent film productions, which, in different ways, are entries into the ways examples and exemplification work. My theoretical conception, then, is also my analytical method, and my method is my theory, in that radical exemplification may open new ways to conceive of sociality and how we make sense of it. The examination of the modelling of sainthood is undertaken as a movement across the chapters of this book, where I take up prayers, sermons, life stories, evidence, pilgrimages, and historical precedent as exemplary for the followers of Our Lady of Soufanieh. I explore the modelling of sainthood and the structure of exemplarity as we move through the chapters from Soufanieh and the practices in the home of Myrna Nazzour to the public domain, where the followers aim to make the message of Our Lady of Soufanieh manifest. In this movement, we are taken from the home of Myrna Nazzour towards the wider location of Christians in Syrian society and the world.

The structure of the argument follows the exemplary in different domains. Each chapter is an exploration in and of exemplification. In the first chapter, we enter the home of Myrna and are presented with the house, people, and message of Our Lady of Soufanieh. The second chapter explores the daily prayers as a particular modelling of sainthood, which is seen as an exemplary Christian practice and is tied to the miraculous oozing of oil from the icon of Our Lady of Soufanieh. The third chapter deals with sermons delivered in Soufanieh and how they invite the listener to become part of an exemplary series. The fourth chapter explores life stories and hagiography and, in this sense, takes us from the exemplary series presented in the sermons to the attempts of the followers of Our Lady of Soufanieh to live as an example. The fifth chapter deals with evidence and signs, looking at how different relations towards Myrna and her persona are nested in the wider society. The sixth chapter concerns the spreading of the message of Myrna during the anniversary in 2009, and how unity and discord are at play in the reception and corroboration of the message of Our Lady of Soufanieh. The seventh chapter discusses a recent film and the relation between Myrna and Paul, and aims to establish broader perspectives of the Christian minority in Syrian society. Lastly, in the conclusion, I present perspectives on exemplarity and anthropology, and the critical themes that emerge from this book.

All along in the book, a movement of proximity and distance will be followed, as we are taken from a close-up in the home and then proceed towards the role in society more directly. In this sense, Catholic and, for that matter, Orthodox Christian sensibility allows for a process whereby people gradually move closer or further away from Mary, Christ, and divine truth. This trajectory is rather different from the portrait Susan Harding (2000: 39) paints of her fundamentalist Christian interlocutors in the United States. For Harding's interlocutors, only two positions are allowed: either you are on God's side, or you are on the side of the devil. While this framing is no doubt important in much Protestant and Charismatic thought, it does not capture the prolonged invitation Mary is believed to send to her children in Catholic thought. So, where Harding rightly argues that no neutrality can be found in an ultimate sense, this outlook still allows for a process whereby people – to paraphrase Hermkens, Jansen, and Notermans (2009) – are moved by Mary. Susan Harding, in her personal narrative, shows how learning the categories of fundamentalist Christians can only come by a situated learning, one she argues comes through the acquisition of a particular language. In the case of the followers of Myrna, learning is not merely about language acquisition; learning is a prolonged process in which a sensibility is trained to see, listen, feel, and smell the divine. Mary is seen to have moved Myrna, and likewise to have invited every single person to follow her. The first invitation in this journey is to open the door to the home of Myrna and Nicolas, and to pay Our Lady of Soufanieh a visit.

# Chapter One

# Closer to Mary

[W]e need to write histories of religion that are not dedicated solely to telling the stories of religious institutions and intellectuals or to describing religion as a social and political force. Rather, and difficult though it may be, we must narrate tales of faith and belief, those intangible yet powerful elements of the human experience. We must allow a role for the supernatural in human history by accepting that it moved individuals and communities in small and great ways – even if it does not move us in a similar manner.

– Akram Fouad Khater,
*Embracing the Divine*

As you enter the door and ascend the steps of Myrna and Nicolas's house, you may not know what to expect. Some will anxiously climb the steps to see Myrna. Others will be curious to meet Myrna, even if they do not know quite what to think. Yet others will be used to coming here, because they attend the weekly masses or daily prayers on a regular basis. In any case, as you climb the steps, you are now on the premises of Our Lady of Soufanieh. This house is also the home of Nicolas and Myrna, their two children, and Myrna's parents. It is quite a standard home in some ways, but in others not. The home, in a particular way, is a dwelling at the intersection between Heaven and Earth. It is the place where the Virgin Mary appeared to Myrna, the place where a message of unity, faith, and love was given to her by Jesus, and a place where people come to pray and see Myrna. In this chapter, I shall lay out the story of Myrna and the apparitions, and invite you on a tour of Myrna's home, placing the rhythms of the week in a broader pre-2011 Damascene and Syrian landscape.

### Dwelling at the Intersection between Heaven and Earth

On climbing the stairs, you cannot fail to see an icon of Our Lady of Soufanieh placed on the wall at the end. Stacks of black plastic stools are stored here. Images of saints, such as Mar Sharbel and Saint George, also cover the walls. Having climbed the steps, on the left side of the entrance you will see two open bookshelves displaying magazines and books on Our Lady of Soufanieh in several languages. The books are noticeable, with their titles in Arabic, German, French, English, and Hungarian. The magazines are displayed differently, some open on the pages presenting the story of Myrna and Our Lady of Soufanieh. Others have a special issue devoted to Our Lady of Soufanieh and are displayed with their title page. Some magazines have photos of Myrna, others of the icon of Our Lady of Soufanieh. The books, magazines, and photos all make it clear to the visitor that the story of Our Lady of Soufanieh has not just stayed in Damascus but has also travelled to countries and devotees far away.

When you turn right after the steps, you enter an inner courtyard typical of older Damascene houses (Keenan 2000; Weber 2009). Here, you enter a second door, most often open but sometimes closed in winter to keep out the cold from the frequently opened outer door. The courtyard measures some five by six metres. On the end wall is an icon of the Virgin Mary holding the Baby Jesus, and above it are engraved golden letters in Arabic that read *Sayyidatu-ṣ-Ṣūfāniyya yanbūʿ uz-zayt il-muqaddas* and in English, Our Lady of Soufanieh. The words "Source of Holy Oil" are not added in the English version. The icon is hand-painted and has been in the possession of Nicolas's family for some generations. It is known as Our Lady of Kazan, named after a most famous Russian icon (see Luermann 2010). However, it is not the only icon of this type. Below it, inserted in a triptych, is a postcard reproduction of the same icon. The triptych is made of brass and has its doors open. The postcard reproduction stands on top of a glass bowl used to collect drops of oil when they are exuded. A glass screen covers the icon. In front of the triptych is a tray with several candles lit. The candles are placed in sand as part of the prayers and petitions said here. As you stand there, an elderly lady comes up, assisted by her two daughters, each with a plastic bag from one of the nearby shops. They all stand silently in front of the icon. In turn, they light candles and place them in the sand. The screen of the icon is touched, and they leave again.

To the right of the icon is a stereo. The speakers are placed higher up the white and black painted walls. The stereo is not always in use, but it is often used to play devotional songs: Arabic hymns in praise of the Virgin Mary but also, more specifically, songs devoted to Our Lady of Soufanieh. At other times, French devotional songs and classical music create an atmosphere of prayer and emotional responsivity. On the wall next to the stereo, a white plastic sign with black letters in Arabic, French, and English announces that no donations will be accepted. Flowers, however, are welcome, and bouquets of various sizes and forms are often placed in front of the icon of Our Lady of Soufanieh as tokens of gratitude.

On either side of the triptych hang icons of the Archangels Michael and Gabriel, respectively. Both are turned in the direction of the icon of Our Lady of Soufanieh. To the left of the triptych, two plastic chairs are located. Next to these is an altar. On the altar is a Bible, open on the reading for this particular day. Two microphones stand on the altar, along with candles and a larger reproduction of Our Lady of Soufanieh. Over the altar hangs a devotional image of Jesus and the Sacred Heart. "Jesus, I trust in you" say the words painted beneath the feet of Jesus. The image of Jesus shows him standing in a white robe, with rays beaming from his chest and wearing a silent smile, as he gazes at the beholder. On each side of the altar, more icons are located.

The inner courtyard is laid with tiles. In the middle of the room is a fountain used as a table. A tablecloth on a wooden board covers it. Here, on a wooden stand, are a book and a pen. As you flick through the book, you will find written petitions, prayers, and words of thanksgiving to Our Lady of Soufanieh. Along the sides of the inner courtyard are couches. High up, a plastic roof covers the inner courtyard.

To the left of the courtyard are two rooms, the bedroom of Myrna and Nicolas, and the room of their son, Johnny Emmanuel. More icons are situated on this wall, including one of Saint Thérèse of Lisieux, as well as a large rosary and two versions of the icon of Our Lady of Soufanieh. Myrna and Nicolas's daughter Miriam also has a room, which is located beside the stairway. In the back of the inner courtyard are a rest room and the family kitchen. Both kitchen and rest room are inconspicuous in size and style, as the house generally conveys an impression of simplicity. To the right of the central icon is the family living room. Here can be found family photos and more personal items, alongside photos of Myrna's now deceased spiritual mentor, Abuna Youssef Maalouli. A television and a landline phone are located in this room, as well as several couches for receiving guests. From this room, it is only a few steps down to the inner courtyard, or you can descend the stairs to the entrance. From there, you can also take the stairs to the right and climb to the second floor.

On the second floor are Myrna's parents. They live here and have a room where they reside as part of the household. Both are integral to the everyday life of the house. Myrna's father is typically part of the daily prayers, and most days he can be found sitting on a chair next to the stereo. From there, he adjusts the fan and the light. Myrna's mother takes part less frequently in the prayers, but she looks after many of the people coming to the house. The family dog, Putchi, a little long-haired mixed breed, is frequently around, but not as part of the prayers and masses.

In front of Myrna's parents' room is a plastic table and some plastic chairs. You can sit there, and many do when the Saturday mass has crowded the house with guests. Over the inner courtyard hang icons of the twelve apostles. You can take a couple of steps to the right and, from there, climb up two steps to reach the family's terrace. The terrace is where Myrna received her first apparition. Standing on the terrace overlooking the adjacent park, the Virgin Mary approached Myrna, who could do nothing but flee. A plastic table and chairs are located there. The reproduction of Our Lady of Soufanieh decorates the wall, the one that can be seen from the street. It is large, an image of Our Lady of Soufanieh painted specifically for this place. A statue of the Virgin Mary in white marble stands in the middle of the terrace. From Mary's hands hang rosaries, and she is standing on top of a crushed serpent. Beneath the statue, letters have been tucked in, as there is a small box for petitions, prayers, and personal messages. People often come to pray here. On the terrace is a budgerigar in a cage. It can frequently be heard singing.

Next to the painted image of Our Lady of Soufanieh on the wall is a closed door. The door has an upper part with a window in it. A white curtain covers what is behind the door. Not that it is any secret, though, as this room is used as a confessional and place of devotion for Myrna. Here, Myrna and priests, such as Abuna Elias Zahlawi, Abuna Elias Saloun, and Abuna Boulos Fadel, can confide. The room is set with an altar similar to the one in the courtyard, if slightly smaller. This room is a sanctuary, a place for prayer. The home more generally is just that, a family home, but also a home and a shrine for the followers of Our Lady of Soufanieh, who come here frequently, and for the curious or passersby who may have more urgent needs to be stilled.

### Rhythms of the Home: Prayers, Mass, Novena

Scrambling sounds can be heard from the kitchen. A woman is cleaning. You may not have noticed her before, but if you had asked for Myrna, she would have said: "I'm Myrna. What can I do for you?" It may come as a surprise to some that the Christian visionary and stigmatic also cleans the house and occupies herself with mundane tasks. Myrna is in her late forties. Her hair is dark brown, shoulder length, and she wears glasses. She is dressed ordinarily, typically in black or grey trousers, a blouse, and a cardigan. The colours worn are mostly grey, black, and white, and give an impression of simplicity. For others, however, it is less of a surprise, as Myrna is a living person, someone they know from the neighbourhood and from a common upbringing; for these people, it is precisely the simplicity of Myrna's character that has made her a chosen vessel. In this sense, people's expectations vary as to what they will meet in this home. This house, in some respects, is just an ordinary home and not that different from many other Syrian households, where three generations live under the same roof (see Rugh 1997). However, in other ways, this home is special. The home is not just regarded as the home of this family but of Our Lady of Soufanieh. The rhythm of the week attests to the joint ownership in the form of daily prayers, weekly Saturday mass, and weekly Tuesday novenas. The visiting hours stated outside on the sheet are also used by friends, relatives, and followers of Our Lady of Soufanieh, as well as by people with more pressing concerns.

The house of Myrna and Nicolas has its rhythms. A steady flow of people come and go here. Some are accustomed to the life of the home and treat it as a second home. Salwa, one of Myrna's closest trustees, comes here almost every single day and has even chosen to live with her own family in close proximity to the house in order to be part of the unfolding miracle of Soufanieh. Salwa often guides foreign visitors who come to Soufanieh. At times, Salwa gives a presentation of the story of Soufanieh, preferably in French but also in English if necessary. In that case, Salwa takes people from the inner courtyard to the terrace and explains how the apparitions started. Salwa and several other women participate in presenting the story of Soufanieh for others and take some of the responsibility off Myrna's shoulders.

Salwa also plays a role in the daily prayers. Each day in the afternoon, the rosary is said in the inner courtyard in front of the icon. Stools from the stacks in the entrance are placed in a few pews next to the covered fountain. Here, the rosary is said in the form of repeated decades of Hail Marys, Our Father, and the reading of and reflection on exemplary scenes from the life of Jesus (see Winston-Allen 1997; Mitchell 2009). Typically, the prayer is led by Pierre, a man in his late seventies. When the time approaches 4.30 p.m. in winter – 5.30 p.m. in summer – Pierre will greet those present, and people will start praying.

Pierre makes the sign of the cross and starts saying the Creed. Everybody follows Pierre's lead, saying the Creed aloud. After the Creed comes a joint recitation of Our Father and three Hail Marys to dwell on the virtues of faith, hope, and charity. Then comes the Glory Be to the Father. Pierre then reads the text of the first mystery. Upon conclusion, one of the people present, Abu Rami, a man in his late fifties, walks up to stand in front of the icon of Our Lady of Soufanieh. Abu Rami lifts his hands, holding a rosary in one hand, and starts saying Our Father. Then follow ten repetitions of Hail Mary and the response from the people present.

> Peace upon you, Mary, full of grace, the Lord is with Thee [as-salāmu ʿalayki ya Maryam, ya mumtaliʿa niʿmatan]. Blessed art Thou among women, and blessed is the Fruit of Thy Womb, Jesus Christ [mubārakatun anti fī-n-nisāʾ, wa mubārakatun thamrat baṭniki, Yesūʿ al-Mesīḥ].

Abu Rami says these words in his own distinct intonation and diction. He ends with a gentle bow.

> Holy Mary, Mother of God, pray for us sinners, now and at the hour of our death [Ya qadīsatu Maryam, ya wālidatu-llāh, ṣalli li ʿajilnā naḥnu al-khaṭaʾ, alʾān wa fī-sāʿat mawtinā]. Amen.

Everybody responds. The prayer is repeated ten times. As Abu Rami prays, others can be seen praying along, letting the prayer beads follow each repetition. Some accompany Abu Rami's prayer with an almost inaudible whisper or with just a movement of the lips; some may at times exclaim an extra "Ya Mariam!" When the ten repetitions have been said, Abu Rami closes the prayer, saying:

> Glory be to the Father, and to the Son, and to the Holy Spirit [al-majdu lil-ab, wal-ibn, wa-r-rūḥ il-qudus], now and all time and until forever and ever[1] [alʾān wa kulla awānin wa ilā dahri ad-dāhirīn]. Amen.

Abu Rami assumes his seat to the left of the altar. Once Abu Rami is seated, Pierre reads the next mystery. As he finishes the reading, a second person walks to stand in front of the icon and say Our Father and the subsequent ten repetitions of Hail Marys.

On an ordinary weekday, there may be ten to twenty people praying. There is a core group who join in as often as possible. Abu Boutros, his wife and three kids, refugees from Iraq, Abu Rami, George, Umm Qusawi, Umm Salwa, Myrna's father, and some other elderly women and men participate, if not daily then every other day or as often as possible. Another group comes once or twice a week. Again, the group of people is diverse in terms of age, social standing, and gender. A third group participating are people who do not come frequently but attend for a specific time and have a specific purpose for coming. These may be people with ailments or concerns; they may also be pilgrims or tourists and travellers from afar. The repeated prayers saluting Mary are seen to be part of an unceasing chain of prayers at work since the inception of this place as a shrine. Prayer beads sift through the fingers of those present. Different styles and intonations can be heard.

The five decades of the rosary last for half an hour, whereupon a second part of the prayer follows, in which readings from the Bible and messages received by Myrna, psalms to the Virgin Mary, and hymns devoted to Our Lady of Soufanieh craft the general line of Christian salvation and particularity of the grace bestowed on this place. Traditionally, some of those closest to Myrna arrive just before the second part of the prayer. Myrna herself, Salwa, Georgette, or some of the other core female members most frequently lead the singing of the hymns. The person leading the singing will usually go to the altar and, opening a drawer, take out a song book of the collected hymns and devotional songs. This song book is not an official copy but a self-made and handwritten one. The song book is decorated with a reproduction of the icon of Our Lady of Soufanieh. Salwa, Myrna, or the person leading the singing will then choose songs, but often with no preplanning, as the second part of the prayer sometimes starts without singing, and someone will take up responsibility during the event. The prayer ends with one of the elders taking the icon of Our Lady of Soufanieh from the stand on the altar and holding it in his hands, allowing the people present to kiss and touch it, as one of the most cherished hymns in the home is sung: Our Lady of Soufanieh.

After the conclusion of the prayer, the core group soon bids Myrna farewell. Pierre, Abu Boutros, his wife and three kids, Abu Rami, George, and Umm Salwa all soon leave, out of respect for Myrna and her family. People with a specific purpose will often ask for Myrna. If she is present, she will talk to them. Often, such as when ailments are suffered and Myrna is asked to pray for healing, people will also ask for cotton pads with holy oil and prayer cards. Either Myrna or Salwa accompanying her will open the drawer in the altar and take out small plastic bags of cotton pads imbued with the oil exuded by the icon or Myrna. Postcard-size prayer cards with the icon of Our Lady of Soufanieh are also distributed. Some are given booklets with a short history of Our Lady of Soufanieh, and if particular interest is shown, a DVD can be obtained with testimonies from central figures around Myrna.

Each Saturday there is a mass in the home. The mass is preceded by the rosary, which, as on weekdays, starts half an hour before the service.

Several people arrive from the start and participate in the prayer. The closer the time gets to the start of the mass, however, the more people appear. Myrna's father, Raif, Michel, and some of the other men usually guide people to seats in the front rows. This orchestration is needed, as the service will often have the courtyard packed with people once the rosary has been said. All the plastic stools will be in use for the Saturday service and so will the second floor, where the plastic chairs of Myrna's parents are put to use. Some people will be praying on the terrace during the service, kneeling in front of the statue, and others will be keenly following the liturgy of the service. During the service, the house is a vibrant place in which people participate and circulate less than can be experienced in many of the Orthodox and Catholic churches during mass.

As the rosary is said, one of the priests will enter from Myrna and Nicolas's living room. Typically, the priest will stop in front of the icon of Our Lady of Soufanieh to say a personal prayer before walking to the altar. The service follows the liturgy of the Greek Catholic Church, and books with the liturgy are available for those whose memories need aiding or those not brought up in the Greek Catholic Church. At times, the liturgy may be following the pattern of the Orthodox Church, depending on guests present. People attentively follow the liturgy and readings from scripture, which follows the church calendar. The reading from the epistles will be read by one of the elders from Soufanieh, whereas the priest will read from the gospels. Children are urged to stand under the Bible as the priest reads and to kiss or touch the book afterwards. The sermon then follows. Abuna Elias Saloun, Abuna Elias Zahlawi, Abuna Boulos Fadel, or another priest will give a sermon, which will typically draw upon the context of the text read from the gospel; the sermon will furthermore address the particular grace of Soufanieh.

After the sermon, to which people listen attentively, prayers and the Eucharist follow. If Myrna has been in the living room for the service until this point, she will assist the priest as the devotees queue to receive bread and wine from the hand of the priest. Myrna holds the tray with bread. The priest dips the bread in the wine and places it in the mouth of the person in front of him. As this ritual involves the movement of a huge number of people in the inner courtyard, the plastic stools are stacked up, and people queue from the left side and walk back via the right. Salwa or one of the other women will lead hymns as the Eucharist is consummated, heightening the spiritual ambience (Engelke 2012; Kaell 2017). Many people will stop in front of the icon to pray, light candles, and touch the screen of the icon. Some of the core members of Soufanieh will ask people to follow the movement around and continue up the steps to the living room, where some take a seat on one of the couches or continue to the entrance or the second floor. Some people can be found talking outside, as the Eucharist will typically last about twenty minutes. Usually, Raif, Tony, Samir, and Ilyas will lead a chat, either on issues related to the topic of the sermon or, more frequently, the talk will deviate into other aspects of life.

Following the Eucharist is the conclusion of the service. The service ends, like the daily rosary prayer, with the priest taking the enlarged reproduction of the icon that stands on the altar and holding it up for all to circumambulate in order to kiss and touch the icon of Our Lady of Soufanieh while singing the hymn in her praise. On the way down and out the stairs, baskets with the remaining bread from the Eucharist are offered for people to take with them. The Saturday service will have people with various degree of proximity to Myrna participating in it. The group of ardent followers will, of course, be present for the service, but people with different, more specific purposes will also participate. Myrna will be asked for as the service ends, and DVDs, booklets, cotton pads with holy oil, and prayer cards will be distributed. Some of the people coming for the first time use cameras or cell phones to take photos or videos of Myrna, or line up next to her to have the moment captured.

For the most devoted circle of Our Lady of Soufanieh's followers, the Tuesday evening novena, *as-sujūd*, is mandatory. The evening of spiritual reflection is not mandatory in the sense that it is compulsory. Rather, it is felt to be a necessary part of the weekly rhythm for the followers of Our Lady of Soufanieh. The program typically lasts one hour. The plastic stools are placed in rows, and people start to arrive a little before eight p.m. in the winter – nine p.m. in the summer. A handout with the topic of the evening is placed on the plastic stools, and the remaining handouts are placed on the covered fountain. The handout is printed on A4 sheets. In the top corner, the icon of Our Lady of Soufanieh is printed, and the three tenets of faith, love, and unity are written below it. The evening will typically be given a title, either from the Bible or from one of Myrna's messages.

Devotional music is played on the stereo, and people will greet each other heartily as they steadily arrive. Around forty people are usually present, although the tally varies. One of the priests closest to Myrna, most typically Abuna Elias Saloun, leads the evening's program. The evening starts with an abbreviated collective saying of the rosary. After this recitation comes a free prayer, said most often by Rita or Salwa. Then follow the readings of the chosen messages and passages from scripture. Abuna Elias Saloun reads aloud, and people listen carefully. In contrast to the Saturday services, the novenas most Tuesdays do not have a sermon in a classic fashion. The priest highlights a topic worthy of reflection among the devoted circle of followers. Whereas a traditional sermon is directed from the mouth of the priest to the ears of the listeners, the novena opens a space for more direct mutual engagement. Typically, the priest opens with reflections on the words printed on the handout. Often the reflections relate to situations that have been pressing over the last week: reactions to the message of Soufanieh, popular support, the value of prayer in individual life, doubt, and faith.

After the opening reflections, people are invited to voice their thoughts. The evening is central, as here a dialogue is what is strived for. The tone is reverential. Different opinions may, however, be articulated and discussed. As the conversation draws to a close, Myrna will frequently have a few minutes to speak. She may tell of miraculous healings, contestation in the local society, or her reception during travel to foreign countries to bear witness and visit churches. This moment is often regarded as the high point, and the followers of Our Lady of Soufanieh marvel at the stories of healings, sigh at the accusations met in local society, and rejoice in being part of the plans of the Virgin Mary at this particular place. Occasionally, a more specific program will be planned.

On the first Tuesday of every month, the evening is crafted as a mass, and at times, the program is planned to entail either a joint confession of sins or the possibility for individual confessions of sins to priests in different rooms of the home. The program always concludes by following the same pattern. A joint prayer is said. The prayer is made up of three different parts, placed in the same sequence. Each part of the prayer has been ordained by the instruction of the Virgin Mary's fourth apparition on 21 February 1983; the Virgin Mary to Myrna on Ascension Day, 31 May 1984; and Jesus in a message given to Myrna in Maad, Lebanon, on 22 July 1987. The prayer is said as everybody stands facing the original icon in the triptych:

> Beloved Jesus, grant that I rest in You above all things, above all creatures, above Your Angels, above all praise, above all rejoicing and exultation, above all glory and honour, above all heavenly hosts, for You are the Most High, You alone are the Almighty and Good above all things. May You come to me and relieve me, and release me from my chains, and grant me freedom, because without You my joy is not complete, without You my table is empty.

Everybody says the prayer by heart and continues with the second part:

God saves me, Jesus enlightens me, the Holy Spirit is my life, thus I fear nothing.

And they conclude by a threefold repetition of the last part:

O Father, through the merits of Your beloved Son's wounds, save us.

The evening ends with people singing the hymn of praise to Our Lady of Soufanieh, while the plastic stools are stacked and placed in the doorway. The followers talk and comment on the reflections shared during the evening. Myrna's reflections particularly are attended to with much anticipation. The talk is very free on these Tuesday evenings. Here, the program is for the inner circle of trustees who all participate in spreading the message of Our Lady of Soufanieh. People such as Fadi, Terese, Said, Rula, Nabil, Rafik, Maia, Reem, and Riyadh all converse. People of both sexes are present for these evenings. In terms of age, there are no children present, and a number of the older people do not attend, as it may finish late, particularly in the summer. Pierre, Myrna's parents, and Umm Salwa will rarely be present for the evening program. Newcomers will be asked their situation and will be accommodated with answers to questions. Nicolas will often adjust the stereo with devotional music. As the conversation grows heartily louder and louder, Nicolas may ask people to lower their voices because the house is a place of worship. People do so immediately or walk outside. Several accompany each other home, some by foot, others by car, and with them, the message of Our Lady of Soufanieh is carried to their homes, families, and neighbourhoods.

**The Start of the Apparitions: Fear Not**

How did it all start? The story has been meticulously crafted by Myrna and her followers, and goes according to their rendition in books, booklets, and on DVD as follows. Myrna, or more formally Mary Kourbet al-Akhras, was born in 1964 to a Greek Orthodox mother and a Greek Catholic father. She went to local schools and displayed no particular signs of being anything special. She left high school one year prior to obtaining the Syrian baccalaureate diploma. In May 1982, Myrna married Nicolas Nazzour, who hailed from a Greek Orthodox background. Nicolas is somewhat older than Myrna; for some time, he lived outside Syria in Germany. However, these details are frequently just laid out as details before what was later to happen. On 22 November 1982, oil started to ooze from the hands of Myrna Nazzour. Myrna was praying for her ailing sister-in-law as the oil began to exude. Not only did oil flow from her hands, but her sister-in-law was cured when the ailments on her body were anointed with the oil. This miracle happened to Myrna's great surprise, and she did not quite know what to think. Nicolas Nazzour, her husband, was also highly sceptical and mocked Myrna in his disbelief; if she could produce oil, it would be of better use in the kitchen! Yet this event was only the start of a series of miraculous incidents that were to happen. Myrna's mother had long had an aching back and now asked Myrna to pray for her too. Myrna did so three days later, on 25 November. Again, oil started to ooze, and Myrna's mother was healed. Then oil started to ooze from a postcard-size reproduction of the icon of the Virgin Mary, an icon Nicolas had brought home from his travels to Sofia in Bulgaria.

The events immediately drew people's attention in Damascus. Within a few days, much commotion had moved the different Christian groups in Damascus to investigate what was going on. Laity, diocesan and religious clergy, ordinary passersby, and officers from the Syrian secret service all – for various reasons – wanted to see for themselves and check what these events were all about. As Nicolas's family adhere to the Greek Orthodox Church, the local Bishop Boulos Bandali and two Greek Orthodox priests were among the first to visit. Greek Catholic priests also came to see, however, as Myrna's family has a background in the Greek Catholic Church. All marvelled at the miraculous happenings.

It is recounted how, after three weeks, on 15 December 1982, Myrna was on her terrace at night. Suddenly, she saw the appearance of a figure like the Virgin Mary looming in the air. "The Virgin, the Virgin!" Myrna shouted, struck with fear. The figure dissipated, and Myrna was calmed down by the Greek Orthodox Abuna George Abu Zakham. The Greek Catholic Abuna Elias Zahlawi arrived not long after and heard what had happened. He gave Myrna advice to not be afraid:

> Myrna, you must not be scared. Nobody is afraid of their mother. No doubt the Virgin wants to give you a message, and when she found you so scared, she didn't tell you anything. You have to be calm and pray to prepare yourself in case of another apparition.

The direction and comfort given by Abuna Elias Zahlawi gave Myrna peace, even if she admitted not knowing why these things were happening. She had not been particularly devoted. In fact, she claimed only to know Our Father and the Hail Mary. She was young, seventeen years of age, and had married Nicolas earlier the same year. In her inexperience, she was chosen, and Abuna Elias Zahlawi's support put her more at peace with what she did not understand. Three days later, on 18 December, Myrna had a second apparition. The Virgin Mary appeared to her in white and blue robes, and gave her a message. The message, delivered in Arabic, said:

> My Children, remember God, because God is with us. You know all things and yet you know nothing. Your knowledge is an incomplete knowledge. But the day will come when you will know all things the way God knows Me. Do good to those who do evil. And do not harm anybody. I have given you more oil than you have asked for, but I shall give you something much more powerful than oil. Repent and have faith, and remember Me in your joy. Announce My Son the Emmanuel. He who announces Him is saved, and he who does not announce Him, his faith is in vain. Love one another. I am not asking for money to give to churches or for money to distribute to the poor. I am asking for love. Those who distribute their money to the poor and to churches, but have no love, those are nothing. I shall visit homes more often, because those who go to church sometimes do not go there to pray. I am not asking you to build Me a church, but a shrine. Give. Do not turn away from anyone who asks for help.

The message, focusing on repentance and devotional zeal, was followed by three more apparitions in 1983, on 8 January, 21 February, and 24 March. In the apparitions, the Virgin Mary was crying and smiling. Furthermore, the messages in the apparitions praised the humble and admonished the haughty and pretentious. The messages urged prayer and forgiveness. Myrna was instructed to establish a shrine, not to build a church, and to work to counter divisions among Christians. The Virgin Mary ended her fifth apparition on 24 March by saying:

> I tell you: "Pray, pray, and pray again!" How beautiful are My Children when they kneel down, imploring. Do not fear, I am with you. Do not be divided as the great ones are. You will teach the generations the word of unity, love, and faith. Pray for the inhabitants of Earth and Heaven.

Having heard these words, Myrna started saying the Creed and added: "Glory to God in the highest of Heavens and peace on earth to men of good will." When Myrna was asked why she added this sentence, she answered: "The Virgin Mary started the Creed, and I continued it after her!"

After the five apparitions, messages followed on many occasions. The importance of the messages is underscored by the followers and by

Abuna Elias Zahlawi. They stress that it is the first time the Virgin Mary has communicated directly in Arabic. More importantly, however, the messages are regarded as being a finer form of divine communication, because the words clearly formulate what is in the hearts of Mary and Christ for this particular place and for the world. The words of faith, love, and unity are repeatedly highlighted, as is the instruction to teach the generations, both in the messages and by the followers of Our Lady of Soufanieh.

Later in 1983, more miraculous features were added to the evolving phenomenon. Myrna started to have ecstasies. The first was on 28 October, when Myrna was praying, and oil started to ooze from her hands, neck, and face. As she was guided to a bed, she reached spiritual ecstasy and was unable to hear, see, or feel anything in the mundane world while she experienced the Virgin Mary. Myrna has been in ecstasy thirty-five times over the years, and has frequently seen Mary, Jesus, or an intense light, as well as received messages, during the ecstasies. Furthermore, the miracle of holy oil did not only happen around the icon in Myrna's home. In October 1983, hundreds of reproductions of the icon also started to ooze oil in the vicinity of Myrna and Nicolas's home. People praying in front of the icon started to report miracles of oil being exuded. The miracle was, so to speak, productive of further miracles.

But more was to come. On 25 November 1983, Myrna's body was marked by stigmata, the wounds of Christ. Wounds opened on her hands, feet, side, and forehead. Later, the wounds closed again. This phenomenon has been documented as happening on four further occasions, when Easter was celebrated jointly by the churches. As the various Orthodox churches follow the Julian calendar but the various Catholic churches follow the Gregorian calendar, Easter is most often celebrated on different days, much to the concern of Syrian Christians more broadly. Christians in general decry the lack of unity that is captured most vividly by the celebration of Easter on different days. Concomitantly, when Myrna has had stigmata during the unified Easters, the followers of Our Lady of Soufanieh have taken it as a clear sign of the importance of unity between the Christian churches in the heart of Christ himself. The four times have been Maundy Thursday in 1984, 1987, 1990, and 2001. The stigmata were carefully monitored by doctors and experts, and the event was filmed for documentation by Myrna's supporters.

The miracles of oil, healings, apparitions, messages, ecstasies, and stigmata led to the inception of devotion to Our Lady of Soufanieh, as the priests closest to Myrna, Abuna Youssef Maalouli and Abuna Elias Zahlawi, started to designate the devotion to the Virgin Mary on this particular spot. The locality, in this sense, gave name to the image and the devotion to the Virgin Mary, as she was believed to have sanctioned this place with a particular grace (see Christian 1989[1972]; Sallnow 1981) and a particular task. The followers see this house not just as a mundane dwelling but as a dwelling chosen by the Virgin Mary and Christ to participate in divine redemption, a dwelling located at the intersection between Heaven and Earth. However, as we shall see over the pages of this book, beyond the circle of devout followers, the general attitude of the Greek Orthodox Christians, clerics in particular, has often been marked by scepticism, while the attitude of the Greek Catholics, lay people and establishment, overall has been more positive, sometimes openly so and other times by a tacit form of accommodation. The challenge as seen from the perspective of the devout followers is to flesh out Myrna's message in order to move people from scepticism and disinterest to become closer to Mary.

The last message Myrna received was on Holy Saturday during Easter 2004. The message was from Jesus, and in it, he stated that it was to be the last:

> This is my last commandment to you: Each one of you return to your home. However, hold the East in your hearts. From here a light emerged anew. You are its radiance in a world seduced by materialism, sensuality, and fame, so much as to have lost its values. As for you, hold on to your Eastern identity. Do not allow your will, your freedom, and your faith in this Orient to be taken away from you.

The precarious nature and situation of Christianity in the Middle East is hinted at. However, an idea of global reach and radiation that emphasizes the importance of this particular place universally is also manifest. The world is invited to come to Soufanieh, and to this day the door has been open to everyone.

### Moved by Mary: Travels, Pilgrimages, and Anniversaries

The door remains open to everyone, and it is, indeed, opened by many. The followers of Myrna and Our Lady of Soufanieh, or the "family of Soufanieh" as they term themselves, frequent the home as often as possible. For some, it means primarily coming for the Saturday mass and Tuesday evening novena; for others, it means coming for the Saturday mass and the daily prayers; and for yet others, it means coming when time allows, albeit less regularly. A time when all participate with a heightened sense of urgency is during the annual celebrations of Our Lady of Soufanieh. The anniversary of the first oil exuded from the

icon of Our Lady of Soufanieh on 25 November and the days immediately preceding and following it gather most of the ardent followers
for masses in the home, although the celebrations have, over the years,
developed to also encompass masses and concerts in the Patriarchate of
the Greek Catholic Church in Harat al-Zeitoun in the Christian part of
the old city. The festivities have over the years attracted pilgrim groups
from France and Germany, as well as from other Arab countries such as
Lebanon and Egypt. Our Lady of Soufanieh can, in this sense, be seen
to attract people from all over the world. The numbers may not be as
impressive as the famous pilgrimage sites of Our Lady of Guadalupe in
Mexico, Lourdes in France, or Fatima in Portugal, where millions can be
counted on an annual basis (see Turner & Turner 1978; Zimdars-Swartz
1991; Apolito 2005[2001]; Maunder 2016), but the intensity of prayer is
underlined by priests and followers alike. Regarding the intensity of
prayers and the messages received, Our Lady of Soufanieh has been
termed "Our Lady of Lourdes in the Middle East." This comparison has
been a source of pride among the followers of Our Lady of Soufanieh,
even if the particularity of the message of this place is kept in mind.

Local devotion and attention to Our Lady of Soufanieh has been
waxing and waning over the years, quite frequently correlating to the
number of miracles said to happen around Myrna and the icon of Our
Lady of Soufanieh. During the time of fieldwork, I estimate that at least
200 persons would come by the house during a normal week. However,
for celebrations, many more would turn up. According to what I was
told, several thousands were taking part when the miraculous events
of stigmata were taking place. In a local conception, Mary is seen to
move people physically from the far corners of the Earth but also to
move people in their hearts and direction of life (see Coleman & Eade
2004b; Hermkens, Jansen, & Notermans 2009; Napolitano 2009; Coleman 2022). Movement is critical, as Mary is understood to affect people,
to move them to a more devoted life. "You have to get closer to Mary,
Andreas," I was gently admonished by Samir, as we talked about the
theme of the sermon one day after Saturday mass. This urgent call is
one that each individual member of the extended family of Soufanieh
sees as necessary, not merely for their own sake but for the sake of Syrian society and the wider world. To the most ardent followers, getting
closer to Mary means being able to more fully participate in divine and
redemptive work. While the members of the extended family of Soufanieh place a great deal of time and energy in prayers aimed at spreading the message of Soufanieh, they are troubled by what they see as a
waning number of people coming since Christ's last message in 2004.
The task, they believe, is now for the extended family of Soufanieh to

spread and corroborate the message of Soufanieh and, indeed, to embody the message of unity, faith, and love. New initiatives have been taken, such as pilgrimages with the icon of Our Lady of Soufanieh during the annual celebrations of 2009 to significant cathedrals in different parts of Syria. If people will not come themselves to see, Soufanieh will have to come to them.

One way Soufanieh can be seen to travel is in the figure of Myrna herself. Myrna is often invited as a special guest to countries all over the world. She frequently visits neighbouring Lebanon, and Jordan and Egypt have also been destinations for her travels. On numerous international journeys to countries such as Sweden, Germany, Poland, Slovakia, Austria, Belgium, France, Canada, and the United States, Myrna has also presented the story of Our Lady of Soufanieh and what has befallen her. These travels are viewed as significant among Myrna's followers, as the message is thus seen to be spread. Quite importantly, the travels are always presented as happening upon invitation, which is perceived as evidence that Myrna is not demanding attention but rather that she is wanted all over the globe to bear witness to the story of Soufanieh. The travels are always undertaken in the company of one of the priests, and at times also in the company of other members of Myrna's family or members of the extended family of Soufanieh. Her travels are amply prayed for in Soufanieh, while Myrna is away, and they are listened to when Myrna and one of the priests tell the details at the next Tuesday evening novena.

The spread of the message of Soufanieh today also takes place via the active propagation that can be found on the website hosted by core members around Myrna. Maia, one of the active women in her late thirties, is integral in placing recent events online on the website https://www.soufanieh.com/. The website is hosted in Arabic, but the language can also be changed to French or English. Likewise, videos and footage from Myrna's travels, testimonies from pilgrims or people cured, as well as activities in the home are documented on YouTube via the official channel https://www.youtube.com/user/SOUFANIEHVIDEOS, where the corroboration of the message of Soufanieh takes place virally with close to 600 videos on display. The greatest number of visitors or users may not be found there, but that is not an issue locally, as concrete meetings between individuals are seen as the most important. However, for the wider acclaim of the devotion to Our Lady of Soufanieh, it is important to stake Myrna and her family's claim to sainthood and the happenings at this place, and modern technology helps traverse time and space, and allows fellow devotees, as well as interested people, to participate or follow in front of their computer screens.

## Syrian Christians: Locations in the Syrian State and Region

Locally, only a few people get their primary information on Soufanieh from the official website or YouTube. The attention Soufanieh attracts is predominantly spread by more traditional means in the form of stories passed from mouth to mouth. The devotion to Our Lady of Soufanieh and the person of Myrna are known by many Christians, but not by all. Part of the reason why some Christians do not know her is that Syrian Christians belong to a great variety of churches. The three largest are the Greek Orthodox Church, the Armenian Orthodox Church, and the Greek Catholic Church. Besides these churches, one can also find the Syrian Orthodox Church, the Syrian Catholic Church, the Church of the Franciscans, the Maronite Church, the Armenian Catholic Church, the Nestorian Church, the Chaldean Church, as well as the Anglican Church and various minor Protestant churches (Abdu 2003: 33; Rabo 2012). The various churches in Damascus and Syria more widely represent diverse theological trajectories taken in the past. And in a time of vulnerability on the part of Christians in the region, the ideal of Christian unity is becoming more articulated.

The inception of Soufanieh as a site for devotion took place in one of the most troubled years – at that time – in recent Syrian history. In the late 1970s, former president Hafez al-Assad and his regime were accused of heresy. As the regime base was and continues to be drawn from the Alawite minority, the accusations – particularly on the part of the Syrian Muslim Brotherhood – led to violent showdowns (see Seale 1988: 332–4; Perthes 1995: 137; van Dam 1996: 111). Most notorious was the massacre in the city of Hama, where an estimated up to 30,000 civilians were killed when the old part of the city was levelled by tanks, soldiers, and bulldozers (George 2003: 16; Lesch 2005: 44; Wieland 2006: 93; Ismail 2018: 131). The regime's crackdown succeeded, and the Muslim Brotherhood was expelled and banned from Syrian soil. Myrna's apparitions started later that year. For her followers and the priests, such as Abuna Elias Zahlawi, that particular vulnerability in times of upheaval is a critical background against which to understand the words of Our Lady of Soufanieh. Marian apparitions have, in this sense, often started in such times of uncertainty (Turner & Turner 1978; Christian 1996; Matter 2001; Davis & Boles 2003; Apolito 2005[2001]; Morgan 2012).

Several of Myrna's later messages likewise underscore the importance of Christians in the region, and priests such as Abuna Elias Zahlawi see other recent wars prefigured in the messages received by Myrna. The first Gulf War, for instance, can in their reading be seen in a brief message in 1990. On 15 August that year, Myrna was invited to Braatschaatt in Belgium, and during the visit, she received the following message from the Virgin Mary:

> My Children, pray for peace, and especially in the East, because you are all brothers in Christ.

This brief message was, of course, seen as an instruction to pray more for this particular theme, peace in the Middle East. However, in light of what happened the following year in Iraq, the message was seen as prophetic. The creation of Our Lady of Soufanieh, in this sense, is also a collusion of expectations, fears, and hopes, in which she is seen as a sign for those with eyes and ears to see and hear (Christian 1981; Apolito 1998[1992]; Morgan 2012; Maunder 2016).

The Christians in Syria likewise were reminded of their precarious situation by the great number of Iraqi refugees who fled the neighbouring country after the coalition removed Saddam Hussein and his regime in 2003, which for many was an acute reminder of what could also befall Syria. The ensuing uncertainty and civil war in Iraq have had a direct bearing on Syrian sensibilities, because more than a million people, perhaps even double that figure, sought refuge in Syria in the years before 2011. Among the Iraqi refugees, one can find many Christians, alongside other minority groups such as Shiites (see Szanto 2012). The situation of the Iraqi Christians was, at the time, seen as a very likely scenario for Syria should the regime fall, a scenario that made Syrian Christians very wary, the dangers of which they have often been reminded, particularly since the killing of Lebanon's former prime minister Rafiq al-Hariri on 14 February 2005. For the remaining part of that year, the international society pointed its finger at Syria and the regime until the Syrian army was withdrawn from Lebanon, where it had been since the civil war and for many years after the war had come to an end in 1990. The civil war in Lebanon stands as another example of the dangers of sectarianism in the region.

The fate of Egypt's large Coptic Christian minority has also been followed by Syrian Christians. There, an escalation of violent episodes occurred in the 2000s, which was seen by many Christians as a worrying sign. Among Syrian Christians and the followers of Our Lady of Soufanieh, it has precisely been Egypt that was known for the famous Marian apparitions of Zeitoun (see Nelson 1973; Jansen 2005; Heo 2013; Matter 2001; Scheer 2013). Over an extended period in the late 1960s, vast masses of both Christians and Muslims saw a luminous figure in blue and white over a local church in Cairo. This collective vision was interpreted differently but was seen by many as a sign of support in troubled times. More recently, in December 2009, a collective vision of the Virgin Mary again appeared in Cairo and was spread virally over YouTube. For Christians in Syria, this apparition was again viewed as a sign of support in troubled times, something that was seen – following the shooting massacre one month later during the Coptic Christmas – as the Virgin's sign of care in complicated times.

With such a general climate in the region during the 2000s, Syrian Christians generally treasured the possibilities that have been ensured by the regime's focus on national unity and stability (Bandak 2013). The strong focus on stability has also made the Christian minorities able to enjoy civil rights as well as the rebuilding of churches and infrastructure, enabling easier access to various monasteries (Poujeau 2010: 178; see also Wieland 2006: 33). The regime of the ruling Ba'th Party, which was developed by, among others, the Greek Orthodox Christian Michel Aflaq, has historically underscored the Syrian Arab nation rather than various sectarian and tribal affiliations (see van Dam 1996: 15; George 2003: 66; Provence 2005: 152; Rabo 2012; Kastrinou 2016). This ideology was still part of the broader Syrian society in the 2000s and allowed the different Christian churches and communities a wide degree of freedom in religious affairs, as long as they did not go against the general idea of national unity. In this regard, Sunni Muslims have often been targeted more harshly (Pierret & Selvik 2009; Pierret 2013). This situation was, in the times leading up to 2011, often contrasted with neighbouring Arab countries, where discrimination was seen as endemic to the system, Egypt being the primary example.

For the followers of Our Lady of Soufanieh, the regime is not seen as an enemy. In the very early days of the phenomenon, officers from the secret service came to examine what was going on. The story of the visit is presented on the official DVD available at no charge in Soufanieh. The three officers examined the icon and tried to disassemble it to see if tubes or other signs of fraud could be detected. As this examination was taking place, oil started to grease the fingers of the officer scratching the surface of the icon, and he ended up convinced of the veracity of the miraculous icon. In other words, the relationship with the state is not troublesome, given that the message of unity, which is so important to the followers of Our Lady of Soufanieh, is not seen as working against the idea of national unity. Even if it is not the same unity, it is not an uncorrelated vision of unity. The state, concomitantly, is not seen as hostile to the followers of Our Lady of Soufanieh and Myrna. There has been some form of monitoring of the message, but as it has been deemed to be within acceptable limits, it enjoys an accepted role in the Syrian nation.

The role of prayer and the message of unity in Soufanieh, in this sense, speak to a longing found among most Syrian Christians. If you go out the door of the home of Our Lady of Soufanieh and into the Christian or mixed neighbourhoods of Bab Touma, Bab Sharqi, Jaramana, Dweila, Burze, Abu Roumane, al-Qassaʿ, and al-Qusour, you will find Christians of various social standing and denominations. The longing is for one common Christian people rather than a plethora of diverse denominations. This longing, however, is not one that is easily transformed into real life, as the churches of the Levant have traditionally had an arduous relationship. The followers of Our Lady of Soufanieh, therefore, feel the need to pray and work for unity even more. In their prayers, they hope more people will be moved to come closer to Mary and that Mary will make sure stability and peace will prevail in Syria. Prayers, as we shall see in the next chapter, are one of the core practices that the followers of Our Lady of Soufanieh hold on to in modelling the sainthood of Myrna and, by extension, their own lives.

# Chapter Two

# Repeated Prayers

Prayer is not an innocent social or psychological activity. It is always situated in specific and discrepant environments of social power, and it derives its meanings, implications, and consequences in relation to these configurations. Indeed, praying is one of the most implicating social historical practices because it is in and through prayer that the self comes into intimate and extended contact with the contradictions and constraints of the social world.

– Robert Orsi, *Thank You, St. Jude*

"The oil oozed from this image!" Umm Salwa confides in me as we stand in her bedroom. On the drawer in front of her mirror are placed several postcard-size images and devotional cards of Christian saints. Some are tucked into the frame of the mirror, while others are placed in frames and stands on the table. A devotional image of the famous Italian saint Pio of Pietrelcina, better known as Padre Pio, has found a place here, as well as an image of Saint George. The image Umm Salwa points to is none of these, though, but that of Our Lady of Soufanieh. The postcard-size devotional image depicts the Virgin Mary holding the Baby Jesus in her arms. "Look at it," Umm Salwa says, as she points out a greasy, crisp brownish trace on the image. One area clearly has a different texture to the rest of the image. "You can see how oil has oozed from it," Umm Salwa emphasizes. I look at the image again and admit that the surface appears to be greasy, and the colours too have waned. "I took it to Abuna Elias Zahlawi, and he approved it as being genuine," Umm Salwa continues, thereby explaining how credence was bestowed on the miraculous event in her home by one of the foremost authorities on miracles in Damascus, Abuna Elias Zahlawi. Zahlawi, one of the most ardent promoters of Our Lady of Soufanieh and supporters of Myrna, inspected the image and sanctioned that a particular grace had been bestowed upon it and, perforce, on the home that housed the icon.

I carry on looking at the cheap reproduction. The image is by now well known, even familiar, to me. It is the icon of Our Lady of Soufanieh. The size is that of a standard postcard, and it is similar to the ones I have been given and have at home. It is a cheap reproduction. Not just that, it is a cheap reproduction of another reproduction, in the sense that this devotional image has been reproduced from the cheap reproduced icon Nicolas bought in Sofia and which, on numerous occasions, has exuded oil. Umm Salwa smiles at me, arresting me in my thoughts, and I am directed back to the living room of the apartment of her daughter, Salwa, and Salwa's husband, Eimar, and their two children. Salwa is one of Myrna's closest trustees and has invited me over this afternoon. I am served coffee as Salwa repeats that I have been sent by God to write this book. Umm Salwa nods. Umm Salwa is almost a daily part of the afternoon prayer in Soufanieh. She walks the short distance of around 200 metres to reach Myrna and Nicolas's home. With her, she brings her prayer beads. She makes the sign of the cross as she enters and assumes a seat, most often on the left side of the inner courtyard. Here, she says her prayers as part of an unceasing chain of prayers, which has been running since the inception of this particular locality as a centre of devotion, as a place consecrated to Mary. Her personal prayers are added to the communal ones said in front of the icon of Our Lady of Soufanieh that first started to exude oil.

In this chapter, we shall examine how a modelling of sainthood and an exemplification of Christian character is nurtured by prayer in front of the image of Our Lady of Soufanieh. Prayer, as we have already seen in the previous chapter, is a fundamental part of the daily life and rhythm of Soufanieh. Our Lady of Soufanieh has instructed people to pray, and an unceasing chain of prayers has been said on this spot. Whereas prayer, in this sense, is one of the core practices at Soufanieh, and for Christians more generally, anthropology as a discipline has only recently started to give sustained attention to the social life of prayers, even if they are a significant way for Christians to relate to God (see Robbins 2004; Bandak 2017b; Luehrmann 2018; Bandak & Henkel 2021).[1] It may come as a surprise that only now have prayers begun to flourish as a theme in anthropological literature – even more surprising, since Marcel Mauss's significant work in the early twentieth century on prayer in his doctoral thesis, *On Prayer*. The thesis, however, was only privately printed in 1909 and went unpublished during Mauss's own lifetime (see Pickering 2003). Only recently was it published in English (Mauss 2003), and much time has thus passed before this particular work – and the world of prayer – has finally been considered anthropologically in its own right (Jenkins 2008). One of the key insights of Mauss's thesis is that prayers need to be understood as inherently social. Prayers are not solemnly effectuated by the individual as "the effusion of a soul" (Mauss 2003: 33). Rather, Mauss continues: "It is a fragment of religion. In it one can hear the echo of numberless phrases; it is a tiny piece of literature, it is the product of the accumulated efforts of men and women over generations" (33). The character of prayers explored by Mauss is social, and prayer expresses the collective concerns of the people praying. Prayer, furthermore, conjoins ritual and belief (22). Prayer is a way of acting in the world, but it is also a way of believing and of formulating this belief while praying; prayer is a form of Credo, Mauss contends.

However, Mauss (2003) also asserts that different qualitative types of prayer exist and that prayers can deteriorate and lose significance: "Very often, prayers which were once wholly spiritual become simple recitations without any kind of personal content. They sink to the level of manual rite. One simply moves the lips rather than moving the limbs. Constantly repeated prayers, prayers in a language we do not understand, formulae which have lost all meaning, whose words are so dated as to be incomprehensible, all these are striking examples of this type of regression" (26). Some prayers may even be reduced to "a mere material object" (26). The rosary, in Mauss's outline, is numbered among such prayers, potentially decaying to mere materiality. Indeed, the rosary can be seen in use in many places around the globe as something that could be framed as a merely mechanical prayer. In other words, the sheer repetitiveness of words works as a charm, or a prayer inculcated for use only to absolve the mind of work, or one that can be said without paying attention to the words uttered.

I shall argue in this chapter that the social character of prayer is captured well by Mauss, but sidelining the rosary as a merely mechanical prayer of repetition is less accurate. Repetition is surely at play in the prayers in Myrna's home, but I will argue that repetition need not be conceptualized as dulling and inhibiting for the devotee. Rather, repetition can be seen like a heartbeat: something that is alive and needs to be pulsating. The rosary, in this sense, is an exemplary practice sanctioned by the Catholic Church and the Virgin Mary. For the followers of Our Lady of Soufanieh, their prayers and petitions are a way of participating in divine labour, where they see the fruits of the prayers in miracles such as holy oil oozing from icons, healings, or changes in people's lives. Their prayers place them in a direct relationship with Our Lady of Soufanieh and allow the individual devotee to look beyond and meet the gaze of the Virgin Mary embodied in the icon of Our Lady of Soufanieh. The repetition of the prayers is not forced; rather, it is a free response that the followers see as a grace (see Pitt-Rivers 1991). Prayers are a response to this grace, and in this sense, repetition is to be understood as re-petition (see also Bandak & Coleman 2019). This re-petition is seen as modelling the individual in the image of the saint and, in this way, exemplifying the saintly character of the devout. Or better still, prayer is part of an exchange between the individual and Our Lady of Soufanieh, an exchange that entails words, emotions, and the ability to see and listen for her response. The response, in an exemplary manner, is seen in the form of oil emanating from the icon of Our Lady of Soufanieh in the home of Myrna and Nicolas or from copies of the icon in the homes of her devout followers such as Umm Salwa.

**Praying to Our Lady of Soufanieh: The Spirit of Prayer**

Umm Salwa's hands are joined on her rosary as she sits in the couch waiting for Pierre to start the afternoon prayer. She knows this place intimately, as she has come here on a frequent basis to pray for the last twenty-seven years. Pierre, George, and Abu Rami arrive together from Jaramana. The three of them usually accompany each other, taking the minibus to Bab Touma and walking to Soufanieh from there. They greet Umm Salwa and take their seats. Myrna's father adjusts the fan and the lights. More people arrive and find a place on one of the plastic stools arranged in front of the icon. Pierre starts by saying the prayer, and all follow suit with the Apostle's Creed, holding the crucifix of their rosaries in their hands. The pattern follows the same standard practice as all days: the Apostle's Creed, one Our Father, three Hail Marys, one Glory to God, the reading of the first mystery, one Our Father, and a decade of Hail Marys with joint responses. Five mysteries are read, and, accordingly, five decades of Hail Marys are said. The standard rosary is also named a chaplet. Each of the regular visitors sits with their personal rosary beads in their hands following the prayer. A crucifix, a medallion, and fifty-nine beads on a string – that is the standard rosary, even if forms and materials vary. The beads are counted as they slowly sift through the fingers following each repetition. Each bead is touched and kept between the fingers as the lips of Salwa, George, Pierre, Abu Rami, and the others present either silently accompany the person leading the prayer in front of the icon of Our Lady of Soufanieh or audibly respond in joint chorus. The numerous repetitions of prayers may indeed, to the outsider, appear cumbersome. Why such repetitiveness? Why not open one's mouth and freely say what is in one's mind and heart?

To the devout followers of Our Lady of Soufanieh, who come here as often as possible, there is a reason for repeating their prayers. However, the spiritual work of offering repeated prayers relates to the spirit of prayer, ar-rūḥ aṣ-ṣallā, as George says one day when I follow him while he seeks a new job in Jaramana on the outskirts of greater Damascus. The spirit of prayer is important because it shows that prayers not only surface as a result of moving lips and moving limbs but also of moved hearts and souls. Indeed, a serious message is voiced in the Bible regarding the issue of lips as opposed to heart. In the gospel according to Matthew (15:7–9), Jesus himself, with reference to Isaiah (29:13), famously castigated the Pharisees for only pretending to worship God: "You hypocrites! Isaiah was right when he prophesied about you: 'These People honour me with their lips, but their hearts are far from me. They worship me in vain; their teachings are but rules taught by men.'" These words are serious, and they express a more general concern that is prevalent among the followers of Our Lady of Soufanieh: prayer should not merely stem from the movement of the lips; it should be directed by the sincerely moved heart. When the heart is sincerely moved, the response ought to be repeated offering of prayers. To understand what we could designate as the pulsation of the heart in this Catholic context, one needs to understand the mystery of the rosary.

### Exemplary Prayer: Object of Devotion, Medium of Presence

The rosary has long been a part of Christian devotion in the Middle East. In various Catholic churches, the rosary is said before mass with five decades of Hail Marys. Most Christian churches have scouts, and here the rosary is often instructed in the Catholic churches and used as part of the activities. In several of the Greek Catholic churches, groups are organized that are affiliated to the Legion of Mary, groups that focus on the spiritual life of the youth and entail participation in the life of the church and parish. In these groups, the rosary is also said as the start of the weekly program. One of the famous Syrian Catholic churches in Damascus is named after Our Lady of Fatima, one of the most well-known modern apparition sites located in Portugal, where the rosary was underscored as a particular devotion for the followers to use in their individual and communal life. In Palestine, Jordan, Syria, and a wide range of Arab countries, the Roman Catholic order of the Congregation of Rosary Sisters exists, which has the mission of propagating the rosary (Jansen 2009).[2]

In her recent work, Willy Jansen (2009) explored how the mission of the Rosary Sisters was initiated in Palestine and later continued in

Jordan by Sister Marie Alphonsine. The rosary, in this context, is not just a random object among the plethora of devotional objects in the Catholic Church but rather has developed to become an exemplary object that allows for participation on different levels. The rosary can function as a devotional item, a marker of identity in the form of pious jewellery and apparel, but also as a medium of presence (Mitchell 2009: 212, 238). The rosary is said in church before mass; it is said in people's homes and individual lives. The rosary, in this sense, is an exemplary prayer, as it is both a material item and a devotion; it is portable, and it aids the prayer of the individual and gives something tangible to hold on to in times of adversity and, most pointedly, at the hour of death. As the rosary is instructed in many official settings, it is a prayer that is seen to capture belief in an exemplary manner; it carries multiple meanings but somehow stands in for the devout as well as for the less devout as a primary way of accessing and pleading with the divine. As the rosary is an item often used in the home and in the family, it mediates different kinds of relationships and emotions in a very material and tangible form.

From a broader view, the inception of the rosary has had apparition legend attached to it: Saint Dominic, legend claims, was instructed by the Virgin Mary in an apparition to start using the rosary (Winston-Allen 1997: 72; Mitchell 2009: 24). In Marian devotion, prayer and also the rosary specifically have been and continue to be mentioned in different currents of visionaries, both in the late medieval period and later in Lourdes and La Salette, from Fatima and Ezkioga and onwards to Medjugorje and Oliveto Citra, as an exemplary way of relating to God (Christian 1981: 142–4, 215; 1996: 20, 267; Turner & Turner 1978: 216; Apolito 1998[1992]: 35; 2005[2001]; Morgan 2009: 50; Scheer 2013). In various apparitions, Mary holds a rosary in her hands and blesses, even urges, people to pray more or instructs them as to how to say the prayer and adds new devotions. The rosary, in this sense, is not tied to the mechanical repetition of prayers alone but to a sustained meditation on exemplary scenes from the life of Christ and the Virgin Mary. For the followers of Our Lady of Soufanieh, as we shall see, it is through the combination of continuous prayers and sustained meditation that a modelling of sainthood is hoped to take place.

### The Story of the Rosary: Devotion, Mysteries, and Visibilities

The history of the rosary has only relatively recently been given more serious scholarly attention (see Winston-Allen 1997; Wills 2005; Mitchell 2009). In the rosary, the Hail Mary prayer is central in its repetitive structuring of devotion for the individual and the collective.

As an iterable practice, the rosary is a prototypical prayer, exemplary of the wider Catholic Church. Historically, the rosary was developed in the early medieval period in Europe under the influence of the *devotio moderna* movement, as well as through Observant reform piety (Winston-Allen 1997: 11, 73) and, later, in the spiritual exercises of Ignatius of Loyola, completed around 1541 (Mitchell 2009: 19, 40). Since the fifteenth century, the rosary has been sanctioned by papal decree as a prayer of the church, and in modern times, various popes have made homilies on the value of the rosary. It could therefore lead to an analysis of the rosary as a technique of the self, as proposed by Michel Foucault (1988).

While such a strategy would render part of the disciplining of the individual through mental and spiritual exercises conceivable, it is nonetheless important to also situate the rosary in another frame, namely one of a community of others.[3] The rosary is more than the prayers of Hail Mary and Our Lord's Prayer, as we have already seen practised in Soufanieh and beyond. The rosary, as pointed out by Anne Winston-Allen (1997) in her seminal *Stories of the Rose*, is characterized by "the combination of oral repetition with serial mental meditations" (3). This devotion has been tied to beads on a string in a relatively persistent form, as Nathan D. Mitchell (2009) writes in *The Mystery of the Rosary*: "The rosary, a ritually repeated sequence of prayers accompanied by meditations on episodes in the lives of Christ and Mary, has varied little in form (round beads strung on cord or wire), structure, or content" (1). Whereas the Hail Mary, Our Father, the Creed, and the Gloria are part of the prayer, and place emphasis on the specific words and reality of the prayer, the series of mental meditations on the life of Christ and the Virgin Mary place emphasis on the image of saintly life.

The joining of the life of Christ meditations with the Hail Mary prayer happened during the late medieval period and was a way of teaching the laity the example of Christ and Christian virtues more generally (Winston-Allen 1997: 16, 27; Mitchell 2009: 30). Christ was the ultimate model, and by reflecting on his life while praying, the individual, it was believed, would be more fully able to conform to the model. Similarly, the Virgin Mary has historically been identified as the model of the Catholic Church and the first bride of Christ, and concomitantly, the model for the individual believer to conform to. Although this historical view points to a classic analogy between Christ and Adam, one in which Christ alleviates the sin of Adam, Winston-Allen suggests a critical double analogy, in that Mary can also be seen as a second Eve: "Just as the name 'Eva' reversed spells the word 'Ave,' so was Eve's sin reversed by Mary, the new Eve" (1997: 92; see also Turner & Turner

1978: 210). In a Catholic landscape, the role of Mary is accordingly pivotal as co-redemptrix but also in her capacity to act as the exemplary mother, the person to relate to *per se* and to beseech for guidance and intercession (Orsi 1985: 164, 172ff.; 2005: 50; Napolitano 2009).

As George, Abu Rami, Umm Salwa, and the others continue letting their prayer beads sift through their fingers for each Hail Mary during the afternoon prayer, they meditate on each of the five mysteries for the specific day or season. The five mysteries belong to one of three sets: the joyful mysteries, the sorrowful mysteries, and the glorious mysteries. Each set of mysteries consists of five exemplary scenes in the life of Jesus or Mary. The joyful mysteries are the Annunciation, the Visitation, the Nativity, the Presentation of Jesus in the Temple, and the Lost Child Jesus found in the Temple. The sorrowful mysteries are the Agony in the Garden, the Scourging at the Pillar, the Crowning with Thorns, the Carrying of the Cross, and the Crucifixion and Death of Jesus. And lastly, the glorious mysteries are the Resurrection, the Ascension, the Descent of the Holy Spirit on the Apostles, the Assumption of the Virgin Mary to Heaven, and the Coronation of the Virgin Mary.[4] As can be seen, the latter set of mysteries contains scenes from scripture but goes beyond the Bible with the scenes of the Virgin Mary's Assumption and Coronation, respectively. The scenes of the life of the Virgin Mary do not stem from scripture but rather from tradition. As the last set of mysteries has been sanctioned by the papal institution, however, they are used on a par with the joyful and sorrowful mysteries. Tradition and the rulings of the Catholic Church have, in this regard, been instrumental in elevating the scenes from the life of Mary so that they are reflected upon on a par with those from the life of Christ.

The three sets of mysteries present exemplary scenes to be reflected upon. They give the devotee a blueprint for pious behaviour and instill patterns for devotional life. Repetition is understood as a reflective and pious act, whereby the scenes from the life of Christ and the Virgin Mary place the individual in a divinely sculpted landscape. The regular visitors are reminded on a daily basis of the exemplary lives of Jesus and Mary, and of their powers of intercession. Abu Rami explains to me, one day when we are talking about the rosary, that he has learned the prayers all by heart and says them both at home and here in Soufanieh. This ritual is important for him, as he is praying to find solace, having fled Baghdad with his family in the aftermath of the destabilization of Iraq following the events of 2003. In his search for a new job, George likewise feels the need to place his situation in the hands of Mary and does so in his daily prayers. Saying the rosary here in Soufanieh and at home helps redirect life, but it also places the responsibility on Our Lady of Soufanieh to find a solution for Abu Rami and his family, and for George. The repetition of the prayers therefore functions as a re-petition, a constant reminder to Mary of the intensity of the devotion of the individual, but it also instills an on-going meditation on spiritual life as embodied in the life of Mary and Christ in prototypical scenes, which is seen as modelling the character of the individual.

### Prayer and Confession: Supplications, Offerings, and Praise

As emphasized by Mauss, prayer is also a form of Credo (2003: 33). The prayers and petitions said in front of the icon of Our Lady of Sou-fanieh also formulate a specific confession of faith. When Myrna, in a symbolic gesture, started saying the Creed after the fifth and final ap-parition, she placed the message in the sanctioned line of the Catholic Church. The messages continue the tradition of the church and need to be remembered, repeated, and reflected upon. The prayers in Soufa-nieh both underscore a specific reality outside the individual and align the individual with this reality and aim to affect it. The daily prayers of the rosary lead to the more specific prayers particular to Soufanieh. Each afternoon, when the first half hour of the rosary is said, readings from scripture as well as messages received by Myrna are recited from handouts taken from the drawer in the altar. Abu Rami usually fetches the handouts during the fifth decade of Hail Marys. By reading and reciting these words, the individual prayers are placed firmly in the community of believers and inserted into the tradition of the Catholic Church, the Melkite Greek Catholic Church. The daily readings from scripture are accompanied by messages given by Jesus and the Virgin Mary at this particular spot. Placing the messages received by Myrna in the same series as tradition grafts an addition to that tradition. The words are recited with the same authoritative force as the words from scripture itself.

Salwa arrives after the first half hour for the second part of the prayer. She leads the singing of the hymns of praise to Our Lady of Soufanieh. Prayers and songs of worship flow from the devotees and back towards the icon of Our Lady of Soufanieh. At the very end, Pierre takes the icon from its stand on the altar and holds it in his hands, his arms stretched out for people to circumambulate in order to kiss and touch the icon. Abu Rami, George, Umm Salwa, Salwa, Myrna's father, and the other people present walk to the icon singing the hymn of Our Lady of Sou-fanieh. Each one, in his or her own way, kisses the icon, touches it, and bows, before walking to the side.

The repetition of the prayers said in turns in front of the icon of Our Lady of Soufanieh, which on numerous occasions has oozed oil, is one way in which the past apparitions are rendered as public commemoration in the same mould as scripture itself. The prayer of the church is said in the home, now turned shrine, in front of the very icon God chose to make into a sign and hence to gesture to the people coming here that God is active and capable of moving hearts. But the very moving of hearts is also a preoccupation central to the core of members around Myrna. Congregants, priests, Myrna's family, and Myrna herself all emphasize the urgent need for a change of heart (*taghyīr al-qulūb*). This transformation is accomplished by emphasizing the need for a Christian life centred on servitude, prayer, devotion, the rosary, the Eucharist, and exemplification of the Christian character in word and deed. Life in general is rendered confessional. And, in this rendering of the life of the individual as confessional, the individual can cross from "I" to "we." The ideal of unity emphasized in the messages of Our Lady of Soufanieh also pertains to the domain of prayer. The daily prayers are said together. This communal prayer does not preclude personal and individual prayer; on the contrary, personal and communal prayers complement each other and allow the followers of Our Lady of Soufanieh to participate intensively in the life of devotion.

Umm Salwa, George, Abu Rami, Pierre, and the others present for the prayer leave the home of Myrna and Nicolas soon after the prayer. When asked why, each one of them responded in their own words that it was to respect the peace of the home. They know Myrna is beseeched by many people, and they do not want to heap further pressure on her. They bring their rosaries and the sense of having been recharged with them. As Abu Rami and George explain, this place must be one of the holiest places in Damascus, so should they not count themselves among the blessed to be able to pray here daily?

## Prayer and Creed: Sacramental Sensibility, Imagination, and Visualization

The addition of the Creed to the rosary in effect means that the prayer was also dogmatically in line with the official teachings of the Catholic Church. The Creed, however, does not stand on the outside of the prayer as a mere frame; rather, it participates in the blend of liturgical and devotional aspects in the rosary as a devotion that expresses doctrine as well (Mitchell 2009: 29, 86). Prayer, as Mauss (2003) reminded us, is closely related to creed. In praying, a Credo is also formulated, particularly when the prayers are sanctioned by the Catholic Church. In the rosary, the Credo takes a particular form as a narrative and image, in which the individual can be involved as a participant. Mitchell (2009) formulates this insight as follows:

> The fifteen mysteries of the rosary were, after all, a *compendium fidei* (summary of faith), a narratively expanded Credo that invited contemplative review of the most fundamental tenets of Catholic belief. In such contemplation, however, *the believer him- or herself becomes a direct participant, an active agent in the mystery being meditated.* (72; emphasis in the original)

In such a use of the rosary, the prayer has the potential to become something more than mere words and oral repetitions; it can point beyond reflection to participation in the mysteries of faith itself. The rosary, in this sense, is a medium of presence and not just a devotion. The drama of human history is intensified as participation presents Mary, Christ, and the saints as real figures with whom one interacts in prayer and life, with whom identification is possible, and for whom things are possible that otherwise would not be. Here, the individual conversation with the Virgin Mary, Christ, and the saints places personal needs at the centre and thus develops sustained relationships in which the holy figures interact and respond to personal needs.

The rosary needs to be understood in a ritual context in which the performance is key; by saying the prayer, the individual participates in a re-enactment of divine reality in the life of Christ and Mary. There is, however, more than ritual to the prayer; it is also part of the everyday routines in the daily life of the individual, and it is here that a sense of self and other is configured. In medieval practice, icons and devotional images formed a sequential narrative, aiding the meditations in prayer (Winston-Allen 1997: 38). In Europe, there was a more general shift in ritual and images as a particular visual culture existed, one in which a specific religious sensibility was fashioned by holy imagery, narratives, and the scenes of the life of Christ tied to the rosary, which all forged a connection between the rosary and visualization (Mitchell 2009: 20, 40, 78). The numbers of prayers are hence placed in a sequence whereby powerful scenes from the life of Christ guide the praying person and community.

The mechanics of prayer, in Joel Robbins's formulation (2004: 253–88), is here not to be understood as mechanistic, as a quantifiable expiation of sin by repeated petitions. It is instead participation in redemptive work that is to be inculcated through prayer in the pious formulation (see also Winston-Allen 1997: 79). In the repeated prayers of Hail Mary, Mary is not simply understood as being called upon when saying the prayers, as pointed out by Mitchell (2009): "Mary is not present to those who pray the rosary merely as historical memory, but as immediate reality" (28). This point is also emphasized by Catholic thinker and professor of social science Andrew Greeley (2000), who, in his work on the Catholic imagination, underscores a general sacramental sensibility as being inculcated from an early age among Catholics, both practising and non-practising. Greeley argues that the Catholic imagination is founded on analogy and metaphor. It is characterized by a general idea of divine presence lurking everywhere in creation (see also Mitchell & Mitchell 2008; Christian 2012). Greeley (2000) contrasts this imagination with a dialectical imagination found among Protestants. The dialectical imagination focuses on absence, the analogical imagination of presence.

The two kinds of imagination are formed in separate traditions with different emphases regarding the role of saints and divine presence. This difference in nurtured awareness is also manifest regarding prayer. Robert Orsi (2005) writes about the social experience of praying the rosary together: "Such imagery was there to assist people in imagining their way into the narrative of salvation history, aiding the inner eye to reconstruct the landscape of the sacred world" (68). Orsi captures this concept well a little later, when he writes:

> The murmuring of the repetitive prayers, the presence of others praying alongside oneself, and the feel of the beads across one's fingers rendered the interior processes of the imagination corporal and moved Mary into the body. So Mary became everyone's contemporary. (68)

The experiences of ordinary people are reflected in Mary's life, as her life course – her emotional states standing in front of her crucified son at Calvary and at his resurrection – can be followed in the mysteries. In other words, an intimate relationship can be fashioned in the prayerful relation between Mary and the devout, one in which mysteries and the repeated prayers allow for the development of sustained affection. Mary is formed in the interplay of devotional art, kitsch, prayer cards, rosaries, and mundane experiences that are all part of the everyday life of Catholics. Mary is searched for, and she is found and likened to the inner image the devotee holds, and evaluated on that basis. In imagery and paintings, Mary comes to be known by particular traits, and this image is influential for the devotees in their individual and collective imaginings and prayerful lives (Morgan 1998, 2012; Mitchell 2009: 69, 79). The individual can, through his or her empathy with Christ and Mary, vicariously participate in their suffering and victory, but in addition, the saints can be petitioned for benevolence out of their sympathy for the individual devotee.

## Instructed to Pray: Prayers to Our Lady of Soufanieh

To participate in saying the rosary and, more generically, to pray on the spot where Mary and Jesus so forcefully appeared is to follow their words and prescriptions. Prayer is a recurrent theme in the messages of both the Virgin Mary and Jesus. In several of her messages to Myrna, the Virgin Mary has underscored prayer:

> 24 March 1983: I tell you: "Pray, pray, and pray again!" How beautiful are My Children when they kneel down, imploring.
> 7 September 1984: Live your life, but let not life prevent you from continuing to pray.
> 14 August 1985: Your prayer is My feast. Your faith is My feast. The unity of your hearts is My feast.

Likewise Jesus, in his messages to Myrna, has emphasized the importance of prayer for her and the followers.

> 26 November 1986: Pray for the sinners, because for each word of prayer, I shall spill a drop of blood on one of the sinners.
> 28 May 1987: Love one another and pray with faith.
> 22 July 1987: Pray, pray, and pray again!

Beyond these general words pointing to the centrality of prayer, the Virgin Mary and Jesus have instructed specific prayers to be "engraved" on the minds of the followers. As we saw in the previous chapter, the prayer used for concluding the afternoon prayers, but also for concluding the Tuesday evening novena and the Saturday mass, was given on instruction. Or to be more accurate, the instruction was clear on the three occasions when the messages were given to Myrna that the following words were to be said as a prayer pleasing to God. On 21 February 1983, the Virgin Mary instructed:

> I would like to request something from you, a word that you will engrave in your memory that you shall always repeat.

Thereupon, she gave the prayer used as the second part of the concluding daily prayer:

> God saves me, Jesus enlightens me, the Holy Spirit is my life, thus I fear nothing.

On two different occasions, Jesus instructed the two other parts of the prayer that are used. On 31 May 1984, Jesus said:

Pray for God's will to be done in you, and say: "Beloved Jesus, grant that I rest in You above all things, above all creatures, above Your Angels, above all praise, above all rejoicing and exultation, above all glory and honour, above all heavenly hosts, for You are the Most High, You alone are the Almighty and Good above all things. May You come to me and relieve me, and release me from my chains, and grant me freedom, because without You my joy is not complete, without You my table is empty."

And on 22 July 1987, Jesus said:

And if you pray, say: "O Father, through the merits of Your beloved Son's wounds, save us."

The concluding prayer of the daily prayers, the Tuesday evening novenas, and the Saturday masses is also given on instruction and hence is seen as a divinely sanctioned prayer in line with the Lord's Prayer that Jesus similarly taught to his disciples. The prayer lifts the individual and inserts him or her into the story of this specific place and into the greater divine history. Abu George, Umm Salwa, George, Pierre, Myrna's father, Salwa, and the others present stand tall and say the prayer with much emphasis:

Beloved Jesus, grant that I rest in You above all things, above all creatures, above Your Angels, above all praise, above all rejoicing and exultation, above all glory and honour, above all heavenly hosts, for You are the Most High, You alone are the Almighty and Good above all things. May You come to me and relieve me, and release me from my chains, and grant me freedom, because without You my joy is not complete, without You my table is empty.

God saves me, Jesus enlightens me, the Holy Spirit is my life, thus I fear nothing.
O Father, through the merits of Your beloved Son's wounds, save us.
O Father, through the merits of Your beloved Son's wounds, save us.
O Father, through the merits of Your beloved Son's wounds, save us.

The words are said with focus and intention, since to pray here is to add oneself to the living chain of prayers. The prayers therefore mediate both individual concerns and the wider communal concerns of the extended family of Our Lady of Soufanieh.

## Pray versus Play: Right Attitude and Prayer

That prayer holds a general purchase was evident in my talks with people both in and outside the circles of Soufanieh. One evening, I had a long talk on Soufanieh, miracles, and prayer with Nabil, a young man in his early thirties. When we touched upon the topic of prayer, he gave a lengthy exemplification of good and bad forms of prayer. "When you pray Our Lord's Prayer, it has to be with reflection, like this":

*Abānā alladhī fī-s-samāwāt* [Our Father in Heaven] ...
*Liyataqaddas ismuka* [Hallowed be your name] ...
*Liya'ti malakūtuka* [Your kingdom come] ...
*Litakun mashī'atuka kamā fī-s-samā'i kadhālik 'alā-l-'arḍ* [Your will be done on earth as it is in heaven] ...
*U'ṭīnā khubzanā kafāfa yawminā* [Give us today our daily bread] ...
*Ughfir lanā khaṭāyānā kamā naḥnu nughfir liman adha ilaynā* [Forgive us our debts, as we also have forgiven our debtors] ...
*Wa la tudkhilnā fī-t-tajārib lākin najjinā min al-sharrīr* [And lead us not into temptation, but deliver us from evil] ...
*Āmīn* [Amen]!

Nabil pauses between each part of the prayer, meditatively thinking on the meaning of the words. As he concludes the prayer, Nabil points out parts of it, those he finds of particular importance: "*Wa la tudkhilnā fiil-tajārib lakin najjinā min al-sharrīr.* This is very important! Who is it that frees us from evil? It's Jesus!" Nabil halts to emphasize the power of Jesus. "It doesn't make sense if you just pray fast with your thoughts in another place," Nabil says. He goes on to show what he means by speed praying one Our Father:

*Abānāalladhīfī-s-samāwātliyataqaddasismukaliya'timalakūtukalitakunmashī'atuka kamāfi-s-samā'ikadhālik'alā-l-'arḍ ... u'ṭīnākhubzanākafāfayawmināwaughfirlanā khaṭāyānākamānaḥnunughfirlimanadhailaynā ... walatudkhilnāfī-t-tajāriblākin- najjināminal-sharrīr. Āmīn!*

Nabil continues straight away with a Hail Mary:

*Al-salāmu 'alaykiyaMaryamyamumtali 'ani 'matanmubārakatunantifī-n-nisā'wa mubārakatunthamratbaṭnikiYesū 'al-Mesīḥ ... YaqadīsatuMaryamya wālidatu-llāhṣal- lili 'ajilnānaḥnual-khaṭa'al'ānwafī-sā'atmawtinā. Āmīn!*

After this impressive display of speed, Nabil has to catch his breath. He smiles, knowing that he has amused me.

It is not merely a funny topic, however; it is serious. "There are many who just say the prayer, but they do not think about what they are actually saying," Nabil says, deploring such an attitude to prayer. Prayer must not be mere words. The words must be said with reflection, intention, and focus. I ask Nabil about his prayer beads, as they are not the standard rosary. "This is an Islamic one. I don't use this for prayer [ṣallā]; this is only for entertainment [taslyya, sallā]!" Nabil, fond of his clever play on words and his distinction between what goes for prayer and what goes for leisure, takes an ordinary rosary from his shelf and points to it. "This is my rosary! This is for prayer, not for entertainment, so I don't walk around with it in my pocket just to play with it in my fingers. If it is only for entertainment, I use this," Nabil says and points to the Islamic prayer beads. Even though the prayer beads have the same function in terms of keeping track of prayers, they function in two different registers for Nabil: one is spiritual, the other relaxation and play. For Nabil, Muslims may pray too, but their prayers are not seen to be efficacious and genuine, as Christian prayer is.[5] The implication is that you do not play with the rosary; you pray with it. However, it is something more than a mere instrument of prayer: it is itself a devotion, something to be treated with respect and a reverential attitude. For Nabil, whom we shall meet again in chapter five, the rosary is not to be used on par with any other material item. This particular item is something more; it is both an object of devotion and a medium of presence.

### Dangers of the Heart and Mouth: Acting as Opposed to Surrendering

In Soufanieh, it is an important concern to ground prayer and the spirit of prayer in the life of individuals. Many will explain how, before knowing of Soufanieh, they only knew the Our Father and the Hail Mary. They had to be taught prayer. In interviews and talks with people such as Hani, Rima, Fadi, and Rafik, it was underscored how prayer as a way of life was learned. Furthermore, even if the spirit of prayer has been learned, your prayer could, yet again, succumb to the level of the lips. The right state of mind must concomitantly be strived for while praying. One of the key dangers, however, is that prayer and the life of the faithful may be merely pretence.

Webb Keane (2007) aptly formulated this insight: "The nature of iterability means one can never be sure; the most earnest deeds and protestations of faith are in themselves but acting, mere words" (288).

This issue, however, is not just a theoretical one but one with practical ramifications. As invariably emphasized by the different priests giving sermons and novenas in the home of Myrna, God knows the heart, whereas fellow man does not. The dangers of acting (*tamthīl*) as if you were a believer or only saying the words of prayer, confession, and creed with no intention (*niyya*) or focus (*tarkīz*) is countered by priests such as Abuna Elias Saloun, Abuna Boulos Fadel, and Abuna Elias Zahlawi, respectively. Myrna also, on occasion, addresses the devotees, admonishing a lack of honesty. The fear, Myrna underlines, is not in regard to Jesus – he is held to be unchanging – but in regard to the believers and the temptation of riches and earthly desires. The most salient voices giving this warning have been Our Lady of Soufanieh and Jesus Christ in their messages to Myrna. In the fourth apparition on 21 February 1983, the Virgin Mary said: "He who pretends to be pure and loving before people is impure before God." Likewise, Jesus, in his message of 14 August 1988, said these words: "It is easier for me to accept that an infidel believe in my name than that those who pretend to have faith and love swear by my name." Pretence is a danger to be countered.

One Tuesday evening, during the joint rendering of the Hail Marys at the beginning of the evening's program, everybody appears to pray out of rhythm. Rita, one of Myrna's closest trustees, brings the prayer of the rosary to an immediate stop and quickly addresses the problem by vehemently criticizing the lack of joint spirit in saying the prayer aloud. "You have to pray with one spirit!" Rita exclaims. The prayer is started over again, and this time the pace is markedly slower, as each sentence is allowed to ring out before the next follows. The spirit of prayer and devotion in the confession is, in this sense, paramount in connecting heart and mouth, and rushing through it mindlessly is not to be condoned. Instead of acting, surrendering (*istislām*) is set up as the behaviour to strive for. Surrendering or giving up oneself is the heartbeat of life as a confession. This heartbeat is aided by the daily rhythms of devotion instilled by the rosary. The daily rhythms ground individual confession in the confession of the community and tradition, and then in the specific location now sanctified by the presence of Our Lady of Soufanieh. The rosary here helps to engrain the devotion in the individual and the community. This concept is what Keane (2007) likewise asserts: the words and creeds may turn from mere words to something more. He formulates it this way: "But there is another side to the story. Citation can become use. Creeds uttered by rote can be taken to heart" (288). The words may turn into life, and the lips may connect to the heart.

## Crossing the Visible: Answers to Prayers

The followers of Our Lady of Soufanieh all have their own reproduced icon in various shapes and sizes. Salwa wears the image of Our Lady of Soufanieh in her necklace and at home has different reproductions of the icon. Umm Salwa, her mother, has her reproduction in her bedroom, the one she showed me marked by the miracle of holy oil. Similarly, all the followers I met had their image of Our Lady of Soufanieh. Personal prayers at home were often tied to the relationship with the image of Our Lady of Soufanieh, as people prayed in front of their icon. "I talk to her every day!" was the formulation Tony, one of my interlocutors, used as he showed me his icons and prayer cards stored on a table next to a mirror. The spiritual conversation and prayerful relation, in this sense, is tied to the image of Our Lady of Soufanieh, and a particular grace is manifest in the holy oil that oozes from her image. To understand this relationship, it is critical to understand the logic of the icon and its reproducibility.

Reproduction, in different senses of the word, is a highly intriguing factor in understanding the workings of the miraculous in the case of Myrna Nazzour and her followers. Reproduction points to the fact that the cheap reproduction from Sofia has been reproduced and distributed free of charge to all who come to Myrna's home. In this sense, what we have is a reproduction of a reproduction of an icon. However, it is precisely many of these reproductions of the icon that have been reported to shed oil, particularly in the neighbourhood of Soufanieh but also in Lebanon, the United States, and different places in Europe. We are therefore taken towards another conceptualization of what it is that is being reproduced. Icons and statues that move, exude liquids, emit a celestial odour, or talk are a central figure in some forms of Catholic and Orthodox Christianity (Carroll 1992; Christian 2012: 48).[6] The little image of Our Lady of Soufanieh handed out for free to all who come to Soufanieh breaks with any modern logic of art as it fractures the distinction between copy and original. What is copy and what is original in such a chain of reproductions? And we likewise find prayer and the relationship between holy figures and devotee operating in two forms of logic, the logic of recognition and the logic of imitation, simulation, and mimesis.

In this regard, it is particularly helpful to explore the notion of visual piety introduced by David Morgan. Visual piety, according to Morgan, is "the visual formation and practice of religious belief" (1998: 1). A visual piety implies that the popular and classic images and icons of the Virgin Mary, Christ, and the saints are seen as a fundamental part of Christian belief and exchange. The images guide understandings of scripture; they open the eyes of the devotee and provide instruction on what to see and look for. In prayer, the images of the Virgin Mary, Christ, and the saints are operative and guided by the visual ideas disseminated in a broader culture. The images in popular culture respond in a personal manner to the needs of the devotee and make the exchange central, which is why no passivity or disinterest is found in the exchange between individual and image (Morgan 1998: 22, 31; see also Orsi 2005: 49). Morgan asserts that this visual piety in Christian history has been tied to a particular visual culture. According to Morgan, images have remained central to devotion:

> People find it difficult, even impossible, to worship comfortably without them. This persistence is, rather, an index of visual piety. The image creates a devotional space, a place to encounter or interact with the sacred. Many say that the picture corresponds to the mental image of Jesus that is present in prayer. Both homes and worship spaces are transformed by the images displayed therein. Images are the means by which a space becomes familiar and personal. (1998: 57)

The home is made into a particular home when icons and devotional images are placed among people's belongings, photos, and artefacts. Morgan continues: "Such images have the power to make a place home by installing there a sacred presence, an icon that listens to believers and watches over them" (57). The sympathetic eyes and ears of the icon allow for a devotional atmosphere in which what happens never falls out of the care and concern of the saint, Jesus, or Mary. The devotee is placed in front of a visual countenance, an interface, whereby the icon is not merely a representation but a presentation. In this sense, looking becomes a devotional activity (see Morgan 1998, 2012; Orsi 2005: 58; Mitchell 2009: 214). Looking entails the knowledge of being seen and of oneself seeing the reality of God.

### Icon and Prayer: Repetition versus Mimesis

The idea that the act of looking can be rendered a devotional activity can also be seen in the work of French Catholic theologian and phenomenologist Jean-Luc Marion. In his work, Marion extends a rather vivid, theoretical approach to questions on perspective (1991[1982], 2001[1997], 2004[1996], 2008[2005]). He argues that vision always exerts a paradox, in the sense that what is visible or revealed rests on a background invisible to the perceiver. Or rather, invisibility is found within visibility. Marion uses the icon as exemplary in this regard, since it does not exert perspective but, in a more radical way, offers the possibility of infinitude to break open the screen of materiality. The icon, in this way, looks back, and through the looking back, two gazes are enabled to meet (see also Luehrmann 2010; Hanganu 2010: 45–8). Marion formulates it thus:

> At the center of the icon, and ascribed to a saint, the Virgin, or Christ, this gaze looks at the one who, in prayer, raises his gaze toward the icon: the painted gaze invisibly responds to the invisible gaze of the one in prayer, and transfigures its own visibility by including it in the commerce of two invisible gazes. (2004[1996]: 20)

In this way, Marion argues that the stigmata of the unseen are opened as traces of the invisible:

> The icon thus finds its logic and its unique legitimacy only in repetition – this time between the face of the face of the resurrected Christ ("colors, mosaics, and other suitable materials") and an irreducible approximation ... – of the paradox of recognition without spectacle which sees the visible tool of torture as the invisible holiness of a Living One, who nevertheless died there. Such a repetition breaks here with every imitation, since the one moves from the visible to the visible by semblance, whereas the other moves from the visible to the invisible by recognition. (2004[1996]: 74)

Marion hence poses the possibility of breaking away from a model of simple imitation to one of recognition. Imitation is here understood as a direct quest for answers and proof moved by visibility, whereas recognition is a process that entails a surrender or giving oneself over to the gaze of the saint depicted and is, in this sense, moved by invisibility. According to Marion, this transformation can only happen in prayer. Marion formulates this insight poignantly:

> So the icon can be contemplated with honor only by a gaze that venerates it as the stigmata of the invisible. Only the one who prays can thus climb from the visible to the invisible (according to the logic of type), whereas the spectator can only compare the visible to the visible (according to the logic of the mimetic). To the saints these things are holy: only the one who prays crosses the icon, because he alone knows the function of type. (2004[1996]: 75)

The icon must lead to confession, and the holiness of the icon can only consist in giving back the prototype to Christ; only by receding to the margins of perspective can holiness be aimed at. An icon in the most radical understanding does not represent, but present: it gives.

## Duplication and Reproduction Reconsidered

Technologies of reproduction are fundamental to the spreading of the story, including the reproduction of the icon of Our Lady of Soufanieh. The duplication and subsequent shedding of oil attest to another way of thinking about the icon, other than that of the original and the copy or of aura, in line with Walter Benjamin (1999[1968]) in his famous piece "The Work of Art in the Age of Mechanical Reproduction." To Benjamin, the duplication or possibility of multiplication of artworks by modern technique threatens the aura of the artwork. Singularity is threatened by a multiplication and hence destruction of uniqueness. This logic is a very modern one, however, and one that is interesting to read through the thinking of icons. The destruction of uniqueness is perhaps only possible insofar as thinking to some extent still rests on the Platonic distinction between copy and original (see Morgan 2009: 60; 2010, 2012). To Benjamin (1999[1968]), the work of art loses something in the mechanical reproduction, which rests on a commodification of what had otherwise been singular (see Kopytoff 1986). Beyond being reproduced, the artwork can be purchased as a commodity. The artwork in the age of mechanical reproduction, in this sense, is supposed to announce the demise of singularity (Benjamin 1999[1968]).

Whereas Benjamin is preoccupied with artworks in relation to novel technologies for reproduction, it is wise to point out that technology is not in itself hostile to the sacred (see Herzfeld 1990; Wojcyk 1996; Coleman 2000: 166ff.; de Vries & Weber 2001; Apolito 2005[2001]; Hirschkind & Larkin 2008; Meyer 2010a). Technology offers prospects of disseminating and spreading what, in a Christian context, are the good tidings, the gospel, and here, the message of Soufanieh. However, dangers simultaneously lurk in technologies that are used for different purposes or for circumventing traditional lines of force and communication. The authority of the church can more easily be challenged when stories and images are circulated with less control (Apolito 2005[2001]: 16; Margry 2009; Maunder 2016). The very portability of messages makes the scale upon which their influence is made pertain to more levels at once; locally and regionally, messages play to particular concerns and policies, but globally, they may conjure up a picture of a general transformation in which messages are thought to hold universal relevance (Turner & Turner 1978: 209; Csordas 2009b).

The question remains as to what is reproducible in the image, at least from the perspective of the icon. What is an icon? In classic Christian theology, an icon was not just a pictorial representation of the divine but any material form by which you are led to God. In addition, one of the terms for distinguishing a genuine icon in the Orthodox and Catholic traditions has been the condition of its making. The making of the icon has classically been by hand during the contemplation and prayer of its maker. In that sense, each icon had its own sphere of devotion as its condition of possibility. Icons were then modelled on specific types and persons singled out for devotion, namely saints. The icon, in this sense, was not an artwork, even if certain aesthetics and rules were critical for it to qualify as an icon (see Herzfeld 1990; Bowman 1991).

The German philosopher Hans-Georg Gadamer spent some time reflecting on the work of art related to the icon in his monumental *Truth and Method* (2004[1960]: 130ff.). In Gadamer, we encounter a problem that goes all the way back to the role of the picture in Platonism. Gadamer finds this problem in the use of the word "image." The image crisis of today, according to Gadamer, is due to modern industry and a functionalized public, and as such, it is an ontological problem. We encounter two problems according to Gadamer: the relation between image and copy, and the relation between image and world: "We are asking in what respect the picture (*Bild*: also, image) is different from a *copy* (*Abbild*) – that is, we are raising the problem of the original (*Ur-bild*: also, ur-picture). Further, we are asking in what way the picture's relation to its *world* follows from this" (132). To Gadamer, it is critical that we reflect on the reproducibility of the picture. No original can be reproduced. What we meet is presentation. The copy is nothing but an attempt at an exact reproduction and is, in this sense, self-effacing. This statement does not really capture the complexity of the picture, though. A picture, according to Gadamer, works back upon the original. It is not just a passive relationship: "The picture then has an autonomy that also affects the original. For strictly speaking, it is only through the picture (*Bild*) that the original (*Ur-bild*) becomes the original (*Ur-bild*, also, Ur-picture) – e.g., it is only by being pictured that a landscape becomes pittoresque" (136). This explanation amounts to a paradox, in that the original cannot exist as original without subsequent reproduction. The reproduction gives life and a broader sphere of existence to the original; likewise, the reproduction works back upon and has a backwards effect on the original: "The original acquires an image only by being imaged, and yet the image is nothing but the appearance of the original" (137). This effect pertains, Gadamer shows, especially to the religious picture, which is in no way a picture of a copied being but rather an ontological communion with what is copied.

**Imitation of Christ: Mimesis and Recognition**

A figure of great renown, not just in Damascus but in much wider Orthodox and Catholic Christianity, is Saint John of Damascus. Saint John of Damascus lived at the time of the first severe currents of icon-oclasms in the eighth century CE. He was the fiscal minister during the Umayyad dynasty but, more importantly, wrote poetry and several important works on theology, including on images and the veneration of saints. Saint John is still an important figure, and several schools and churches, both Catholic and Orthodox, are named after him in Damas-cus. A classic discussion of the import and value of the icon was given by John in his famous *Three Treatises on the Divine Images*. In the face of accusations of idolatry in relation to icons, he discusses at great length several distinctions that nuance the way in which relations, to author-ities, are mundane, clerical, and divine. The series he makes consist of distinctions between prototype and copy, veneration and worship or adoration, or more generally the distinction between idol and icon (John of Damascus 2003[726–30]). The problem is not things, relics, saints, and so on in themselves but rather the status they are given in social relations. In other words, misjudging veneration as worship is the mistake inherent in iconoclastic tendencies. Although an icon can be used as an object through which one reaches for the divine, if it discloses the reaching beyond, the transfer, the icon turns into base material and becomes an idol. Whatever material leads you to God is not despicable, however, but deemed useful in the eyes of God as well as the believer. Similar treatise was later given by Saint Theodore the Studite (1981[816–19]) in his *On the Holy Icons*, where the reality of the icon is precisely the gaze, or a "looking beyond," as the formulation has been put more recently (Hourihane 2010). In the case of the fol-lowers of Our Lady of Soufanieh, however, the gaze is but one aspect of the reality of the icon. An even more radical kind of stigmata of the invisible is revealed when the icon not only opens to the believer in a gaze but actually sheds oil – when the screen or flatness of dimension-ality is broken in what the follower of Our Lady of Soufanieh takes as a sign of grace and favour. Here, not just the sense of sight and looking but also olfactory and tactile sensing of the divine is in play in the form of oil and incense. All the different senses give a synaesthetic experi-ence of the divine (see Ditchfield 2009). The gaze of the saint, in other words, is haptic and crosses over ordinary vision at the touch of the saint (Meyer 2010b).

Prayer, in this sense, opens the eyes of the individual to the world of Our Lady of Soufanieh and to divine reality. The individual life is in a transfigured world in which the devout see the answers to prayers in the most mundane acts. This world is encountered in the reality of the presence of the icon for the person praying. What the copy retains of the prototype is the reality of a world of grace, not lost, and divine seeing (see Freedberg 1989; Belting 1994; Maniura & Shepherd 2006; Hourihane 2010). In the world of the devotees of Our Lady of Soufanieh, it is not a question of losing out through duplication, since the copies also have grace bestowed upon them, and even the base material of which the reproduction is made is sanctified. It was not the old hand-painted icon in the home of Myrna and Nicolas that oozed oil; rather, it was the cheap copy Nicolas brought from a trip to Sofia. This is pointed out on several occasions, as it is used to evidence the power of God to act in his own way. And it is from copies of this copy, or reproductions of this reproduction, that oil can also exude, as in the case of Umm Salwa, Raif, and many more. The power of the image, then, is to effect stronger and more courageous prayer, and to allow the individual to participate in divine work in the exchanged and transformed gaze of the saint. Our Lady of Soufanieh with the Baby Jesus on her lap holds the intercessory power to affect divine will, and the individual is invited to participate in realizing God's plans. In one register, imitation is impossible; in another mirrored effect, it is the only viable response. Recognition must lead to imitation. It is in this process that the critical movement from models *of* sainthood to models *for* sainthood – so important for priests, the family, and followers around Myrna – is believed to come about.

**Stories and the Story**

The icon of Our Lady of Soufanieh exuding oil is seen as a response to prayers and petitions. However, prayers and petitions can never guarantee such miracles as a response. Prayers can effect a change of heart in the person praying, and this change is understood as central among the followers of Our Lady of Soufanieh. Umm Salwa's icon and the many other icons exuding oil manifest to the devotees the power of the Virgin Mary to intercede on their behalf. In this sense, it is not only Umm Salwa but almost all the followers of Our Lady of Soufanieh who will be able to tell of miracles of oil being exuded from the icon or from Myrna's hands. Raif, another regular follower, showed me a picture he kept in his wallet that carried the same traces of greasy liquid he took as an unfathomable token of Mary's grace and favour. For others, like George, these miraculous signs had not – or had not yet – been seen with their own eyes. George did not take this absence as a sign of a lack of favour, however, but rather understood it as a sign of his stronger faith. Referring to the exhortations of priests such as Abuna Elias Zahlawi and Abuna Elias Saloun, George emphasized the figure of Thomas, the doubting disciple, reproached for wanting to see.[7] For George, not having seen the miracles of oil was understood as a way of God wanting to keep his faith in a state of purity.

It is not only followers who have these kinds of stories, however; at several places in Damascus, you can hear similar stories of icons or statues shedding oil or even, in some instances, bleeding. In this sense, the distance between news and story remains critical, and only the becoming of the listener challenges the loss of story to news (see Benjamin 1999[1968]: 90–1). Abuna Elias Zahlawi would, in his sermons, inadvertently stick to this refrain: "You might think that you have heard this one hundred times, but the gospel is always new! God wants to change you!" And this instigated change opens the interstices between a proposed piety and the problems in living and getting it right. Often-heard criticisms of devotion and lack of understanding, not just in society but also among the followers of Soufanieh, offer an understanding of the tensions inherent in the impossible demands of the holy life made workable in practice, at least sometimes. God's grace by the intercession of Mary can be seen more fully in the mistakes of an imperfect life – in other words, to the eyes, which have been bestowed to see, and the ears, which have been bestowed to hear. In the next chapter, we shall explore the sermons and the structure of exemplarity that these establish for the listeners; for now, suffice it to say that the unceasing chain of prayers, for the believers, opens perspectives of what cannot be seen, of the invisible, albeit real, character of grace. The rosary as an exemplary practice functions in the iterability but also in the communality in shared practice, both in and across time. This collectivization is countered by the individuation in the response from the heart of the individual as part of the community of believers. In this joint practice of re-petition, there also exist the joys of the experience of flow (Turner & Turner 1978: 122, 139). What I have argued in this chapter is that a genuine anthropological understanding of prayer must encompass its inherently social nature. However, prayers work for the devout, such as the followers of Our Lady of Soufanieh, as an exemplary practice that instills in the individual a combination of repeated words and images for sustained meditation. We have seen that the relationship between prayer and the image of Our Lady of Soufanieh is one in which all her copied and reproduced images allow the devout – through prayer – to look beyond and participate in her grace. Her favour is manifest in the signs of oil exuded from her image, most significantly in Myrna's home but also in various reproductions of her image. The exemplary character of the image of Our Lady of Soufanieh corroborates her power of intercession, made possible by the petitions and prayers said in front of her very image. In the daily prayers to her, she is seen to model the followers. In front of her image, heart and mouth potentially meet. This meeting needs to be bestowed upon the praying person, however, and by extension on the confessing congregation. For the followers of Our Lady of Soufanieh, this transformation is a mystery more than a mastery; it is a logic of love, which works only by re-petition.

# Chapter Three

# Exemplary Series

How are we taught the word "God" (its use, that is)? I cannot give an exhaustive systematic description. But I can, as it were, make contributions toward the description; I can say something about it and perhaps in time assemble a sort of collection of examples.

– Ludwig Wittgenstein, *Culture and Value*

"The gospel is always new!" Abuna Elias Zahlawi emphasizes in his always eloquently delivered sermon. The eighty-year-old priest looks at the congregants through his heavy glasses. "The gospel is always new, even if we have heard it one hundred times before," he continues, making a rhetorical pause to let the effect of his words be felt. The whirring sound of the fans on the ceiling can be heard. A couple of youngsters wriggle around on their plastic chairs, which make a noise as they scratch on the tiles. The inner courtyard of the Nazzour family's house, where the weekly service is held, is packed this Saturday. People of all ages are present: children, young men, old ladies, and even whole families are assembled in the house. During the last decade of Hail Marys of the rosary on this January Saturday in 2010, Abuna Elias Zahlawi slowly descends the steps from the living room and walks past the people sitting there. He halts in front of the icon, where he silently says a prayer. People touch his white gown, decorated with a cross in red satin. He takes some steps further and exchanges a few words with two of the elders before assuming his stand in front of the altar. A microphone is switched on by one of the two elders, who walks to the side of the room and adjusts the sound on the stereo. Abuna Elias Zahlawi is silent for a moment as the congregants all await his initiative. Abuna Zahlawi then leads the liturgy and thereby signals the start of the service proper. Some know the liturgy by heart, while others use books, following the liturgy of the Melchite Catholic Church to aid the memory of the patterned practice. Later, Eucharist hymns and devotional songs in praise of the Virgin Mary, Christ, and the happenings in this very house add yet another layer of words to those already uttered. The words of prayers, hymns, liturgy, Bible, and the sermon delivered by Abuna Elias Zahlawi all emphasize the role of words in the formation of the Christian character.

In this chapter, I shall address the formation of character as a modelling of sainthood. I explore the specific models and exemplars presented in sermons as prisms for lives to be imitated. The framing of these lives is made through entextualizations, whereby the lives of some are made into texts that others are told to emulate. The process of making life into text and text into life is explored in the production of examples at the weekly Saturday sermons in Soufanieh. While directly related to lives as lived, such sermons also stand for a broader class of lives as *forma vitae*, that is, lives to be followed. I thus explore the example as an exemplum, a particular moral story used for edification and didactic purposes, one that situates the listener at the centre of the story by integrating the miraculous happenings in Soufanieh with the response of the individual. The sermons here serve as a particular aspect of my examination of exemplification and modelling of sainthood in contemporary Damascus.

### Readings from Scripture

Leading the liturgy of the service, Abuna Elias Zahlawi follows the typical structure of the Saturday services in the home of Myrna. Various prayers are said and responded to by attentive people. As is mostly the case here, Michel, one of the trusted males, reads the epistle, today from Paul in his letter to the Ephesians (4:7–13). Abuna Elias Zahlawi introduces this reading by saying: "We are told." Michel assumes a stand in front of the icon of Our Lady of Soufanieh and says: "This is the reading for the family in Ephesus by the Apostle Paul." Abuna Elias Zahlawi responds: "The wisdom we are told." Michel then starts the reading in an almost sing-song voice:

> But to each one of us grace has been given as Christ apportioned it. This is why it says: "When he ascended on high, he led captives in his train and gave gifts to men." What does "he ascended" mean except that he also descended to the lower earthly regions. He who descended is the very one who ascended higher than all the heavens, in order to fill the whole universe. It was he who gave some to be apostles, some to be prophets, some

to be evangelists, and some to be priests and teachers to prepare God's people for works of service, so that the body of Christ may be built up until we all reach unity in the faith and in the knowledge of the Son of God and become mature, attaining to the whole measure of the fullness of Christ.

Abuna Elias Zahlawi wishes peace on Michel. Michel takes his seat, and a prayer is said jointly before the reading from the gospels follows. "Let us listen to the wisdom which is revealed to us in the Holy gospel. Peace be upon you all," Abuna Elias Zahlawi says. "And on your spirit," everybody responds. The next reading is from Matthew (4:12–17), which as always is read by the priest, today Abuna Elias Zahlawi. "Listen to the gospel according to Matthew," he says. All respond in unison: "Glory to You, oh Lord, glory to You!" Abuna Elias Zahlawi goes on:

> We are told: When Jesus heard that John had been put in prison, he returned to Galilee. Leaving Nazareth, he went and lived in Capernaum, which was by the lake in the area of Zebulun and Naphtali, to fulfil what was said through the prophet Isaiah: "Land of Zebulun and land of Naphtali, the way to the sea, along the Jordan, Galilee of the Gentiles – the people living in darkness have seen a great light; on those living in the land of the shadow of death a light has dawned." From that time on Jesus began to preach, "Repent, for the kingdom of heaven is near."

All respond again: "Glory to You, oh Lord, glory to You!" The liturgical part of the service with readings from the Bible now makes way for the sermon.

### Exemplifying the Gospel: Repentance and Change

Abuna Elias Zahlawi begins his sermon this Saturday by clearing his throat. People are all ears. Abuna Elias Zahlawi clears his throat once more and starts with the words spoken by Jesus. "If we listen to what is in the gospel today, Jesus says: 'Repent, for the kingdom of heaven is near.'" He pauses briefly before continuing: "Perhaps you think that this is something Jesus said two thousand years ago. And perhaps you think that this was probably fine for those living then, but we … What should we change? Or perhaps, that nothing changes in our lives." Abuna Zahlawi glances out over the people assembled. The narration goes on in a steady pace without the assistance of a manuscript. Abuna Zahlawi holds the microphone in his hands, which are joined in front of him. The hands shake slightly, but no shaking is heard in the voice of the experienced priest. If people are reluctant regarding the message of Soufanieh, it is difficult not to be – if not persuaded – at least affected by the work of words undertaken by this priest. From the outset, the importance of change is underscored as the theme for today.

"When I discuss with some people, they say to me: 'Abuna, what do you want from me?' I say: 'How long is it since you confessed?' 'Uff, pihhh … I haven't confessed for a very long time.' And the person is old. 'Very well, so there is nothing problematic in your life?' 'No, not really.'" By giving this brief description of a person who does not confess, it is possible for Elias Zahlawi to address a more general problem: "Man's problem is that he wants to see his situation as from afar … If one stands in front of a mirror, even if it is a pretty person, the closer he gets, his reaction is 'Uff, is it me?!'" Steadily and engagingly, Abuna Zahlawi builds up his sermon and frames the importance of the gospel for today. The first move is to situate the problem of mankind as such. From there, the relevance of the gospel for today can be assessed. His line is very clear as he takes his listeners on a tour of the scriptural context; from this context, he proceeds to examples in Damascus and finally ends in this house, with the grace God bestowed upon it and perforce on the listeners: God wants change! He has done it in history, and history has been made on the very soil where people are now present.

"I don't know if your situation is like this," Abuna Zahlawi continues. "The problem in us is that our life feels distanced." He continues this line of thought and relocates the problem in relation to Jesus a little later: "Jesus is in our hearts, but very often, we don't let this reality enter our families or our behaviour. We pray. We go to church … We go to the Eucharist far away from other people, and everybody goes to Eucharist without confession." The problem now is addressed in moral terms, that a life devoid of attentive listening and ensuing action is dangerous and that the very moment of the sermon is precious for each person present.

"Believe me, we need time to see the daily importance of this sentence from the gospel, because there is very much in our lives that needs to be brought into being [takwīn]. Jesus's words – 'Repent, for the kingdom of heaven is near' – are not just for those living two thousand years ago. It is here, too!" Apart from stating that the basic problem is still the same, Abuna Zahlawi now couples Jesus's first recorded public message with the first message the Virgin is reported to have said to Myrna: "'Repent and have faith, and remember me in your joy.' In the first message! Who of you know the messages? … I want you all to know the messages. Let us pause and examine some of the words the Virgin and Jesus said. Repent. From what should we repent?" He repeats the sentence: "From what should we repent? … I and you. There are things in our lives that he wants us to repent from." The doubling and crafting of the relationship between Jesus's first message and the Virgin's first message here in Damascus adds weight to the proximity of God in this location and to the focus on personal change as tied to repentance.

"Repent, for the kingdom of heaven is near." Abuna Zahlawi recursively repeats the first public words of Jesus, before centring on the role of Soufanieh and Damascus yet again. "We may think that God is far away, even if we know that he is close. Sometimes we can feel as if he is far away ... God is closer than we imagine! And Jesus is closer than we imagine! And the demonstration [al-burhān], the happenings of this house twenty-seven years ago. Who of you would have expected that? Not me," Abuna Elias Zahlawi explains, as he includes this very locality and the characters in the very house where the sermon is delivered in the divine plan of redemption. The listeners include people who have been part of the extended family of Soufanieh from the outset, and they all have vivid memories of the first time when it all happened. Abuna Zahlawi places himself firmly in the chain of events. He recounts how he was told of the first apparition. "I rejected it," the experienced priest explains. He underscores his personal scepticism when the rumours of the first apparition spread and how he rejected their veracity, not just once but three times.[1]

## Exemplifications: Crafting the Series

"I don't know each of you. God alone knows what is in your hearts," Abuna Elias Zahlawi says as he glances over the congregants. He takes his time, while attentively looking at specific people and not just at the crowd. Abuna Zahlawi, at once mildly and fervently, turns his almost bald head from the left side of the courtyard to the right. "However, I am convinced that most people live as if God were far away from them." The focus on the distance between personal experience and God's reality is addressed in the part of the sermon that follows, where Abuna Zahlawi first emphasizes God's love for the individual person. He ties this love to the message of the Virgin at this very locality: "The Virgin says: 'Remember God, because God is with us!' This means he loves all of us. There are no exceptions. The words of Jesus in the gospel for today are 'Repent, for the kingdom of heaven is near.' We need to attend to this." To make it simpler, Abuna Zahlawi underscores how God sees the individual: "He is with me, but am I with him? And if I died, in what condition [wad'a] would I arrive? How would he see me? In his eyes, how would I fare? This could happen to us at any moment, whether we are big or small, no one knows." The implication of these words is that the focus on God's vision is tied both to the comforting voice of the Virgin here in Soufanieh and to an afterlife with or without God. However, the sermon does not dwell on these aspects of the afterlife, but rather the choice and situation of the moment are underlined: "We in particular know that the Lord is with us! You are children of Soufanieh. Here in Soufanieh, we are closer than so many other people who don't know Soufanieh." Zahlawi continues his exhortation: "This is the secret of Soufanieh, the love of Soufanieh, the existence of Soufanieh in our lives."

Now Abuna Elias Zahlawi starts to focus on another part of the section read from the gospel: "The second word from the gospel for today says this: 'The people living in darkness have seen a great light; on those living in the land of the shadow of death a light has dawned.'" Abuna Elias Zahlawi now fashions another important series resting on locality. "In the gospel for today, Jesus approaches Capernaum from Nazareth where they tried to kill him. They tried to kill him! Because of this, Jesus once said: 'No prophet is respected in his own country.'[2] Do you know these words?" Abuna Elias Zahlawi repeats Jesus's words: "'No prophet is respected in his own country.'" The words here are important, as one of the issues difficult to grapple with is that many locals do not care about the miracle of Our Lady of Soufanieh. In the sermon, this situation is mirrored in that of Nazareth and Capernaum. The reluctance is a sign of futile minds not wanting to change. Abuna Zahlawi continues: "In Damascus, to this day there are people talking badly about Soufanieh. They talk about those who believe in Soufanieh. But people are travelling from the ends of the world to pray here." The global relevance is hence inscribed to counter the local lukewarm attitudes. It is a matter of seeing things from God's perspective: "We hope that the Lord will open their eyes," says Abuna Zahlawi. To make this point even more pertinent to the listeners, Abuna Zahlawi uses a recent incident to mirror the importance of Our Lady of Soufanieh and, by extension, Myrna. He recounts a trip just undertaken to Amman, the capital of Jordan, where a plenitude of people wanted to see Myrna and where, more significantly, many of them had travelled from Nazareth to do so: "Recently Myrna was in Amman. One hundred and four persons came from Nazareth. From Nazareth, from the town of Jesus!" He explains the details of the meeting and continues: "They wanted to listen; they wanted to understand. From the first to the last moment, we were with them. And here, this is not necessarily the case. 'In the shadow' means hidden from the world. God will open our hearts. Each one of us wants from Jesus the change to become messengers. Ask Jesus to change you. And try from your home. Then you will become his apostle. And today he needs messengers." What Abuna Zahlawi accomplishes is to craft a series whereby the villagers from Nazareth, who rejected Christ, now accept Myrna, whom many in Damascus still do not endorse.

## Change and Saintly Models: Seriation Performed

Damascus is mirrored in Nazareth, in the lack of receptivity in Nazareth in the past but not today, which allows Abuna Zahlawi to create one last series that attests to change as possible. He uses specific lives to frame this idea:

> We know Saint Augustine. He died in the year 430 AD. His father was an officer and lived in Tunis, in North Africa. His mother believed very strongly. His father was very rich. He was very handsome and very clever. His mother was crying. His mother was crying: "What are you doing with your life?" And it so happened that his uncle became a Christian and tried to form his faith. And it happened in the area where he lived he heard that in Milan there was a bishop who was a wonderful speaker. So he said: "I want to go to his school." He was just a youngster. He went to Milan and asked where this man was. The name of the bishop was Ambrose. He was close to the emperor and had taught him everything. And, therefore, he had been given the seat as bishop of Milan. At that time, it was the capital of the Roman Empire. Ambrose felt that something was going to change. They had a conversation, and the conversation changed Augustine's mind. He wanted to live the life God wants. Now he wanted to live it. Here began a complete transformation. He went back to the home of his uncle. He read the Bible for a year. And, after this year, people wanted to see him; they knew him as he had been famous before. After a year, the local bishop died. At that time, it was the people who decided who was to become bishop. The greatest priest among the priests would ask who they wanted to be the next bishop. They would say, "We want this one or that one." Thus was the opinion of the people. But there was a child who said: "We want Augustine." Augustine, however, doubted that this would be the right choice. Me? Never, me. I'm the last human to do so! But, in time he became a priest, he became a bishop, and so the Lord can change people. But patience, patience. If you feel your situation is weak. If you are tempted by sins.

Abuna Elias Zahlawi now forcefully adds several new people to the series by focusing on the possibility of change for God: "As he changed the disciples, as he changed Mary Magdalene, as he changed Thomas, as he changed Augustine, as he changed John of Damascus." Having presented this series, Abuna Elias Zahlawi explains: "John of Damascus was head of the ministers among the Umayyads. The ruler of the

Umayyads was in his hands; he was responsible for everything. He left and went to Bethlehem. And there, he used his time in prayer and writing. The church today still uses his hymns and his poetry and theology. How long has he been dead, and he is still influential? God's change really transforms a person. And in Soufanieh we know how he changes people. Each of you knows what he has changed in you. In truth, he wants you to change more." He pauses and later elaborates: "We ask Jesus for healing, and the Virgin changes us." The work of the sermon here is to establish a formative series, where the listener is enabled to be touched by the Virgin and Jesus. As they have changed the lives of so many others, so they can change the life of the receptive listener.

**The Logic of Seriation**

Abuna Elias Zahlawi is frequently on national television and even received a prize from the Syrian First Lady in the summer of 2009 for his work for Syria.[3] The fame Abuna Zahlawi has in a Syrian context is also manifest in the attentive listening with which his sermon is received in Myrna's home this specific Saturday. Abuna Zahlawi elaborates on his theme, that he himself would be able to discern only some of the faces of those present but that God, the all-knowing, would know not only all the faces but all the hearts as well. He goes on to talk about many Christians in Syria who are not confessing and the problems that evolve in abstaining from this sacrament. Abuna Zahlawi continues with the topic of change. He recounts the life and change of Augustine and continues with John of Damascus. Change in every single person is thus underscored as urgent and necessary. He brings in Soufanieh and the first message as well as other features of particular importance to his exposition. By bringing these themes together, people are placed in a particular time-space whereby personal change is tied to God's planning and human response.

Not all are well trained in reading practices, but all have the faculty for listening, and listening is here emphasized as a profound way to relate to God. The different lives presented in the sermon all embody the qualities of a changed and charged life, and in this sense, each is exemplary of a certain type of sanctified life. As these figures were moulded by God, every single listener is challenged to let his or her life be changed, just like Saint Augustine, Saint John of Damascus, Saint Francis of Assisi, or local types in contemporary Damascus, Myrna being the foremost example. These examples are used by the priest to flesh out the Christian character to be strived for. Not – as the priest emphasizes – because each person necessarily so wants it, but because

God wants it. Personal change, in this sense, rests on dual ground: the divinely ordained and inspired life, and the human response. Life can become charged and sanctified, and used as an example to follow for others. The examples given do not rest on human perfection but on divine election and sanctification.

The saintly exemplars, modelled by the words of the skilled Abuna Zahlawi, are placed in a series of divinely inspired figures, all of whom were changed, perforce allowing the listeners to see themselves reflected and challenged to become part of the same series. Even the story of Myrna has the classic motif of her wanting to flee upon the first apparition. It fits, or is fitted, into the biblical standard, which has a host of such examples whereby the chosen prophet either reluctantly or, stricken with panic, is seized by the Lord (for example, 1 Samuel 3; Isaiah 6; Jeremiah 1). This model renders credible the source in that it could not be made up, as it were, by human imagination, but was a task enforced upon the individual against his or her previous knowledge or anticipation. In this regard, only the way the election is received can be lauded, as in the case of the Virgin Mary, who in peace and quiet received the words from the Archangel on the annunciation of her becoming the mother of Christ (see Luke 1:26ff.; more generally see Christian 1981: 200).

## Example and Exemplar: Ex-sample and Ex-sampling

To understand the working of the example in the sermon, it is instructive to note that, in Arabic, there exists an intricate relation between representation, example, ideal, model, parable, and resemblance, all of which derive from the three root letters m-th-l (mathala). In general, the root designates what stands for something else. According to Abraham Mitrie Rihbani (2003[1922]), mithāl is sociable and carries the meaning and weight of storytelling (90). Persons, stories, proverbs, and sayings can stand for and sum up human conditions.

It is precisely this quality of standing for something else that has been examined by Nelson Goodman (1981, see also 1976). Goodman lists several forms of reference, one of them being exemplification, which he terms an overlooked but extremely important form of non-denotational reference (1981: 124). Exemplification is not a simple denotation but rather "reference by sample to a feature of it" (124–5; see also 1976: 52–67). A part of a whole is taken to stand for the whole, to express it. Exemplification is, in this sense, to use a part, which is made to stand for the whole. Extending this concept in a series of examples, each of the parts may not be understood as identical, but they are subsumed in a category, which they are made to represent, and in this process, they are juxtaposed.

Saint Augustine is not identical to Saint John of Damascus, but they are both used by Abuna Elias Zahlawi to point to a particular reality. On Goodman's understanding, exemplification implies reference between elements in both directions (1976: 59). Exemplification emphasizes the capacity of particulars to relate to universalities, albeit in very different manners.

However, the quality of the example to stand for something else has, from the inception of Greek thought, resulted in two markedly different approaches to the category and status of examples and exemplarity. As argued by Alexander Gelley (1995), Plato, on the one hand, thought of *paradeigma* as a model or exemplar, whereas Aristotle, conversely, thought of *paradeigma* as an instance from which inductive conclusions can be derived. The relationship between the example as an instance or instantiation and the exemplar as the ideal form highlights a certain tension in the way particularity and universality relates. As a mere example, nothing much is to be expected, and a reduction to the specific case seems possible. As an exemplar and model, conversely, everything is to be expected. Jacques Derrida (2001[1978]) writes of the two different senses of the example in *Writing and Difference*: "It is an example as a sample and not as a model ... To pose the problem of its exemplarity: are we concerned with an example among others or the 'good example,' an example that is revelatory by privilege?" (51). To Derrida and to the classical tradition, what we are presented with appears a choice. Either we go with the "mere" example, or we go with the exemplar. What if there is no choice to be taken, however, but rather lines of force to be followed?

In the sermon, Abuna Elias Zahlawi crafts a crucial series of examples. He is, in other words, *ex-sampling*, taking something out of the sample – that is, drawing from the stock of divinely ordained figures to paint with words particular characters to emulate. The series does not, however, indicate that the samples are merely singularities, as they add up to a larger field in which each instantiation is worthy of attention in its own right but also adds to the divine glory in and through human response. Here the sample is also the model. Seriality is modelling. Abuna Elias Zahlawi, accordingly, is not merely adding more examples of the same but is modelling a series, which opens up and extends so that the listener can become a part of it.

### Examples and Words: Fleshing Out Examples

In the exposition of the sermon above, central features of genre and authority conjure up a specific configuration of practices. As pointed out by Eric Hoenes del Piñal (2009: 88), the Catholic sermon may very well function as disciplining within the universal church, following the same calendar and biblical readings, but the exhortation may depart a good deal from the reading, allowing different interpretive modulations. In the sermon by Abuna Elias Zahlawi, a particular interpretive modulation consists of linking models past and present to personal change in imitation of these models. By drawing on both highly acclaimed persons already authorized as saints, such as Saint Augustine, Saint John of Damascus, and Saint Francis, as well as on Myrna and ordinary people from Damascus, the purpose of the sermon is to mould the character of the listener. Presented with these examples, each person can test his or her own life. Examples and models are used as evidence for sanctity, both on a mundane and extraordinary basis, but also as instigators of life change. The basic insecurity – that only God knows the heart – can be used to let God mould the character both in the joint prayers and confession of faith, and also in the labour of living oneself as an example and confessing one's sins in not being able to live up to the model.

The use of words, in this Catholic formulation, relates to a particular understanding of the Word as Christ incarnated. In this vein, the Christian tenet from the opening of the gospel according to John is significant. In the very opening of this gospel, John (1:1) says: "In the beginning was the Word, and the Word was with God, and the Word was God"; later, John (1:14) says: "The Word became flesh and made his dwelling among us." Words are, in the logic of Abuna Zahlawi and among the followers of Our Lady of Soufanieh, not conceived as just surface or letters devoid of spirit but as holding the capacity to change hearts – both in sermons and in the example of life made text and text made life. Here is where stories of Christ, Mary, and the saints merge with mundane persons, and flesh and blood participates in divine labour. Words are a distinct way of human action in the world, one that Hannah Arendt (1998[1958]), who was also deeply inspired by Augustine (Arendt 1996[1929]; Bandak 2012), claimed holds the potential for opening the space of appearance for natality, where something new can be initiated. To Augustine – one of the figures used as exemplifying God's change in Abuna Elias Zahlawi's sermon – the memory was critical, in that it opened up the scrutiny of the self, albeit not in the modern sense as a life regarded as unique and individual but rather as an *exemplary* life (see Arendt 1994[1930]; see also Hartog 2015[2003]: 41ff.; Lowrie & Lüdemann 2015). Life testifies to the fact that it is possible for everybody to change: some people have been changed, so it is possible for others to be changed too. Memory and grace are hence intertwined, as life can be separated into a clear before and after having been called to change. Repentance and new life are seen as part of a living tradition to which the listener can add him- or herself.

## Example, Exemplar, Exemplum: Webs of Exempla

A central way to conceive of the Bible and the Christian tradition is as a web of *exempla*. In addition to recent studies of reading (Boyarin 1993; Reed 2011) and the social life of scriptures (Bielo 2009; see also Engelke 2009; Tomlinson 2014), I will argue that the Bible, more than being mere letters read and used in social contexts, is a web of exempla, of figures to imitate and reflect upon. This web is then, in effect, extended in the sermons delivered by Abuna Zahlawi. The specific examples given, however, are not just positive. The scriptural edifice or repository abounds with examples not to be imitated.

One of the most severe examples is given by Abuna Elias Saloun in one of the weekly Tuesday evening novenas in the home of Myrna. Abuna Saloun here refers to Ananias and Saphira who, according to the Acts of the Apostles (5:1–11), were both struck dead when they lied in front of the disciples. This rather dark tale is used as an admonition to the followers of Our Lady of Soufanieh neither to lie to themselves nor to God. The examples, in this sense, do not just comfort and sooth but critically challenge the lives of the listeners. Normally, the examples given would be of emphatic virtue, as in the lives of Saint Augustine, Saint Thérèse of Lisieux, Saint Bernadette Soubirous, and Saint Francis of Assisi or Saint John of Damascus. Precisely because the transmission of the words to individuals is not simply direct but fraught with danger, we often hear criticisms of those who hear without hearing in the biblical record. Rather than just one series, two series are crafted in the sermons: one extending the logic of the bad listener, the other the logic of the good listener. A critical aspect of the work of word found in Soufanieh is to present examples that people can see through and hence mould their own character after.

It is precisely due to this tradition that Caroline Humphrey (1997), in her work on exemplars, appears not to take her conclusion far enough. In asserting that general moral rules and not exemplars govern Western and Christian practice, Humphrey places greater focus on rules than has typically been the case. It may be that moral rules appear to govern in fast formulations of ethics, but in practice, Western traditions abound with exemplary figures giving content and form to moral rules (Warnick 2008). From the antique world onwards, human learning has been focused on exemplars, be they in Greek or, later, Roman formulations (Koselleck 2004; Lianeri 2011; Hartog 2015[2003]). The Christian innovation was to place a centre in the series. As historian Peter Brown (1983) writes of Christianity, its novelty was the proposed central figure: "the Exemplar of all exemplars, a being, Christ, in Whom human and divine had come to be joined" (6). The saints were conceived as exemplars, not necessarily perfect ones, but mediators and intercessors between God and men (Gudeman 1976: 712; Kleinberg 1992: 134; Forbess 2010: 142–3).

The importance of the series in a Christian sense was the extendability from past to future and the double constitution of exemplar in relation to Exemplar. The exemplar was rendering the Exemplar credible, and conversely, the Exemplar was rendering the exemplar credible. This doubling was, in a particular way, captured by John of Damascus – whom Abuna Elias Zahlawi draws upon in the sermon. John of Damascus (2003[726–730]), in a formative way, formulated the relation between archetype and copy in his defence of holy images and icons: "An image is a likeness depicting an archetype, but having some difference from it; the image is not like the archetype in every way" (25). The image bestows glory upon the archetype by way of transfer, which in a Christian tradition means prayer. Later, Hans-Georg Gadamer, in *Truth and Method*, argued that the copy never merely reproduces the original but rather adds to it, given that the first is seen through the latter and vice versa (2004[1960]: 130ff.).

In hagiographical writing and sermons – as Derek Krueger (2004) has emphasized – the importance of the double constitution was profound. Krueger's point is that, not only is the sanctity of the saintly prospect invigorated by the text, but the author also assumes a particular relation to his subject by the very act of writing. By writing the life of the saint, sanctity is bestowed upon the author (9). Writing and holiness, therefore, mutually follow and accomplish each other. Accordingly, a whole *typology* exists in biblical and saintly tradition whereby biblical and saintly figures, as in a series, bestow credence upon each other. This is a classical pattern, which precedes the Arab conquest in the first half of the seventh century and which, in early Eastern Christianity, has been reflected in the discussions of the importance of the Christian as made in God's image (see also Mitchell 1986: 31–6). Here, the Greek term originally used was that of *graphein*, which carries both the meaning of writing and painting. This dual meaning, in an eminent way, attests to what the relation between word and image in a Christian tradition crafts as exemplary: the word paints an image, a story, a narrative as the divine ordeal is fleshed out in types across time and space, which, in Catholic and Orthodox traditions, is very tangible in the form of statues and icons that materialize and make tangible the words of the sermon in physical form (Morgan 1998; Orsi 2005). But it is also the opposite: images and icons render the word of God accessible as a scripted story to become a part of. More than example and exemplar, we here encounter the exemplum, the moral tale used for edification, and it is to the exemplum that we shall now turn.

## Filling in the Gaps: Exemplification and Interpretation

John Lyons has, with great erudition, traced the genealogy of the example in rhetoric. In his elaborate tracing of the various roles allotted to the example throughout a primarily European tradition, Lyons points to the word "exemplum," and how it came to be associated with the Greek *eikon* just as much as *paradeigma* (1989: 10). This point is significant, as it attests to a broader movement between words and images, such as the one just noted above. Lyons asserts:

> This movement, which is entirely consonant with the rhetorical function of example in Aristotle, permits the spread of example from linguistic to non-linguistic forms. At the same time the visual form of the example leads to the ontological consequence that examples have the quality of seeming rather than of being, they are associated with *species* and *imago*, and are therefore within the realm of all that is specious and imaginary. (10)

The example as exemplum had its origins in Greek and Roman tradition, but found a particular Christian form as a moral tale to instruct the masses (see also Demoen 1997: 126). In Christian tradition and, in particular, in the medieval usage of the exemplum, it was a tool for didacticism. As argued by Jacques le Goff (1988[1985]: 78–80, 181), the exemplum was a specific genre that was developed in medieval Europe. The exemplum was now rendered as a narrative that crafted a particular form of persuasiveness alongside biblical exhortation. Wholesale collections of exempla were circulated for use in sermons (Kemmler 1984: 12; Kleinberg 1992, 2008; Gelley 1995: 4). The lives of the saints used as exempla played a crucial role in the sermon, where they could be appropriated as a particular, condensed genre, as short moral stories used for instruction and edification. In Joseph Mosher's words, "the exemplum may be briefly and conveniently described as a short narrative used to illustrate or confirm a general statement" (1911: 1). More recently, however, this view has been challenged, in that, more than merely a genre, the exemplum is a device (Lyons 1989: 9; Kaufmann 1996). As a device, the example is more powerful than the designation "genre" allows for. As a device, the exemplum is used to effect something in the listener, to illustrate, persuade, and convince. And, as such a device, the exemplum is a powerful tool that asserts power and authority both in and through a narrative modelling (Scanlon 1994).

The exemplum is a device used to train certain sensibilities, but also and more importantly, it is a device that places in the listener a responsibility of judgment. Abuna Zahlawi deliberately places the listener at the centre as he or she is presented with various examples of change. The listener is to pass judgment, and by this judgment, he or she will be placed in the series of the good or the bad listener. In his exploration of rabbinic readings of the Bible and the use of examples to corroborate understanding, Daniel Boyarin (1995) has made a strong case for a dual working of exemplification. Boyarin asserts that word-pictures denote something that again exemplifies a label, which, in turn, denotes and exemplifies something else: "The process of interpretation by exemplification is thus a picking out of the feature to which the exemplification will refer" (35). This process is what I have designated as a series, and what, in various ways, can be seen to be put in action in the sermon of Abuna Zahlawi. Abuna Zahlawi uses the different persons in distillated versions, where each feeds back into the series. The action rests on concretion, not abstraction, as the part relates to other parts.

The exemplification, then, works not only by being set in motion in and of itself but by making other wholes feasible as both model and part. Exemplifications can, in this sense, be highly productive for other exemplifications, because the example is not as much stabilizing as it is setting things in motion, inviting action on the part of the listener. The reading by example produces and procures knowledge and asks the listener to fill in the gaps (Boyarin 1995: 35). It is precisely this process of filling in the gaps in narratives that Susan Harding (2000) has argued characterizes the art of language of the fundamentalist Christians surrounding Jerry Falwell's Baptist community. Harding addresses the use of biblical figures in witnessing and preaching among fundamentalist Christian Baptists in the United States. Harding shows what I have designated the logic of seriation. In an interview with Reverend Campbell, one of her interlocutors, Campbell places Harding in a mirrored relationship with biblical figures such as Moses, Nicodemus, Isaac, Adam, Eve, Jesus, John the Baptist, and himself as preacher. Harding writes:

> Narratively, that is, looking at the form his argument took on the surface of his whole juxtaposition of stories, Campbell emphasized the importance of spoken language, of dialogue, in making the passage from one world to the next. He repeatedly relied on dialogue – between Jesus and Nicodemus, himself and me, Isaac and Abraham, John the Baptist and the disciples – to set up the dilemma of human choice. (50)

Biblical figures are placed in a sequence, and Reverend Campbell attempts to insert the listener, Harding, in the series – that is to move her from being a listener to being a speaker. The example in this case not only points to precedents but also to a structure of fulfilment (Harvey 2002: 93), which rests upon a particular dialogue that the listener and, more broadly, the audience is made to participate in. The links made are, in this sense, "typological" or "figural," as Harding later writes (2000: 55, 85; see also Auerbach 1984[1959]). The series breaks off with the invitation and demands the filling in of the gaps in the stories by the listener adding to the series. In other words, the stories, figures, and examples presented by Abuna Elias Zahlawi fulfil each other but only in soliciting interpretive action on part of the listener.

As Abuna Elias Zahlawi approaches the end of his sermon, he carves out the gravity of the listener's response. Having established the need for change through different figures by biblical precedent and authority, he uses the words of Jesus to enforce a choice on the individual listener: "Jesus says in Revelations: 'You are neither hot nor cold, but lukewarm.'"[4] Abuna Zahlawi stops and looks out over the faces inviting a response: "Who knows the continuation?" He pauses again and sees the finger of a young boy go up. "Hana!" Abuna Zahlawi invites him to answer. Hana answers with the clear and high-pitched voice of a child: "So I am about to spit you out of my mouth!" Abuna Elias Zahlawi repeats the sentence: "I am about to spit you out of my mouth!" Abuna Zahlawi pauses a moment and then repeats the words again: "You are neither hot nor cold, but lukewarm, therefore I am about to spit you out of my mouth!" The gravity is felt, even if he is not adding to it in terms of gestures, and neither is he taking any kind of joy in the dire consequences. The words are allowed to effectuate their own weight before he elaborates: "Who of you wants to be lukewarm, who of you wants to be cold? *Inshallah*, no one. *Inshallah*, everyone of us wants to be hot. But in the power of the Lord and by your spirit." The weight of the address is felt, as every listener is now placed in the centre. What will the response be? The series is to be extended. Abuna Elias Zahlawi glances yet again over the assembled people of all ages, and then adds his "Amen!"

**Forma Vitae**

The sermon Abuna Zahlawi delivers allows us to reflect on the use of lives as formative examples for others. Pivotal work has been done by Giorgio Agamben in elaborating on and formulating a theory of the example. Agamben's first formulation of a theory of the example is found in his book *The Coming Community*. Here, Agamben (1993[1990]) very aptly locates the example between the particular phenomenon and the universal class:

> One concept that escapes the antinomy of the universal and the particular has long been familiar to us: the example. In any context where it exerts its force, the example is characterized by the fact that it holds for all cases of the same type, and, at the same time, it is included among these. It is one singularity among others, which, however, stands for each of them and serves for all. On the one hand, every example is treated in effect as a real particular case, but on the other, it remains understood that it cannot serve in its particularity. Neither particular nor universal, the example is a singular object that presents itself as such, that *shows* its singularity. Hence the pregnancy of the Greek term, for example: *para-deigma*, that which is shown alongside (like the German *Bei-spiel*, that which plays alongside). Hence the proper place of the example is always beside itself, in the empty space in which its undefinable and unforgettable life unfolds. This life is purely linguistic life. Only life in the word is undefinable and unforgettable. Exemplary being is purely linguistic being. Exemplary is what is not defined by any property, except being-called. (9–10; emphasis in the original)

Where Agamben rightly asserts the radical singularity, he does not focus on the formative role of the sample. Exemplary being may be linguistic, but, in a Christian sense, such being transcends the letter and fleshes out God's image refracted in personal life. The example holds the potential to flesh out, illustrate, and persuade. Accordingly, in the working of the sermon by Abuna Zahlawi, the example is tied to both identities and properties – here as Christians and followers of Our Lady of Soufanieh – as both are modelled in a particular and not a general series. The modelling of life by words and words by life are two series of effects that bridge the world of the listener and God's reality, and let it become inhabitable. The examples given by Abuna Elias Zahlawi are, in this sense, all part of the same sequence, but they do not point only in one direction. The virtue of particular examples is, of course, to be emulated, but some aspects, more than imitation, demand awe and wonder (Kieckhefer 1988; Woodward 1990; Macklin 2005: 3). Myrna's piety may well be imitated, whereas her stigmata conversely are believed vicariously to stand for the community in a sacrificial economy. Likewise, saints such as John of Damascus, Augustine, Padre Pio, and Francis of Assisi are all part of a series which, at the same time, is extendable. The relationship with the saint is specifically crucial, therefore, as friend, benefactor, intermediary, and intercessor.

Agamben later returned to the example to give it a much more exquisite rethinking in his book *The Signature of All Things: On Method*. Here, Agamben (2009[2008]) devotes the first essay entitled "What Is a Paradigm?" to questions on the working of the example. Of particular interest is Agamben's outlining of monastic orders and their foundations in a Catholic tradition. Agamben asserts that monastic orders, through the ages, have been formed around the life of the founder. In this regard, the life of the founder was moulded as a *forma vitae*, an example to follow, where "the founder's life is in turn a sequel to the life of Jesus as narrated in the gospels" (21). A formalization of the life of the founder would, however, often find its penultimate form in the meaning of a written text. In other words, life is turned to text. The life of the individual monk or novice is moulded upon the example set by the founder: "At least until Saint Benedict, the rule does not indicate a general norm, but the living community (*koinos, bios, cenobio*) that results from an example and in which the life of each monk tends at the limit to become paradigmatic – that is, to constitute itself as *forma vitae*" (22). The paradigmatic relation does not merely occur between sensible objects or between these objects and a general rule; it occurs instead between a singularity (which thus becomes a paradigm) and its exposition (its intelligibility). In a very significant move, Agamben contrasts the working of the example with that of the exception. Where the exception works by exclusion and thereby is included, the example works by exhibiting its inclusion, which makes up for its exclusion. The working of the example, the ex-sampling, renders intelligible a series of phenomena that would otherwise have been unaccounted for.

**Extensions of the Series: To Catch the Drift**

The extendability of Christian exemplary series, therefore, goes beyond the work of words undertaken by Abuna Elias Zahlawi. The exemplary series works as a paradigmatic typology, its logic resting on the very seriation whereby each instantiation, as well as the series as a whole, embodies the Christian logic. Furthermore, the logic of the series works by having an adversary series of anti-exemplarity (see Needham 1985). Figures such as Ananias and Saphira are used as admonition by Abuna Saloun, and in apposite form attesting to the importance of the singular listener's response.

However, Abuna Zahlawi himself is also rendered a part of the exemplary series, as he is often used in media on Christian topics. The priest is known as a confessor of Myrna and a prime intellectual, but also as a man of exemplary stature with regard to piety (Bandak 2015b). The role of the priest is therefore evaluated by the listeners, and the priest is moulded by the sermons he delivers. Where recent work on the role of charismatic preachers has underscored the transgressive nature of their social persona as constitutive of their reputation (see, for example, Harding 2000; Coleman 2009), exemplary piety is shown by the humility of Abuna Elias Zahlawi in his sermon. By effacing himself as nothing but a witness, he assumes the saintly character of the confessor. Moreover, when adding his own corresponding deeds and actions to his words, Zahlawi is admired as a priest to be listened to. This character is contrary to that of many priests and even bishops, who are criticized for not following their own words, thereby making them devoid of exemplary force.

The series, however, extends to the individuals, rosaries, prayer cards, and the whole family of Soufanieh, which are believed to have an exemplary role in the Middle East and the world. The series opens up as it refers to other examples: Myrna as another Mary or visionary such as Bernadette, as another stigmatic such as Francis of Assisi or Padre Pio; and Soufanieh as another Lourdes or Fatima, famous locations for Marian apparitions; and hence, the listener as another Myrna, another Mary, another Christ-carrying exemplar. The challenge to the listener then is to catch or "guess" what Wittgenstein (2009 [1953]) in his *Philosophical Investigations* called the "drift" of the series (90). The series and the motion of the example then open up and ask for the responsiveness and judgment of the individual. Jacques Derrida (1994) says in *Specters of Marx*:

> An example always carries beyond itself: it thereby opens up a testamentary dimension. The example is first of all for others, and beyond the self. Sometimes, perhaps always, whoever gives the example is not equal to the example he gives, even if he does everything to follow it in advance, "to learn how to live," as we were saying, imperfect example of the example he gives – which he gives by giving then what he has not and even what he is not. For this reason, the example thus disjoined separates enough from itself or from whoever gives it so as to be no longer or not yet an example *for itself*. (34; emphasis in the original)

The purpose of the sermon, then, is not to be an example of itself but, rather, to capture and move the listener to a change in which novelty, natality, is bestowed upon him or her as a *forma vitae* for others.

## Exemplifying Soufanieh: On the Social Production of Examples and Types

A paradigmatic typology is highly relevant to thinking through the methods with which both anthropology and Soufanieh produce examples. Persuasion rests in both fields on the creation of viable examples that move us in such a way that we take the actual instantiation up, as it reflects both its particularity but is also used to say something more about social phenomena. In this chapter, the rhetoric of exemplarity in the form of the sermons delivered in Soufanieh has been explored. Centrally, I have argued that a logic of seriation is used to craft two exemplary forms of life, one in line with God, the other with his enemy. In this logic of seriation, I as an anthropologist was addressed very early on by several of the ardent followers of Soufanieh and advised as to whom to talk to and whom not to talk to. I was told not to interview divorcees. I was led towards Myrna, her family, and other "good" examples. And even I was addressed as an example to become. "You didn't choose to come here yourself," Salwa said one day after a service in the home of Myrna. "God chose you! He wants you to spread the message with your book." After these words, Salwa went on to paraphrase some of the messages Myrna had received, emphasizing the last one received from Jesus on Easter Saturday, 10 April 2004: "This is my last commandment to you: Each one of you return to your home. However, hold the East in your hearts. From here a light emerged anew. You are its radiance in a world seduced by materialism, sensuality, and fame, so much as to have lost its values." Emphasizing that a light from the East will emanate and spread to the West, the general interpretation among the followers of Our Lady of Soufanieh was that the light was this particular location. To Salwa, I was the obvious answer to this prophecy and was urged to become a part of the series and extend it in even wider circles. More than extending the series, however, the anthropologist here was also functioning as an example of the importance of Our Lady of Soufanieh beyond Syria proper.

In anthropology and the social sciences more broadly, Max Weber's work on ideal types can help us situate the production of examples. Both in his methodological essays and in his analysis of the Protestant ethic and the capitalist spirit (2003[1905]), Weber used a framing of certain characteristics to describe developments of a certain Christian character (see Cannell 2006). The character Weber (2003[1905]) crafted was that of Calvinistic Christians, used to frame a broader Northern European work ethic. The ideal type Weber thereby presented was a distillation of traits into a single figure of a very general purview.

But by this crafting of an ideal type, Christianity was encapsulated in a particular form, which rendered other forms more opaque. Recent attempts in anthropology to explore Christianity have shared similar tendencies in that a great number, with Joel Robbins (2007) as the prime proponent, have transposed the focus on Christianity from a basically Protestant ideal type, and Calvinistic at that, to a novel ideal type of Christianity that is essentially Pentecostal.

This characterization is not in itself a problem, since Pentecostalism is numerically the most expansive form of contemporary Christianity. The issue, though, is whether Pentecostal types of Christianity are taken to embody Christianity as a whole. The questions raised by Pentecostal ideal types are worthy of investing analytical labour on, but they need to address the varieties of Christian formulations. An examination of types in churches as well as in anthropology, therefore, needs to critically engage types or examples as informative but in different domains (see Weber 2003[1905]; Schmitt 1996[1923]; Agamben 2005[2000]). In this sense, which types are used in research, as well as in the life of the church, is as much a theoretical as it is a methodological question. This viewpoint – as argued throughout this book – offers a way of exploring how different worlds make use of examples and exemplification, even if the goals may be a better understanding in the one domain and the salvation of souls in the other. Roman Catholicism, or the varieties of Eastern Catholicism and Orthodox Christianity as found in Damascus and Syria, need to be read as culturally more nuanced in their formulation of types as opposed, both deliberately and unconsciously, to Protestant varieties. Here the promulgation, discussion, and development of types in the Catholic Church can be seen as a significant inventory of different ideals and examples as they have percolated throughout history and persist to this day. The modelling of sainthood in words and images has its exemplary force in the extendability and spread in and of a series. Here, in different ways, anthropologist, interlocutors, and Christian tradition all appear to be participating.

# Chapter Four

# Life and Story

The young man *says what is true*, but the old man has verified it, has *made that true* which yet is eternally true. The only difference here is that which in these times has been overlooked, when with all this proving and proving it has been forgotten that the highest thing a man is capable of is to make an eternal truth true, to make it true, to make it true that it is true – by doing it, by being himself the proof, by a life which also perhaps will be able to convince others. Did Christ ever undertake to prove some truth or another, or to prove the truth? No, but He made the truth true, or He made it true that He is the Truth.

          – Søren Kierkegaard, *Christian Discourses*

In the previous chapter, we discussed the rhetoric of exemplarity in the form of the sermons delivered in Soufanieh. It was argued that a logic of the series is used to craft two exemplary forms of life, one in line with God, the other with his enemy. Where chapter three thereby deliberately focused on rhetoric and sermons in the modelling of sainthood and the fleshing out of examples to emulate, this chapter will extend this focus by attending to the life stories interwoven with Myrna and her life. Exemplarity for the ardent followers of Our Lady of Soufanieh is not merely a matter of rhetoric and sermons one listens to; rather, it is a constant concern with very practical and quotidian consequences for how they see and narrate their own lives. But how is it possible to place oneself in the story of Our Lady of Soufanieh and to make one's life conform to her model in a truly exemplary life? How does one imitate a saint, or even the Virgin Mary or Christ? How do life and story intersect?

In various formulations across Eastern and Western Christian traditions, some of the most lasting popular imprints have been in works on the imitation of Christ and the saints. One of the most famous works among these is Thomas à Kempis's *The Imitation of Christ*, which for centuries has been formative for a particular type of pious centring on a virtuous life in pursuit of spiritual perfection through imitation (see Carrithers 1985; Cannell 1995; Aubin-Boltanski 2014; Bautista 2017). Kempis (1953[c. 1420]), in a paragraph entitled "Of the Examples of Holy Fathers," thus writes:

> Behold the lively examples of holy Fathers and blessed Saints, in whom flourished and shined all true perfection of life and perfect religion, and thou shalt see how little it is, and nigh as nothing, that we do now in these days, in comparison. O what is our life, if it be to them compared! (31)

What we here encounter is the role of imitation and emulation for the life of what Kempis calls "a true religious person" (30).

The example of the saints should stir devotion and perfection of Christian virtues, such as meekness, obedience, prayer, charity, patience, and service of God, as the life of the true religious person is compared to that of saints, martyrs, and Christ himself. Accordingly, the lives and examples of these saintly figures produce a formative invitation to compare, live, and mould one's life on theirs. A central insight is that such an invitation rests less on a formal idea of prescription or rules than on what historian Catherine Sanok (2007) has described as a form of comparandum (3). Sanok, in her work on exemplarity and the use of female saints' lives in late medieval England, argues:

> Saints were understood to mediate between Christ and ordinary Christians, not only as intercessors but also as ethical models: the saint imitates Christ typologically and in turn provides a tropological (that is, moral) exemplar to those who hear and read her story. (2)

Hereby, we are pointed towards the central insight that exemplarity serves as an interpretive structure, a mode of interpretation, where ethical and – in various Christian formulations – devotional practices are worked out (see Elgin 1996; Kleinberg 2008; Rogers 2009; Lambek 2014; Daswani 2016; Naumescu 2016; Pop 2017). Of further significance, we see that imitation demands labour, as there is a tension in how to actually live up to the example (see also Bandak & Bille 2013a; Mayblin 2014). In this sense, we see here how anthropological engagements with ethics and morality may benefit from a careful working through such concerns with exemplarity and a notion of the intersection and interweaving of life and story, of biography and hagiography, in a religious tradition.[1]

A central feature of the followers of Our Lady of Soufanieh is that they live their lives as witnesses or messengers, as Abuna Zahlawi phrased it in the last chapter. A witness is a person who, through his or her life, testifies to the divine reality by changing that life. As will be noted in chapter five, witnessing is understood as part of a process of evidentification, of corroborating the claims of veracity on the part of Our Lady of Soufanieh, Myrna, and the extended family of followers. The truth of the whole family is to be made evident in and through words and actions, so that one's life, but also that of the collective, to refer to Kierkegaard's words above, "perhaps will be able to convince others."

For all the devoted people I encountered, this process was one that demanded perfection of character in words and deeds. Some of the followers of Our Lady of Soufanieh, however, were seen to embody the spirit of Soufanieh more fully than others. Myrna was seen as the fullest embodiment of the ideal. She, in their perception, had been chosen (Matter 2001; Davis & Boles 2003; Hollander 2008). For the followers, however, some were seen as on their way and others as only at the very beginning of their wandering towards spiritual perfection. We hereby touch upon the topic of exemplarity from the angle of imitation and emulation.

Whereas choice can be underscored in many traditions that focus on learning from exemplars (see Warnick 2008; Humphrey 1997; Laidlaw 2014: 74, 82ff.), the issue is more complicated for the followers of Our Lady of Soufanieh. People will have to make decisions in their lives. And people, as we saw in the previous chapter, will have to choose whether to belong among the good or the bad listeners. These apparent choices and decisions, however, rest on the idea of a calling. The Virgin calls the individual to pay attention. Jesus calls the individual to follow him. Here, choice is to be rendered as a response, not a decision taken on the part of the individual him- or herself. This structure of call and response fits very well with Erich Auerbach's seminal analysis of God's work on ordinary persons in both the Old and New Testament in his monumental *Mimesis* (2003[1953]). Here, Auerbach presents the continual work God undertakes on his chosen subjects as a "formation undergone by those whom God has chosen to be examples" (18). Auerbach continues: "He has not only made them once and for all and chosen them, but continues to work upon them, bends them and kneads them, and without destroying them in essence, produces from them forms which their youth gave no grounds for anticipating" (18). On Auerbach's reading, God's work plays on the themes of humiliation and elevation, where ordinary persons can grow and mature, and where "their greatness, rising out of humiliation, is almost superhuman and an image of God's greatness" (18). As we will see, several of these features also pertain to the way followers of Our Lady of Soufanieh understand their devotion. They hear the Virgin Mary and Jesus calling them personally, and they attempt to craft their lives accordingly. Among the extended family of Soufanieh, each person is urged to embody the spirit of unity, faith, and love, both as individuals and as part of the same collective family. There are different roles in a family, but in a family as envisioned in Soufanieh, every member is meant to attest to the same message in his or her own way. The goal is not to make every single member of the family the same, but to let every single member of the family shine according to his or her own nature. To shine, one has to assume the role planned for the individual, a role that is patterned on gender, age, and social position. Life for the followers of Our Lady of Soufanieh is, accordingly, a matter of learning and becoming. Italian philosopher Alessandro Ferrara (2008) has captured a similar property in the field of exemplarity in the difference between *what is* and *what ought to be the case* (2; see also Lambek 2010a: 6). The exemplary example aligns these two concepts and therefore forcefully renders a particular way of seeing things. The example here is to be seen as a process of becoming, one where *what ought* and *what is* merge in the successful example.

My aim in this chapter is to delve into the rhetoric of exemplarity reflected through two different life stories. I was urged to collect the life of Rima, as she was seen as a good example, a person embodying the spirit of Soufanieh. By contrast, I was admonished not to collect the life of Fadi, as he was seen as a bad example, one who did not embody the spirit of Soufanieh, even though he was very active in promoting her message of faith, love, and unity. Both people are deeply concerned with how to live a virtuous life, how to follow the examples set by Myrna and the Virgin Mary, and how to live up to the ideal. The two life stories are exemplary in different ways, as they both attest more widely to the prevalent concerns of the extended family of Our Lady of Soufanieh – not just in a prosaic sense of having to do better but, rather, as a central impetus to get more people to join the family of Soufanieh and thereby God's family. The concern, therefore, is to make the miraculous happenings in Soufanieh known to the wider society and attract more followers; in this mission, one's own life is an important testimony. Or perhaps – better said – it ought to be an important testimony. Accordingly, for the followers of Our Lady of Soufanieh to follow the example involves a radical sense of participation in divine planning, which is theoretically best conceived of as what Nelson Goodman (1981: 128) calls a "co-exemplification." It is to play an active role in making known and visible the message of Our Lady of Soufanieh in life and deeds, and thereby, how one lives can add or subtract from the story of Our

Lady of Soufanieh. However, people are seen to embody the message of Soufanieh to different degrees, and action therefore remains tied to the work of words. Imitation is never simply straightforward; rather, it is something to be learned, since one of the great dangers is that a person merely acts as if he or she is a believer without making the work and deeds correspond to the message of love, faith, and unity that is so central for the extended family of Soufanieh. In this chapter, then, I present two different life stories.

**The Creation of the Mother Teresa of Damascus: The Good Example**

Rima is one of Myrna's trusted individuals, and she is responsible for alleviating the suffering of many poor people in greater Damascus. She sees other people and their needs, I was frequently told. Myrna even dubbed her "the Mother Teresa of Damascus," and I was urged by Salwa and other central figures in the extended family of Soufanieh to record her life story and to make sure that they also could be allowed to hear it. Salwa described Rima as being too shy and uninterested in publicity, which had made it a challenge for them to obtain her life story. I recorded the interview with Rima over several days. The first two parts were recorded in the inner courtyard of Myrna and Nicolas's home, and the third interview in the home of Salwa. The chosen location for the first two parts of the interview was deliberate on Rima's part, a way of both emphasizing the proximity to the location chosen by the Virgin Mary and of pointing to the relationship with Myrna and her family.[2] The third part of the interview was conducted in the home of Salwa due to activities in Myrna's home and the proximity of Salwa's home to Myrna's. Conducting an interview with Rima, I was soon to learn, was not aimed at focusing solely on her but rather on the common story of which she was but one part. This sense of participation in a larger and unfolding narrative with a divine plot was corroborated by Rima's life story as she narrated it.

Rima's life story is remarkable. It is interwoven with the location but also with the people who have been at the core of this place: Myrna, Abuna Elias Zahlawi, and Abuna Youssef Maalouli. It is crafted as an invitation that took her from a misguided life on the brink of total failure to a life of virtuous servitude. The line of the narrative is not presented as a radical change but rather as steps that gradually have made it possible to live a sanctified life.[3] Rima is late for our first interview as she has been serving poor and needy people in Dweila and Jaramana. As she arrives in front of Myrna's home, she apologizes for her delay; we enter and, after brief greetings, find a location on a couch in the inner courtyard. Rima is at home here. She unbuttons her black coat and places it and her handbag on the couch next to her. Rima is in her mid-fifties, and her hair is black with some grey. Devotional music is playing on the stereo next to the icon of Our Lady of Soufanieh and creates a devotional atmosphere. The Tuesday evening novena will start later, and people are already, one hour before the start, beginning to come and pray in front of the icon. I switch on my recorder, and Rima starts to recount her life, quite dramatically:

> Before I started coming to Soufanieh, I was in a situation where I was about to leave my family. Honestly, I was about to leave my family, to take my children and live on my own. The problem in my family was enormous! I mean, nobody understood me and what I wanted. I wanted respect [iḥtirām], I wanted love [maḥabba], I wanted God to be in my home … But I didn't know that for these things to happen, I would have to carry the cross.

She pauses for a moment. "I rejected the cross!" Rima looks at me and gives what throughout serves as her interpretive key to her narration. She starts her narrative in her family, which was about to be torn apart by conflicts and problems. Her pious aims could not survive in this unhealthy environment, and she had decided to leave her husband. The problems were experienced as insurmountable, and even petitions for help to the wider family were declined.

In order to highlight the general nature of family life problems, Rima uses the messages of Our Lady of Soufanieh as an interpretive key right from the start of our conversation: she refers to a part of the message received by Myrna in the fifth and last apparition on 24 March 1983. "The Virgin said: 'Do not be divided as the great ones are.'" Rima states what she finds to be the implication for her situation: "It means that they are marked by egoism." The division due to egoism in her family had, in other words, left her bereft of any idea of how to continue living in her marriage. On the brink of this drastic decision, she goes to sleep, intending to leave with her children the following morning for the village of Saydnaya, some thirty kilometres away. Rima makes sure to emphasize that she did not have any previous knowledge of Soufanieh: "I didn't know Soufanieh. I had heard of it, but I didn't know it. I didn't know Myrna or anybody else in the home." Rima explains that some of her siblings had been to Soufanieh, but she had never been interested. However, she also reveals that this situation was all to change.

That night Rima receives a dream (ḥulm), which, she makes sure to underline, is very rare as she never dreams. The dream lasts for only five minutes, but something very significant is foreshadowed in the dream.

> The important thing is that, during the night while I was sleeping, I was praying the rosary. I had the first bead in my hand – on the work of unity as I knew it – but I didn't know the gospel, and I didn't know anything. I knew the rosary from the nuns that I had taken lessons with. I knew I had to pray the rosary, and I had liked it. When I had the first bead in my hand, I felt mixed in my desire to take my children and go to Saydnaya in the morning.

The dramatic start to the narrative is important as it frames Rima as a person with a good heart, even if she did not know how to pray properly. It frames the misguided life in a family close to disintegration. This frame is important as a part of the grander narrative of Our Lady of Soufanieh, since the message of faith, love, and unity addresses family life specifically. It does so by focusing on aspects of the received messages but also by mirroring the life of Myrna, Nicolas, and their two children. The individual life story is hence made to corroborate the larger story of Our Lady of Soufanieh.

"At night I saw myself and the mother of my husband in a dream. We were walking on ground that was all pitted." Rima's mother-in-law is not able see how they will be able to get up and searches for a staircase. Together, they search for the staircase and find it, only to realize that there is a huge distance between each step. Rima explains that the stairway was impressive and that she had difficulty climbing it. In trying to climb, she loses track of her mother-in-law and ends up climbing the steps on her own. In other words, she was left alone and exposed, with no possibility of breaking out of her misery. Rima explains her exhaustion at recognizing that she was unable to help herself escape. In her despair, she pleads to the Virgin Mary: "Oh Virgin, Oh Virgin, help me!" Her mother-in-law hears her plea and asks why she is pleading to the Virgin for help. Before managing an answer, Rima explains how a lady, all dressed in white, appears sitting on the ground. "Give me your hand," the lady says. "And she helped me ascend the steps," Rima continues. After waking from the dream, Rima narrates how she explains her situation to the family, telling them that she will leave for Saydnaya with her children the very next morning. The meaning of the dream has not yet dawned on her and has only left her in further despair.

The next morning, Rima is ready to leave for Saydnaya when her sister arrives from Abu Dhabi. Hearing of Rima's destitute situation, the sister pleads with Rima to follow her to Soufanieh to pray. This meeting took place on 7 September, and the sister said something might happen at Myrna's home. At first, Rima did not want to go. However, her sister persuades her to go there, as something might happen on that particular day. For both Catholic and Orthodox Christians in Syria, 7 September is one of the most important celebrations; it is the day of the public celebrations preceding the next day's much celebrated Feast of the Nativity of the Virgin ('Īd as-Sayyida). Rima continues:

> It was in 1987, and it had all started in 1982, that is five years after the beginning. As I arrived, there was no space at all. It was packed with people, and I had to stand outside on the street. Here they had placed a television so that we could follow the events. I didn't watch it, but I could hear the priest saying that Myrna was in ecstasy [inkhiṭāf]. And I didn't know Myrna or anything … I asked my sister what ecstasy was. Then she told me that oil was oozing from Myrna and that she would start talking and to give us a message.

Rima then started to pray fervently with her sister. Rima wanted to obtain one of the prayer cards from Myrna to use for prayer in the home. Because there were so many people, it was initially quite difficult, but Rima and her sister manage to see Abuna Youssef Maalouli, who recounts the message Myrna had just received from Christ. "What was the message?" Rima asks, and immediately answers by reciting the words she has learned by heart:

> Mary, is it not you that I have chosen, the quiet girl with a heart full of love and sympathy? I have noticed that you cannot endure anything for Me. I shall give you a chance to choose. Know that if you lose Me, you will lose the prayers of all those around you, and know that bearing the Cross is unavoidable.

Rima continues: "This message wasn't for Myrna, it was for me! Right in my heart I felt that this was a hand for me."

What is at stake here is an interweaving of narratives. Rima goes reluctantly to see Myrna, and she is met by a message she believes is aimed directly at her. This trait of feeling the Virgin or Christ pointing at an individual is a general feature for the followers of Our Lady of Soufanieh. It was iterated time and time again in the interviews and is a feature that has also been observed at other shrines of other visionaries (see Apolito 1998[1992]; Christian 1996; Davis & Boles 2003; Scheer 2013). In the general conception, this message was a specific message for Myrna, advising her to follow the straight path through suffering and pain, to carry the cross in order not to lose the favour of Christ. In Rima's conception, it was just as much a message to her, a message that *she* was seen by Christ as the quiet girl with a good heart and that *she* had to carry the cross. Here, more general concerns in tune with a larger devout sensibility are articulated, namely that suffering and grace are worked out in a dialectical relationship, where participation in redemptive work comes about not in a life devoid of pain and suffering but in an embrace of it (see Orsi 1985; Cannell 1999; Mayblin 2010; Jansen 2011).

Rima and her sister wait for Myrna to ask her for prayer cards of Our Lady of Soufanieh. Finally, Rima is able to enter Myrna's home. Rima and her sister enter the inner courtyard and want to go to the terrace to see where the apparitions were initially received. They have to climb the stairs, and the steps are very steep. The stairs cause some problems for Rima, but suddenly a woman who is standing on the stairs says: "Give me your hand." And Rima continues with excitement: "Then I remembered her from the dream!" The figure who helps Rima climb the stairs is revealed as Myrna. Rima underlines her fear of the steep staircase and then conjoins the dream with a fulfilment:

> "Give me your hand," she said. "Give me your hand." If you recall the dream! ... I started to cry. Then Myrna asked: "Why are you crying?" I said: "I saw you in a dream yesterday, and my story is such and such – that I would leave my home and take my children."

The scene from the dream is now replicated, and Myrna is revealed as the figure able to alleviate Rima's troubles. This move is very significant for the narrative. Rima is being inserted as an exemplar in the greater story of Soufanieh as one of the figures who not only hears and listens but is called upon by the Virgin and prepared to meet Myrna and hear her message. What we see here is a narrative that is doubled. Myrna receives messages and apparitions; Rima receives a dream that points her towards Myrna. The dream functions as an exemplary form of communication in the narrative and works to sanction and prefigure both the divine election of Myrna and also that of Rima.[4] What's more, Christ's words address problems the individual refuses to face, problems pertaining in particular to the reluctance to embrace and willfully meet suffering. The narrative implies that a response needs to be made if Rima is not to lose the grace of the Virgin and the ability to pray.

At this point in the interview, I am no longer the only person listening. Dina, a lady in her early forties, has joined us and exclaims "Glory to God!" as she hears Rima's "magnificent" testimony. The alignment between Rima's own life trajectory and the happenings in Soufanieh attest in several ways to the grace of God. It confirms Myrna in her role as a divinely ordained figure and, in this narrative, creates for Rima the role of a chosen assistant. It corroborates the Virgin's care in preparing Rima for meeting Myrna at the darkest hour of Rima's life. However, this meeting is not the end of the narrative. On the contrary, it is only the beginning. A process of learning and imitation ensues.

## A Process of Learning and Imitation

Rima takes her story onwards by pointing to the two central priests and their role in educating her, first Abuna Youssef Maalouli and then Abuna Elias Zahlawi. Rima's family problems were not resolved from one day to the next. Even though Rima visited Soufanieh every day and prayed more and more fervently, a sorrow was harboured in her life, and she was always crying. One day, seeing Rima's frustration, Abuna Maalouli addressed her. Rima recounts the wise words of Abuna Maalouli: "Jesus is joy. Why are you crying?" Rima explained the many problems in her life. "Come and talk with me. I'm your father, I'm your brother, I'm your mother. Whatever your problem is, I want to help you" was the response from the experienced priest. As Rima does so, Maalouli gives direction and meaning to Rima's suffering: "This is a test for you, and it is very difficult. But the Virgin is with you and will help you! This is the lesson of the Cross." Rima thereby draws the line to the opening of her life story. She was rejecting the cross, and only by accepting it can genuine fulfilment be found. The solution is not one in which all troubles vanish, but one in which the Virgin, in the midst of human suffering and frailty, allows the situation to be endured for her sake.

What we here encounter may be seen as a transfiguration of pain into suffering, a transfiguration where what hurts is rendered purposeful and to be embraced for the sake of Christ and the Virgin Mary but also as an imitation of the example of Myrna. The Virgin herself is also emulated in her ability to bear suffering and help alleviate the needs of others.

The process of learning is one in which Rima follows Myrna and is directed by Abuna Maalouli. The relationship between Rima and Myrna develops as Rima starts coming to the home every day just before the daily prayers of the rosary. She receives a prayer card from Myrna with the image of Our Lady of Soufanieh on it, which she takes home for her personal prayer. Rima was immediately drawn towards Myrna's home as it felt like somewhere very special. In time, Myrna starts to designate Rima as her sister. "Myrna said: 'I'm like your sister.' I'm eight years older than Myrna. She said I'm like your sister, but I learn from her." And so it happened, Rima explains, that little by little she forgot the problems of her marital life with the help and assistance of Myrna and Abuna Maalouli. Dina enquires as to this process and if the problems just vanished. Rima explains her workload in the home and how the change was gradual and had to start with herself: "I learned from Myrna and Abuna Maalouli to carry all my duties, even the cumbersome ones." The process of learning as well as change in this narrative is hence rendered as a gradual one; Rima had to learn to carry the cross, which did not just happen overnight. However, her life course was changed, and the cumbersome tasks were rendered in a new light.

Whereas miracles occupy a central position in many of the narratives of the followers of Our Lady of Soufanieh, it does not mean that miracles happen in a steady stream. A long time may pass during which no miracles occur. However, the absence of miracles or the time waiting for miracles is significant. Some make sure to underscore the Virgin's personal address through specific miracles. In Rima's case, she did not see a miracle her first year of coming to Soufanieh. She heard about the miracles of healings and exuding oil but did not experience a miracle herself. When she did, however, it was a noteworthy one. As Rima was redirecting her life, she decided to celebrate her daughter's birthday, but this year without dancing, focusing on praying instead. The devotional aspect was not contrary to celebration, and Rima had made a cake and wanted to invite Myrna to come for the birthday. However, she was afraid that it might cause a stir if Myrna were to come for a birthday at her home, as it would entice others to want to do the same, increasing pressure on Myrna. Rima explains how she asked for permission from Abuna Maalouli, which was granted. As the late Abuna Maalouli, at this point, preferred to stay as much as possible only in Myrna's home now turned shrine, it was arranged that Abuna Elias Zahlawi would join Myrna in his stead. It was planned that he and Myrna would come at eight o'clock.

During her preparations, Rima discovered that she needed to have flowers, and she asked her daughter to fetch some from a nearby shop in Tijara. The daughter did so but also spread the news that Myrna was coming. "She said: 'I need this because Myrna Soufanieh is coming to our home, but my mother has told me not to say this to anybody.' She was just a little girl!" Rima smiles at the innocence of her daughter revealing the event. So it happened that many of the neighbours heard of the visit and were curious to see Myrna. All but a few in the neighbourhood are Muslims, Rima explains. Myrna started to pray, and oil began to flow. "At first I didn't see it and thought that people were joking, when they said: 'ya Rima, oil is oozing.'" Rima explains the situation:

"The Virgin celebrated my daughter because of the flowers and the people." Rima then continues and recounts how Abuna Elias Zahlawi seized the possibility and asked everyone present to bear witness to this miracle. So it happened that Rima's home was anointed by holy oil, and ordinary persons, even Muslims, were made witnesses to divine grace in her home. What the story accomplishes is to craft Rima's life course and Myrna's as increasingly intertwined. Rima comes to regard Myrna ever more highly as she attests to holiness on a daily basis. Rima concludes the interview with emphasis: "Myrna is a saint!" The music from the stereo plays softly into the narrative: "Alleluia, Alleluia, Alleluia." Violins create an elated atmosphere, corroborating the miracle of Our Lady of Soufanieh at this very location and in Rima's life.

From this point on, Rima recounts that she started learning from Myrna about how to follow her and to pray and emulate saints such as Thérèse of Lisieux and Don Giovanni Bosco. Myrna points to other more established saints, which are part of the wider Syrian Catholic devotional landscape. By pointing to these authorized saints, Myrna is laying the ground for firmer recognition and emulation, as it is not by her words alone but by her deeds that she attracts a following. In following Myrna, Rima becomes a significant trustee but also a model in her own right, as she is now one of the responsible people who make sure that poor people receive medicine or donations on which to survive. Several of the younger members follow Rima on her rounds, distributing help and learning from her. What is happening here is that Rima's individual life story is interwoven with Myrna's life and the message of Soufanieh, and Rima's very process of learning and devout imitation renders both Rima and Myrna as exemplars for central virtues such as humility, servitude, patience, family, and willingness to bear suffering but also to alleviate the suffering of others. Both Rima and Myrna are now rendered exemplars of virtues worth imitating, and for the devout followers, they model how a perfect example should be. Here life – as proposed by Ferrara (2008) – *is* as it *ought* to be. Rima's life story, more than mere biography, is rendered as hagiography; her life is sanctified by her participation in the divine narrative of Soufanieh, where her weaknesses and family problems gradually make way for service and thereby corroborate Our Lady of Soufanieh's message of faith, love, and unity. Her life story unfolds, however, in a gendered universe in which her role is that of the suffering mother who learns to accept the cross and endure suffering in emulation of Myrna and, ultimately, the Virgin Mary. Here, we see how the modelling of sainthood takes place and how it makes Myrna and the Virgin Mary work as a source of both empowerment and acceptance of a given situation (see Orsi 1985, 1996, 2005; Hermkens, Jansen, & Notermans 2009: 4–5; Jansen 2005; Mayblin 2010). Suffering is not happening in vain; rather, it is rendered purposeful as a form of agency in and upon the world.

## Salwa and Right Examples: Representations by Types

The focus on the right way of life was marked for all in the extended family of Soufanieh. Their interest in my writing was concomitantly evident for some of the people closest to Myrna. Rita and Salwa made sure that I had access to the right people and would find out whom I had met with and interviewed. In this sense, they tried to use me and my anticipated book as testimony to the story of Soufanieh. To portray the miracle of Soufanieh, I had to be led to the most important people. Neither Salwa nor Rita placed themselves at the pinnacle of importance; however, they made sure to direct me to people healed by the grace of God and the intercession of Our Lady of Soufanieh. Both directed me to people who had recently either experienced miracles or had been changed. Rita would point to a young girl, who had been cured of cancer, as she returned with her parents to Soufanieh. Salwa would point to Bashar, a young man who had become more and more devoted to Our Lady of Soufanieh. However, Rima was the person I was above all pointed towards as a prominent example embodying what Joel Robbins (2015) would call the core values evident in flourishing form: servitude, care, humility, and a story of a changed family life through prayer and devotion. Rima was, in other words, a good example. She was a good example in that she referred back to Myrna and co-exemplified the core values so important for the devout followers, not by becoming Myrna but by embodying a process of sanctification and sacrifice attesting to the power of Our Lady of Soufanieh to allow change to happen.

The interest in my work also meant that I was advised not to speak to particular people. Fadi was one of them. This proscription became evident one day in a conversation with Salwa. That day, as I turn from Sharia al-Qassaʿ and approach the home of Nicolas and Myrna, I meet Salwa walking towards me. She explains that Myrna and Nicolas have just left for Saydnaya and that an interview she had tried to set up for me with a local priest has failed to materialize. We turn direction and walk towards her car parked some minutes away at Sahat Burj Arouz. As we start walking, Salwa asks: "Did you talk to Abuna Elias Zahlawi?" She follows up: "You should give your testimony to Abuna Elias Zahlawi regarding what you have experienced here in Soufanieh." I am a bit surprised, as I usually see myself in the role of the person listening and recording people's reactions here, not the opposite. For Salwa, my interest in the devotion to Our Lady of Soufanieh is not coincidental but rather a part of divine planning, and she also wants me to become a witness and a living testimony. In other words, Salwa aims at soliciting not just any reaction but a particular and devout one from me: that I give my testimony. "It would be collected for a new book," Salwa explains in order to convince me further.

Sensing my hesitation, Salwa changes the topic: "Do you need any help with appointments?" She pauses. "Do you need to talk to Rima again?" I say that I have already interviewed Rima twice this week. I continue explaining to her that I have done interviews every day this week and am quite busy currently. I also relay that I have an interview with Fadi later today. "Fadi who?" Salwa asks. I explain who it is. "I think you should ask Myrna whom to talk to," Salwa says with a concerned expression on her face. She continues: "You should talk to people who live right, and not just speak ..." She pauses and leaves the words hanging with a clear, albeit understated, message. At this point, I do not want to back away from the topic, so I explain that it is important for me and my research to have a broad sample of people. "You can and should speak with many, but ask Myrna about whom to go to," Salwa pleads. As she feels that I am still not shying away from the planned interview, she continues: "You should talk to Myrna before you talk to Fadi ... You know he is separated." Salwa looks at me before continuing: "You should speak to people like Rima, people who live the life of Soufanieh and not just talk about it." The sense of gravity is felt here. Salwa wants good examples to speak and display genuine, in her eyes, images of Soufanieh, not bad ones.

Having arrived at Salwa's car, we talk briefly about different errands. I make a final attempt at explaining that it is important for me to talk to different people who come to Soufanieh and that Fadi comes here every week. Salwa looks at me again: "I see, but you need to speak to people who haven't got ..." Salwa pauses and then says in English: "two faces." I look at her, sensing the gravity of the implied accusation. I make one last attempt to salvage the enterprise by saying that, for me, it is interesting not just to see how unity is lived but also why it is difficult to live it. Salwa walks towards her car, the key in her hand. She turns, and then she says: "You know ... the problem with unity starts in the family."

Salwa's interest in the life story of Rima is evident. She urges me to record it and even to pass the recording on to her for later documentation. Rima and her life story highlight and corroborate the image of unity, love, and faith that is important for the extended family of

Soufanieh to present. Moreover, the very idea of the family as a model for life and society is rendered by the lives of Myrna and Rima. Their lives are seen as exemplary in that, in different ways, they have both succeeded in living the message of unity, even in, or perhaps exactly in and through, adversity. With his unsolved marital problems, Fadi is seen not to embody the spirit of unity, which, as Salwa bluntly puts it, always starts with the family. Truly exemplary life is not just talk. Truly exemplary life is practice. The point here is not that such a life is devoid of iniquity, failures, and problems; what is critical is how such problems are overcome and how suffering in the face of such issues is carried and presented.

Salwa's attempt at directing my attention towards particular people could be understood as general image control on the part of the members of Soufanieh. However, rather than conceiving Salwa's plea as an outright monitoring of my research and thereby as a containment of darker sides of the story, I see that, from Salwa's own perspective, her direction is rather a way of guiding me to divine reality. People only talking, or presenting different faces, are putting the whole story in jeopardy. The story needs to be corroborated by life. And in this light, Fadi apparently does not fit. Examples, in other words, need to be chosen carefully in order to show what needs to be shown. To present Rima as an example renders the process of change towards embodying the spirit of Our Lady of Soufanieh most fully, whereas to present Fadi as an example would be wrong, as he, in Salwa's conception, does not elicit the same exemplary qualities as Rima. To Salwa, the example should not be chosen because of its qualities as a representation, in the sense of it being the same as other instantiations; rather, the example must be chosen because it most fully embodies the qualities strived for.[5] The example is thus not understood as a flat representation but as the ideal, the highest form.

### The Bad Example: Fadi and How to Make the Message of Our Lady of Soufanieh Visible

Salwa did not succeed in persuading me not to talk to Fadi. However, she pointed me in a particular direction with her concern and admonitions. When talking to Fadi, some of the same concerns came to the fore, albeit in a different fashion. Fadi was well aware that his life is not perfect. His longing to see the message of Soufanieh spread throughout Syria and the world, however, is a burning one. Fadi is in his late forties. He is always well dressed and tidy. He visits Soufanieh regularly, particularly the Tuesday evening novenas and the Saturday services, and has been a part of the extended family of Soufanieh since 1984. I met Fadi regularly in Soufanieh and, over time, started also to see him at one of his places of employment and in his home. The conversations I had with Fadi always centred on the importance of Soufanieh but also on the scant attention Soufanieh – in his opinion – receives. Over time, I conducted several interviews with Fadi in his home in the old city. The interviews lasted several hours each, and Fadi prepared himself thoroughly for each of them. For Fadi, the topic of Soufanieh was too important to be left to mere chit chat. For the first interview, he read aloud a handwritten page with the three most important things he has learned in Soufanieh.

Fadi marvels at the many miracles he has seen in Soufanieh. He lists them: oil, the divine smell of incense that only God can bring forth, healings. "I have seen the stigmata [al-juruḥāt] three times ... in 1984, 1987, and 1990." Fadi briefly goes over the years to see if he remembers correctly. "The stigmata point man towards Myrna, to look towards her and see her pain ... The stigmata have such deep meaning: they are the pain of living the eternal life of Christ," Fadi explains. Clearly, for Fadi, Myrna is seen as "a living icon" (see Belting 2010), a person most fully moved by God, who participates in the pain of Christ bodily (see also Kleinberg 1992; Morgan 1998; Orsi 2005). Fadi continues: "I saw so many things, so many things ... However, I don't want to talk only of what I have seen – so many people talk and talk. I want to talk about what I have learned through Soufanieh." Fadi looks at me, inviting me to ask the obvious question of what he has learned. He has opened a bottle of local wine and toasts with me after inviting me to join him. "Do you mind if I smoke?" Fadi asks. I say it is his home, whereupon he opens a packet of cigarettes and lights his first cigarette of many during the interview.[6] I prompt him to continue. Having waited for this cue, Fadi immediately seizes the opportunity: "I have written some things down that I want to share with you," he declares and clears his throat. "This is what I learned in Soufanieh." Fadi reads from his prepared document:

> Firstly, I learned prayer and how to pray. The Virgin said: "Remember me in your joy" ... Through the Virgin, I learned to pray in times of joy. To pray in an atmosphere of joy, which leads to what is good. She taught me to become one with my fellows praying in Heaven and on Earth, living and dead, in front of His throne. I have learned not to ask for anything, as God knows what I need. I learned to magnify God through my prayer, to ask for the will of God, to keep God's beatitude in mind. And to see that God is the only thing I need. This is the prayer I learned through Soufanieh.

Fadi closes the first point, and reads his second one:

> Secondly, I learned love. I have learned that love is everything ... We need love and grace in order to serve. It moves us ... Love is a difficult way, but we need to attend to it even in our wounds, even if we have to give up our earthly dreams. We need to give our love for others.

Fadi pauses briefly, before he reads the last point:

> Thirdly, I learned donation, how to give, not just earthly giving, not just the giving of one's riches, but to give from one's poverty, to give with joy.

He expands on this idea, pauses, and then says:

> The good example of this form of giving is Myrna. She gives all her time, spirit, thought, and all her work to whoever needs it. I learned from the Virgin when she said in the fifth apparition: "That night, the Angel told me: 'Blessed are Thou amongst women.' And I was only able to tell Him: 'I am the servant of the Lord.'" This is a very great sentence, a very great sentence. I learned that there is no power but the one granted by God. Jesus our Lord said: "I am among you as your servant." This is the culture that I learned from Soufanieh, to live because the Holy Spirit enables me to say: "Jesus is my light, and God is my salvation, so I do not fear!" This is what I learned in Soufanieh.

Fadi ends his reading from his pages on that note.

The well-composed words attest to Fadi's occupation with Soufanieh. He crafts a line between the importance of Soufanieh and Myrna for his individual life and the need for others to hear about it. He is thus not merely crafting himself as a person striving to live a pious life; more importantly, Fadi is contributing to the modelling of Myrna as a saint. The learning of prayer, love, and giving is central, because these are virtues that constitute both the good life as well as its fruits. Fadi is clear on this point. Myrna is the good example, the example that fully embodies the message of Our Lady of Soufanieh. Fadi underscores God's choosing of Myrna as conditioned by his supreme knowledge of the times and the heart of each person. I ask if Myrna is a saint and will be considered one in the future by the church.

> That's certain! She is an example as I told you. She is an example in every regard. She gives to everybody without exception and without knowing if they need. She gives herself to the Virgin and to Jesus. That is sanctification, and she is a saint ... There is no doubt in her. She is a saint!

Fadi says these words with much emphasis. As if mirroring himself in Myrna and his own evaluation, he continues: "I am not a saint, and I am not in a position to judge others. Everybody is better than me. I am the last of men." Fadi, in this sense, assumes the position of the unworthy person in need of help, which at the same time is the spiritual way of humility.[7]

However, this humility also rests on the knowledge of not having been able to fully live up to the example himself. During the interview, Fadi explains that his wife, who is Rima's sister, now lives with his daughter and son. He is separated. It is a cardinal issue for the Catholic Church, for the ideology of Soufanieh, and also for Fadi personally. It is a major issue and one that he admits is troubling him and tearing him and his well-being apart. "I used to look much better," he says, pointing to his grey hair and wrinkles. His own explanation is that the distance in his relationship with his wife crept in during eight years working in Saudi Arabia. It was hard to live in such a country devoid of fellow Christians and churches. Back in Damascus again, he now does all in his power to promulgate the message of Our Lady of Soufanieh. He is very frustrated that only a few people attend, given that many, many more ought to do so. Everybody needs to help Myrna, Fadi claims. Myrna has been chosen by God from his knowledge of past, present, and future, and she needs support.

With Salwa's words still ringing in my ears, I ask him about the meaning of unity. Fadi is quick to say: "This is unity of the hearts. If this is not in our hearts, there will be no unity among the denominations, churches, and so on." He quotes Our Lady of Soufanieh: "The unity of your hearts is My feast!" The Virgin said in a message: "Jesus told Peter: 'You are the rock, and on it, I shall build My church.' As for Me, I tell you now: You are the heart in which Jesus will build his unity." Fadi continues: "See the magnificence of this sentence!" From the question of unity, Fadi slides directly to the topic of propagation of Our Lady of Soufanieh's message. This task is a prevalent concern for most of the followers, in particular Fadi. In emphasizing that action is tied to the Virgin Mary herself, Fadi refers to Abuna Maalouli: "You don't know him, but he used to say: 'Don't do anything, let the Virgin lead us.'" In this sense, action in this articulation is placed on the Virgin Mary and not on the individual proponents. In practice, however, the followers are the able hands and mouths that make her message known. Fadi would like to do more to carry out this mission, to make people talk and think more. "If one hundred were present and just twenty received the message, or if only five, it would still be plenty." I refer to the gospels, where only one out of ten gives praise to the Lord. "Yes, and I said only five out of one hundred." Fadi laughs.

Fadi is also honest about the discrepancy between what he would like to be able to accomplish and the reality. In terms of prayer, he would like to go to Soufanieh every single day to pray, but it is not currently possible. "I wish I could pray in Soufanieh every day. I did this before, but not now," Fadi explains. His desire to see plenty of people pray the rosary in Soufanieh every day goes beyond himself. "There ought to be hundreds in the home every day," Fadi says. The prayers are important, as they inculcate core values such as peace and simplicity. "How beautiful is this place!" Fadi exclaims, citing the message from Jesus Christ given to Myrna on 26 November 1986. The locality is again underscored as graced by the Virgin Mary and, in a distinct way, making knowledge of God accessible. One can know the will of God through the gospel and the messages of Soufanieh, Fadi explains. And his words have a more dire implication: one can accept the will of God, or one can choose not to. I ask Fadi why he believes all these things happened in Damascus. "This is a particular grace! Al-ḥamdulillāh, it happened in Damascus, but at the same time, this is a great responsibility."

A central concern reverberates throughout the interviews with Fadi: do people want to come? As Fadi lights yet another cigarette, he sighs, and says: "They have Soufanieh, so why don't they come?" There is an internal frustration that, while witnessing the miracles of Our Lady of Soufanieh, so many remain indifferent to the message. Fadi continues with the idea of doing mission work. "It is necessary to do mission ... It is said in one of the messages Myrna received." During the afternoon, Fadi talks about fifteen points he has formulated with regard to spreading the message of Soufanieh. He tells me that he travelled some five months ago to different parts of Syria to explain the message. Unfortunately, the trip did not bear the fruits he had hoped for. He has detailed plans on how and where to spread the message. He pauses for a moment and makes sure he is not asserting his own persona too strongly in his narration. "It is not important to me where the idea came from ... The most important thing is that, if people will not come to Soufanieh, Soufanieh must come to them." Fadi says.

As we are talking about the topic of unity, I ask Fadi which church he is from. He is from the Greek Orthodox Church, he says. However, the next moment Fadi says to forget this, as it is not important. "I can pray in every church. I am a child of Soufanieh." In this regard, Fadi was on par with a great many in Soufanieh. All would precisely underline the importance of unity and downplay their denominational belonging. At the end of the talk, Fadi draws us back to what he finds most important, namely what has changed through Soufanieh. And change, Fadi asserts, happens over time, but the followers of Our Lady of Soufanieh today carry a huge responsibility for bringing her message to the world. "Before, the Virgin and Jesus were working; today, this is our task. But what are we doing today? This is the topic we ought to be discussing. Not between you and me, but in Soufanieh." Fadi thus, yet again, asserts the importance of action as following on from learning.

## Mirrored Sainthood: It All Starts in the Family

As life goes on, experience and learning are expected to grow and ensue for the followers of Our Lady of Soufanieh. Processes of learning are still ongoing, and each day people expect the individual to be able to learn new sides and aspects of and from the Virgin. The followers of Our Lady of Soufanieh expect a process of maturation, and in this regard, they are more understanding when it comes to less experienced people's misgivings as opposed to more senior people (see Mayblin 2017; Napolitano, Norget, & Mayblin 2017).

For Rima and Fadi, learning is central. When we consider the two life stories, it is clear that both see their lives as marked by the grace of the Virgin Mary and her presence in Soufanieh, and both see Myrna as a saint and an example to emulate. However, they are not on equal terms, as they embody the exemplary life to different degrees. Rima captures the story of Soufanieh more fully in being taken from misery towards a life of servitude, prayer, and unity in family life. In this regard, Rima was more easily incorporated into what Robert Orsi (1985: 222) has designated as a Catholic dialectic of suffering and redemption. She had to accept the cross, the suffering, and turn it into a willed sacrifice for the sake of Our Lady of Soufanieh. As expressed by Hannah Arendt (1998[1958]: 175), with recourse to Isak Dinesen, one of Karen Blixen's pseudonyms, much sorrow, or in the case of the followers of Our Lady of Soufanieh, much suffering and pain, can be borne if it is inserted in a story.

The central lesson for Rima to learn was that suffering was not to be taken away but rather to be borne. In the second interview, this lesson is addressed head on, thereby tying into the first interview in which Rima underscored that she had rejected the cross.

> I was rejecting the cross. But Myrna helped me. I learned from Myrna, but not through talk. She didn't say to me: work like this or do like that. I saw her, how she lives, and learned from her. How she lives with people. I saw how she lives with her husband and the home ... Most importantly, I learned that nothing can happen without prayer.

Rima explains how prayer is the remedy for many human frailties and the solution to problems in the family, in the neighbourhood. The importance of prayer is emphasized in the daily practices of Soufanieh in which the rosary, as we saw in chapter two, is a central devotion. As a patterned devotional practice, it imbues the place with unceasing prayer but also conjoins a material practice with this locality.

In my talks with Rima, I asked how she learned to pray. "Abuna Maalouli taught me this." Rima explains how she was taught to pray to the Holy Spirit, Jesus, the Virgin Mary, and the saints; how she was taught to pray the Hail Mary with focus and intention. "This is the cross and the glory. The Virgin creates change in my family, in my children, in my husband, and in my neighbours." Change and prayer are seen as interlinked, and here, the individual can participate. In Rima's case, the change has happened from love of this house and from this house. From this location, she has been transformed to a figure who helps the poor every day. This transformation is not a source of self-pride, however, as Rima repeats that she is weak and must continuously ask the Virgin for guidance and assistance. "This is all the work of prayer ... Believe me, Andreas, I feel it if I don't pray," Rima explains as she looks me straight in the eyes. I comment that I have heard she is called "Mother Teresa of Damascus" by Salwa and others. "Oh, how I wish I was like Mother Teresa!" Rima exclaims. "But I learned everything from Youssef Maalouli and Myrna." Myrna passes us as we talk, and Rima turns her head, saying: "Here she is; she is our story!" Myrna is the story, but it's a story that Rima herself is a part of and one she lives in her daily chores.

As we conduct the interview, Myrna's son John is rather unsatisfied with the food offered for the evening – macaroni – and he starts yelling. Myrna answers him with laughter. Rima immediately points out: "See, see how she handles the situation with laughter!" The tension in the central family is to be rendered, if not normal, then in a light whereby Myrna's handling of it does not allow human imperfection to be seen. Some moments later, Myrna says to us: "What happened? I don't know what happened?" She smiles, and John's voice can be heard from the first floor. Even in a holy family, tensions occur. But here, the situation is rendered in the light of Myrna's sanctity. "What patience, what patience!" Rima exclaims as, with eyes filled with love and adoration, she looks at Myrna who is working in the home preparing the food as we talk. The life story I obtain from Rima, in this sense, is not just a narrative unfolding; in its practical unfolding, it also crafts a story that presents Myrna as a saintly figure who embodies heroic virtue through the handling of what could appear to be the minutiae of everyday life and, by extension, allows Rima to become saintly too.

## Examples and Representativeness: Good and Bad Examples

Rima is considered to fully embody the saintly virtue of humility and servitude, and I had therefore been urged to interview her. This recommendation was also given because Rima's life mirrors Myrna's in many ways. Rima's life has been touched and marked by the example of Myrna. As Rima notes, it is not primarily due to Myrna's words but to her life and deeds. The repeated framing of Rima as a Mother Teresa by Myrna reflects one of the fruits of the work here: a person drawn in from a personal crisis with a crumbling family who is now herself seen as an example of servitude and simplicity, embodying the spirit of Soufanieh.[8] Rima's actions to help the poor render her a reflection of Myrna and living proof of the message of Our Lady of Soufanieh. Nelson Goodman has aptly termed this particular process "co-exemplification" (1981: 128). Myrna stands out as an example for followers such as Rima and Fadi, who both amply attest to the importance of Myrna's exemplary life for their and others' lives.

However, it is not merely Myrna who stands out as an example for others. As Myrna exemplifies specific virtues in and through her life, so Rima can pick them up and imitate Myrna. And by Rima's imitation of Myrna, Myrna's example is proven efficacious. The one example serves the other. Imitation is seen to lead to further imitation, not in the production of sameness but in what could be termed approximations.[9] Myrna and Rima, in this sense, mirror and co-exemplify each other and, by extension, the workings of Our Lady of Soufanieh. The mirroring does not mean that the exemplarity of Myrna and Rima are equivalent; parts of Myrna's claim to sainthood such as stigmata, her visions, and the apparitions cannot be imitated, as these traits attest to her divine election. However, what Vlad Naumescu (2016) has called the ordinary exemplar in this context can also conform and construct the sainthood of the extraordinary exemplar by co-exemplifying her importance. The story of Rima, in other words, is chiselled to fit the image of Our Lady of Soufanieh.

Likewise, Fadi can be seen as a dangerous figure by a person such as Salwa. Fadi does not display the same exemplary process in his own life, which his failed marriage is ample evidence of. For Fadi, his sense of not being able to live up to the example is manifest. But it does not work to the detriment of his conscious labouring to make the message of Our Lady of Soufanieh known in Damascus and beyond. In this sense, failure, misgivings, and doubt are all figures that may also be productive for sustained moral work and ethical labour (see also Lambek 2010b: 53; Bandak & Boylston 2014: 26–8; Laidlaw 2014: 87).

Gendered aspects of the two lives may be one relevant prism to look through. For many devout women, suffering for the family as the good mother is easier to accept than for the father (see Scheper-Hughes 1993[1992]; Orsi 1996; Maunder 2012). Across a wider picture in Syria, there may be the same pattern of gendered religious labour (see also Gallagher 2012). However, it would be a misreading only to view these two stories in terms of such a gendered prism. Myrna herself may be a woman, but alongside Myrna, her family is also used as a model of sainthood. My argument is that a continual interweaving of life and messages underscores the importance of both Myrna as the primary exemplar as well as each individual as a potential co-exemplification. Lives are interlinked, as each person holds a personal relationship with Myrna and aims, with different levels of success and accomplishment, to live life as a witness. As Roland Barthes has underlined, texts are like weavings: they borrow and use threads from different pieces in their own fabric (1977: 159). This insight, in a particular way, holds true for the modelling of sainthood among the followers of Our Lady of Soufanieh; the life of the individual is interwoven with the life and story of Myrna. Here is where biography and hagiography meet. Here, Myrna's life is exemplified in the life of her followers who, through their lives, add to or potentially subtract from her story. The apt formulation of Robert Orsi says it clearly:

> Hagiography is best understood as a creative process that goes on and on in the circumstances of everyday life, as people add their own experiences of a saint to his or her vita and contemporaries get woven into the lives of the saints. Such storytelling was one of the ways the communion of saints became real in people's experiences and memories. (2005: 113)

However, the followers of Our Lady of Soufanieh do not merely live on their memories and past experiences; they feel that they are participating in a continuous modelling of sainthood.

Individual narrative and what Paul Ricoeur (1984) calls "emplotment" within a wider narrative make both individual life and the larger story of Soufanieh true. As in the words of Søren Kierkegaard with which I opened this chapter, the followers of Our Lady of Soufanieh can render the larger story true with their own lives, because the larger story has already given them a plot to be a part of. However, beyond emplotment in a narrative, as Michael Jackson has pointed out (2002: 31; see also Carrithers 1994), we also find an emplacement here. The individual is seen as part of a divine narrative, but this narrative is tied to a particular location where the Virgin Mary has appeared to Myrna. A central feature of the lives presented in the interviews I conducted was a change that happened and took people from ignorance of Christian practices to knowledge and enlightened understanding. Common to many were comments such as, "Beforehand, I did not even know how to pray the rosary." This transition from relative lack of knowledge to fullness is significant, as it shows that the individual corroborates the larger narrative of Soufanieh.

Another common feature was to render the individual's confessional background irrelevant or forgotten. Although that would hardly be the case, it would be the ideal way to underline the engrained character of unity in the life of the individual, the family, and the community of Our Lady of Soufanieh. Here, different stages and degrees of maturity could be found. Rima was seen as a good example, whereas Fadi was not. Yet others, like Nabil and Hani, were seen to be on their way.

If piety is to be used as an interpretive frame, I would argue that piety not only rests on a sense of perfection in oneself but also entails a process of becoming, where life and story is integrated in a larger hermeneutics of grace, which renders parts of life relevant and other parts irrelevant. This contention is similar to what is found in the work of both Thomas à Kempis (1953[c.1420]) and Kierkegaard (1940: 44): a (good) Christian, rather than merely being created in God's image, will have God as his ultimate ideal and pattern, and during his or her life, will strive to become more and more like him. Even bad examples, as Fadi was taken to be, can work to promote the same end, perhaps even more consciously so in the light of the acknowledged gap between life and story, between the ostensible and the subjunctive. For Fadi, the general story of Our Lady of Soufanieh needed to be introduced to all of Syria, and the annual celebrations of Our Lady of Soufanieh, as we shall see later in chapter six, were to make way for a pilgrimage from Soufanieh to the rest of Syria. Mere talk was not sufficient; action was needed. This fervent view may be a form of atonement for his lack of perfection in family life. Yet, as a failed example, Fadi wanted to point in the direction of Our Lady of Soufanieh, modelling her sainthood in Damascus and beyond.

# Chapter Five

# Signs and Evidence

Examples always exceed or subvert the general rule they purport or are assumed to exemplify: the particularities of the example will always threaten to qualify the ostensible universal rule it demonstrates.

– Catherine Sanok, *Her Life Historical*

In recent anthropological writings, a new and more profound focus on evidence among anthropologists has seen the light of day (Hastrup 2004; Engelke 2008). In this chapter, I reflect on the nature of evidence as it is negotiated among the Christians of Damascus regarding Myrna and the alleged miracles in Soufanieh. I examine the relationship between the example and evidence. Is Myrna the perfect example, or is she an example of something quite different – of fraud and human pretentiousness? Is she a *mere* example, or is she an exemplar? This very tension informs the chapter. In *The Art of Rhetoric*, Aristotle had already pointed to the role of the example as an instrument in locution, one which – through inductive logic – could fashion persuasion as a "proof common to all" (2004[1991]: 76–8). Here we will go beyond rhetoric, though, and see how discussions of the miraculous take place in Damascus in practice, both for the followers of Our Lady of Soufanieh and for those who, in different ways, are not persuaded to follow her. In this sense, what I will explore in this chapter points to the unruliness of the example (Gelley 1995). The example is seen as evidence for some, while for others, it is denigrated and seen as something else.

In this chapter, I argue that the often-found lack of attention from local society towards seemingly miraculous events necessitates different strategies to make what the extended family of Soufanieh experience as the gift of God visible and audible. I examine this attitude as a cross-field of indifference and knowledge, where mixed motivations exist in the relationship with Soufanieh in that most Christians know of the place and Myrna, but only a few frequent it regularly. For some, this scant frequenting, if at all, reflects an enmity in which Soufanieh and Myrna are suspected to be a source of evil, but for most, a lack of attention or even outright indifference is the typical attitude. Here, I focus on the explanations and justifications both inside and outside of Soufanieh's extended family for sustaining or suspending relationships with the divine. Instead of separating Damascus into a multiplicity of fields, such as that of many denominations, families, and areas, I contend that the ideas of unity Myrna propagates animate general concerns and must subsequently be treated as a single field rather than a diversity of fields (see Hage 2005). The local negotiations over Myrna's person lead us to a discussion of Christian claims to sainthood and saintliness, and the inherent fragility of such claims.

The French radical phenomenologist and Catholic theologian Jean-Luc Marion, whose work was addressed in chapter two, has perceptively reflected on a number of these themes and establishes a basic paradox as follows: "The holiness of anyone remains for us (*quo ad nos*) undecidable; the saint consequently remains for us formally invisible. The question of the saint's holiness paradoxically begins to be raised from this invisibility" (2009: 705). The basic conundrum, according to Marion, is that a saint can never say that he or she is a saint since, in the very act of so doing, the transfer of attention would be severed, and any claim to sainthood would be rendered fraudulent. Holiness, on the other hand, must be performed or attested to by the faithful in the act of imitating Christ or the life of venerable saints. Bearing witness, in this sense, is the difficult but not insurmountable task bestowed upon the followers of Soufanieh. The critical category of evidence is hereby opened, in that various Christians negotiate the status of the events. In this chapter, I therefore explore the nature of evidence as it relates to forms of knowledge, an exploration that equally involves the opposite, indifference and ignorance. I shall start by describing at some length a heated discussion on Soufanieh that took place among a Greek Orthodox family. From there, I go on to consider other responses from perspectives that are both supportive and suspensive of Soufanieh.

### New Year's Eve with Tony and Hanan: Negotiating Sainthood and Saintliness

I got to know Tony in 2005. He is a devout Christian and a highly intelligent engineer. He is now working for an American company in the Gulf and often visits his in-laws in Damascus. His wife, Hanan, is also a devout Christian and works as a lawyer in a leading company in al-Malki, one of the most prestigious areas of Damascus (see Salamandra 2004). One evening, Tony and Hanan saw standing on my bookshelf the three-volume work *aṣ-Ṣūfāniyya khilāl khamsatin wa 'ashrīn 'āmān, 1982–2007*, a 1,500-page opus on the first twenty-five years of Soufanieh, written by Abuna Elias Zahlawi (2008), the cherished Catholic priest and proponent of Our Lady of Soufanieh and Myrna. I handed the heavy volumes to them, and after a brief examination, sifting through the pages, Tony soon pointed out how expensive the glossy pages and hardcovers must be. His gestures and way of handing the volumes on to Hanan showed an expression of disdain. The comments on the work by Zahlawi and the price of it were only the first reactions of a much deeper resentment towards Myrna that I was to find among many Greek Orthodox Christians. Tony was quick to say that, to him, the veracity of the miracles and their fruits was the most important thing. Hanan fell silent on this point. Contrary to their otherwise standard behaviour, Tony and Hanan did not embark on a long discussion but instead pointed to the great hostility Myrna had provoked. At the same time, both of them admitted to not knowing much about the details of Myrna's life and deeds. In this sense, even as devout Christians, Tony and Hanan are indicative of much broader structures of knowledge and ignorance.

Some months later, on New Year's Eve 2009, I am invited by Tony and Hanan to celebrate the occasion with her family. My thoughts are barely with Soufanieh as I enter their home that evening. Nothing seems to indicate that a heated discussion is about to occur as we enjoy the splendid food and whisky placed on the table. During the evening, the talk revolves around the year that has passed, and many comments are made about the witty programs on television and the weight gained by some of the male members of the family. At some point after midnight, one of Hanan's aunts wants to know what I am doing my research on. On hearing that it focuses on ideas of unity among Christians in Damascus and Syria, and that I am using Soufanieh as a case study, one of the aunts instantly exclaims: "Why Soufanieh?!" She is joined by her sister and Umm Hanan, the lady of the house: "Yes, why Soufanieh?" All express visible disdain in both their voice and facial expressions. "There are many miracles that are prettier than this ... Why then Soufanieh?" Hanan's aunt continues. I say that I find Soufanieh interesting because the story always leads to conversations on the topic of unity among Christians in Damascus and Syria. I remark that I am not for or against Soufanieh and that my aim is to be neutral. "I am against Soufanieh!" the aunt states vehemently, in opposition to such a stance. She continues by expounding a story about the house in which

Myrna lives in order to render it suspect. Immediately following the story, she continues: "Do you know that, at first, the icon was taken to Kanīsat al-Salīb [the Greek Orthodox Church of the Holy Cross], but nothing happened, nothing!? After this, the Orthodox Church opposed it, this was already in the first year ... You know the icon was taken to Kanīsat al-Salīb, but it did not shed oil?" Hanan's aunt reiterates this part of her comment as if to prove her point. Mereh breaks into the conversation: "We went there in the very beginning when all the stories were circulating, and we didn't see anything! So, I don't believe it." The aunt takes up the cause: "All churches but the Catholic Church renounce Soufanieh." After a short pause, she continues with renewed force: "You know, they were really poor before, but see how they are now ... They have a house in Saydnaya, where they give parties! It is the same with Abuna Zahlawi. He was poor as well, but because of his ties with France he is well off now. They have gained a lot from this ... Everybody in Saydnaya knows this!" The aunt hereby transposes her attack onto other domains. The other aunt, who is still eating, supports this view. "Yiiihh, they have a lot of parties in Saydnaya." The onslaught develops ever more fervently, attacking both the family and Abuna Elias Zahlawi: "Once Myrna was asked to see a sick person, and she was very rude. Do you know what she said? She said: 'I can see this person another day, not now' ... She ought to have seen her!"

After this first series of attacks and incriminations, the aunt steps up yet again: "And why go making it public like that? There are many places where similar miracles have been kept for the home ... I have experience of other such miracles where icons have shed oil ... in Saydnaya and in our family, but people do not just go and make their home a public place. Now, they are making it into a church!" She continues: "And why film it and make DVDs? Why make it public like that?" The aunt thus implies that the very form of publicity is only intended to gain something personally and is therefore, concomitantly, a highly suspect enterprice.

"And the relationship with the state, do you know about that?" The aunt is again backed up, but this time by Nabil, Hanan's father, who says: "You do know that they are on good terms with the state?" This point is not continued, but it is very interesting that it is raised, since Christians typically hold ambivalent sentiments towards the Syrian state as both a guarantor of security and, at the same time, a strict regime (Wedeen 1999; Bandak 2013, 2015b; Anderson 2013). It is significant to note that the first apparition and miracles happened the very same year, 1982, in which the infamous atrocities occurred in Hama, where several thousand members of the Muslim Brotherhood were killed by the Syrian regime (Perthes 1995: 137; van Dam 1996: 111; George 2003: 16; Lesch 2005: 44). Even though there may not be a direct link, this event is one of the critical backdrops against which the apparition of Our Lady of Soufanieh and the stress on unity must be understood (see Turner & Turner 1978; Christian 1996; Jansen 2005). Even members of the extended family of Soufanieh see the beginning of the whole phenomenon in 1982 as God's and the Virgin Mary's way of signalling God's path in a time of turmoil and fragility. The idea of fragility does not just pertain to the perception of Syria at this particular time but rather to the whole region. This political turmoil is what made the later messages Myrna received intelligible, and which members of the extended family believed foretold, as we saw in chapter one, the first Gulf War and what was to come.

For some Christians, such as the aunt, the acceptance *qua* non-intrusion of the Syrian state casts Myrna in a dubious light. Is the message of unity promulgated by Myrna on a par with national unity? The aunt leaves this suspicion as an insinuation but continues after just a moment's respite: "Myrna has had something in her psyche [*nafs*]. Where and when have you heard of stigmata in the history of the church?!" The aunt goes on, assisted by several of the others present, especially Hanan's sister and father, who ask: "What is the benefit of stigmata?" At this point, Tony and Hanan attempt to explain that she is most definitely not the first person in the history of the church with stigmata: "Saint Francis was the first to have stigmata, and that isn't contested, is it?" they interject. The aunt makes to continue, but this time Tony manages to make himself heard: "Wait a moment, there are others, for instance Father ... Pio, wasn't that his name, Andreas?" I confirm that he was one of them, but that several more had been reported as having had stigmata.[1] "These are all Western saints!" the aunt retorts, thereby emphasizing the difference between the Orthodox and Catholic churches, which in Arabic are designated as Eastern and Western. "But who would argue that Saint Francis's stigmata weren't genuine? It was due to his faith that these marks were revealed on his body," Tony insists. Tony's certainty of this revealed message is not returned by the others. What is revealed, however, is the difficult idea of unity. This difficulty rests with the history of Catholic intrusion into the Levant, first, following Pope Clement V, who replaced military conquest with conversion (Degeorge 2004: 159), and then Pope Gregory XV, who in 1622 established the *De Propaganda Fides* congregation to promote mission in the East (Masters 2001: 68ff.). The mission and proselytizing were initially directed at Muslims, but finding that too difficult, it was soon redirected at the Orthodox churches, with the ensuing implication of sedition. As a lasting consequence, to this day, the idea of unity (even if lauded by many, the laity in particular) is difficult to achieve due to a trajectory of animosity between the establishments of the various churches (Salibi 1988). Furthermore, this underlying history ties into the idea of unity propagated by Myrna and the extended family of Soufanieh. Myrna herself is from a Greek Catholic family, whereas her husband, Nicolas, is from a Greek Orthodox one. Her followers believe their marriage gives substance to Christian unity, whereas her opponents are more concerned with her morals, public image, and the interest the Greek Catholic Church has shown in Myrna's case.

The aunt goes on to recount how miracles – for instance, miracles of the scent of incense or of icons exuding oil – arise in a home. "I don't think that there are such things in Soufanieh," she says. I listen, and then give the example of a miraculous healing I have been told of by the Frenchman Gérard Challet. Challet was allegedly cured of severe cancer, while in a coma, by having a photo of the icon placed on his stomach.[2] "That's different! That's the icon – it's not Myrna as a person! We believe that God can heal and can do so through icons … We believe in Our Lady!" the aunt says, assisted by Hanan's mother. The aunt refers to a somewhat similar miracle of a young child being cured. At this point, I choose to introduce what the people from the extended family of Soufanieh often refer to as the critical point of distinction, the messages Myrna claims to have received, messages of unity, love, and faith. But this is not something that the aunt knows anything about. "They are all about faith, love, and unity, right?" Hanan states in response, which is just as much directed at me to correct me. This lead is not followed, and Tony tries to broaden the perspective by saying: "For me, I am just a Christian!" Both Hanan's mother and the aunts have their eyes wide open after this comment. "Of course, we are all Christians, but there are differences," the aunt says.

**Accusations and Responses: Sinner or Saint**

What we learn here is that miracles as a general phenomenon may not be rendered as problematic, but their actuality always conjures up wider discussions on the source of the miracle, whether it is credible or not. The heated talk that New Year's Eve, in this sense, signals the explosive material contained in the talk of unity among the Christians of Damascus, and of Soufanieh and Myrna as well, particularly among the Greek Orthodox. Of course, not all are as learned or as vehement regarding the issue as the aunt we just got to know, but many do hold a profound scepticism towards Myrna. Even a lady such as the sceptical aunt, however, is unaware of what many in Soufanieh regard as the most significant part of what has happened, the messages Myrna has received. On a popular level, many other accusations circulate that entail Myrna allegedly frequenting public swimming pools dressed only in a bikini. This charge is presented by some Greek Orthodox as the ultimate token of a lack of modesty on Myrna's part. In addition, the fact that Myrna does not cover her hair and is a married mother of two is seen as problematic and less than conducive to the corroboration of Myrna as a living saint. The image of a Christian saint for many is and has been tied to the image of the young girl, virginity, or a monastic life, and there are very, very few women who have entered the number of those officially blessed and sanctified as mothers (see also Christian 1981: 198; 2012: 71; Woodward 1990: 337; Macklin 2005: 6, 20). Some would not just insinuate that the miracles in Soufanieh are false or made up, as the aunt does, but would even suggest that this trickery was brought about by placing tubes in the frame of the icon from whence the oil was then able to flow. No such fraud has ever been proven directly. The lack of proof does not lessen the accusations, however, as they flourish on moral issues such as extravagance, illicit economic gain, and immoral behaviour, all of which summon up a somewhat different image of Myrna and Soufanieh than what is strived for from within. Furthermore, the paradox we already encountered in the introduction to this chapter on sainthood and visibility is played out regarding the publicity Myrna has attained. Too much visibility would amount to discrediting Myrna; too little and she risks being forgotten altogether. As Marion (2009) has aptly demonstrated, it is from the very invisibility and undecidability that issues of sainthood are raised. Consequently, when the aunt so vehemently opposes the public presentation of the miracles by Myrna and her followers, it shows the precarious nature of any actual claim to sainthood. Polemics and incriminations, however, appear to accompany all claims to sainthood, not just as mere happenstance but as a productive force (Elsner 2009). It is precisely the lack of recognition that is a driving force in claiming the saintliness of Our Lady of Soufanieh and Myrna on the part of her followers.

The negative backdrop of persistent claims of extravagance, immodest behaviour, and illicit economic gains exists and is quite frequently addressed by either Myrna or the people around her. If I brought these accusations up in interviews or conversations with the extended family of Soufanieh, they would quite quickly be put down or silenced. Salwa, whom we met in the last chapter and one of Myrna's confidantes, would derail such accusations quite easily, but not without being troubled, if not saddened. A couple of days after New Year's Eve, Salwa is taking me to the office of the official photographer hired to document all the events of Soufanieh. On the way, she asks me if I had a nice New Year's Eve. In fact, she had already asked me if I wanted to celebrate the evening with her family, but I had declined due to the prior invitation from Tony and Hanan. I tell her how we ended up in a heated discussion over Myrna and Soufanieh. Instantly, Salwa asks for details of how the topic was framed and my responses. I recount the position of the aunt and her sceptical stance. Salwa retorts with a saddened look: "And they have never been there to see for themselves, have they?" In saying this, she gets more worked up at the criticisms, and before I get a chance to answer, she continues: "What is it? Some like you travel from the other side of the planet just to see this, but people here in Damascus just don't care!" I venture upon the line I have heard given in sermons in Soufanieh, one that Abuna Elias Zahlawi used (as seen in chapter three) to paraphrase Jesus – that a prophet is never accepted in his ... But Salwa concludes the sentence: "Assuredly, I say to you, no prophet is accepted in his own country."[3]

As we continue our walk, I bring up the topic of expenses with regard to Abuna Elias Zahlawi and the money for his most recent book, namely where the funds come from. "They come from certain highly trusted persons," says Salwa. She pauses and remains silent, as if withholding information. "Whenever something is needed, it can be asked ... They are of enormous importance to Soufanieh." Money, in this sense, is an important factor but a problematic and even dangerous topic, as the accusations uttered in the Greek Orthodox family attest to. In the home of Myrna, signs announce that donations are forbidden. Pilgrims and guests are typically asked to give donations or votive gifts to churches, not to Our Lady of Soufanieh. The secrecy surrounding the followers' economic support, however, only leads to further suspicion on the part of the sceptics. In interviews, Salwa would emphasize the costs of giving up an ordinary life for Myrna and her family. "Imagine," she ventured, "that you are put under scrutiny all the time, that people notice the slightest thing you do ... that people come at all times of the day and even at night expecting you to be only happy and welcoming." In stressing Myrna's demanding life, Salwa at this point designates the real miracle: that the home has been open for twenty-seven years. Emphatically, Salwa renders Myrna's acts in a light whereby the saint, and not the sinner, in her can be seen and heard. In this sense, Salwa and many others from Soufanieh's close circle do not simply testify to the veracity of the happenings in Soufanieh; an important part of their task is to challenge the spread of slander and gossip from people aimed at vilifying Myrna in her act of witnessing. And this task, at times, may seem to border on insurmountable.

## Bearing Witness: Testimony as Proof

A critical task for the extended network of followers of Our Lady of Soufanieh is to become a witness. This is what Salwa strives to be in word and deed. It is worth expounding on the act of witnessing at some length. By testifying to what the individual believer has seen and heard, that individual becomes a witness and living proof to others of what has happened and can happen in Soufanieh. What you are supposed to see in miracles is directed by what you hear and listen to, and therefore you must tell and be told what has happened in Soufanieh. The act of witnessing can also be seen as a defence against the forgetfulness and neglect that easily refashions what was initially taken as a miracle and sign into mere coincidence or a stroke of luck – as Walter Benjamin neatly captured in the image of Penelope's thread, which has to be started over again every morning (1999[1968]: 204).

The miracle, which is taken to be such a transformative source of evidence, is prone to reinterpretation. There is a particular vulnerability related to the conceptualization of the proof in that it is never fully sufficient to waylay doubts completely. This vulnerability is not necessarily problematic in practice, however, where doubts and misgivings can be productive and creative, as the conditions upon which beliefs are formed (Taussig 2006; Shenoda 2012; Bandak & Jørgensen 2012). Acts despite a lack of belief or an impossibility of belief are, in a certain sense, ways of extending the effects of a continuing reinscription of the importance of Soufanieh. The miracle, then, is not just a miracle by mere chance but as much by its reinvigoration in the form of both individual and communal practices of retelling.

The act of witnessing therefore works precisely as a collective form of what I would term "evidentification": an identification of evidence properly suited to attest to the divine workings in and through Soufanieh. By this definition, I wish to underline that not every happening counts as a divine working but must be tested and discerned to find out the proper source – if it is from God, man, or the devil.[4] Human expectations may, in this sense, override divine plans, and only careful examination and the search for a particular message genuinely reflect the Christian spirit as promulgated in Soufanieh. In an interview on miracles, Fadi, whom we met in the previous chapter, explains how he heard of an alleged miracle in the suburb of Dweila. Fadi, not satisfied with only hearing of the miracle, goes there to see it for himself. His assessment was that it was not a genuine miracle but that a natural explanation could be given. Furthermore, no message was pronounced, which to Fadi epitomizes the utmost mark of divine intention. By downgrading this incident in Dweila, Fadi yet again makes a comparison or rather, as Jaś Elsner (2009) has aptly phrased it, places Soufanieh "beyond compare" (see also Zimdars-Swartz 1991: 57–67; Harris 1999: 91–109; Taves 2012: 64; Candea 2019). The message of Soufanieh is taken by Fadi as proof of the veracity of the miracles, which, through their absence in Dweila, cast the alleged miracle into doubt. Soufanieh, in this sense, is regarded by most of the followers as not just any ordinary Christian revelatory phenomenon; rather, it is a contraction of the Christian message in and through Damascus, which they all see prefigured in the conversion of Saint Paul on his way to Damascus some two millennia ago. Fadi is therefore an active proponent of Soufanieh and goes out of his way to tell of the miraculous happenings, both in his own neighbourhood and in other areas, where he has great plans to also bear witness.

Everyone in the Soufanieh family, like Fadi, are instigated to participate in spreading the message. Raif, whom we met in chapter two and shall meet again in the next chapter, used to emphasize that every single person would be used by Our Lady in terms of the gifts he or she had, whether it be producing web pages, driving an icon of Our Lady on trips for veneration purposes, recording and distributing DVDs and booklets on Soufanieh, or decorating Myrna's home for celebrations. The status of witness is thereby transformed from being a mere passive recipient to an active proponent and hence a part of divine history as it manifests itself over time. The witness is participating in making divine history.

As with saintliness in a general Christian formulation, it is the imitation of Christ in his life and death that has been the diacritical mark throughout history, both when heroic virtue has been emphasized and when the thaumaturgic efficacy and capability for wonderworking have been highlighted (Kieckhefer 1988; Woodward 1990; McBrien 2001). Christ, in this sense, is a model for imitation, and all witnesses are seen to partake in the model by modelling their life upon his by emulation. As already pointed out in the introduction, it makes sense to paraphrase and reformulate Clifford Geertz (1966) when he says that, for the Christians of Damascus, there exist both models *of* and *for* sainthood. The first involves recognizing certain forms of saintliness and holiness, which, as we have already seen, is not a problem for many Syrian Christians. The difficulty arises with the model *for* sainthood, since it is deliberately used to form specific lives and characters. Here, people are drawn into apologetics and defence, or into polemics and a lack of desire, in that the model is something only some adhere to, not all. Bearing witness, to the believer, encapsulates in a particular way the ultimate reality that has marked individual life with a divine touch and that, by being conveyed to others, renders credible what goes beyond human understanding. The act of bearing witness, in this Catholic devotional landscape, is to testify to what has happened and is hence a way of proving the veracity of the miraculous deeds that took place in and through Soufanieh; it presents the possible transition from the model *of* to the model *for* sainthood.

## Objects of Evidence in Anthropology and Beyond: Signs and Evidentification

If we turn back to the miracles, one critical observation is that they have a fundamental ambiguity about them from a Christian tradition. On the one hand, miracles are important and taken as evidence of a certain reality to which they point. On the other hand, miracles lack ultimate force, since they will never be able, once and for all, to settle the matter; some people will always contest the veracity of the miracle. It is not a novel phenomenon to render people of previous times more superstitious; rather, as the anthropological record amply demonstrates, certain thresholds exist across time and cultures, after which no solid explanations can be given (Evans-Pritchard 1937; Douglas 2002[1966]: 74; 1970). Even Christ, in his sayings in the gospels, appears to have a dual stance towards miracles. In the gospels, miracles are designated as signs, as something given to the populace to convince them, but at the same time, something one cannot demand. Some people will not be convinced, but will stop short at the wonder and not see the divine and invisible, to which the miracle as a sign is believed to point. It is precisely this dilemma that is negotiated by the followers in Soufanieh. Whereas the miracles are constantly referred to as a source of joy and happiness by my informants, several of the core members criticize the tendency of the world, a designation of Damascus and Syrian society, to show up only if they hear about miracles that they want to see for themselves. Miracles, in this sense, are not seen to produce conviction but joy. If only a marvel is seen in the miracle and not a sign, then the miracle is happening in vain for the believer. This attitude is also the reason why Robert Shanafelt (2006), in his review of the literature of miracles in anthropology, stops short of arriving at a satisfactory explanation. Shanafelt rightly asserts the anthropological problem with miracles. When he makes the easy transposition of miracles into marvels, however, he cannot aid an understanding of the miraculous as never arriving at certainty. Miracles rather produce chains and logics, which, with perseverance, must be reasserted. However, precisely because the miraculous could have happened, it is not easy to discard miracles altogether.

Again, the central miracle is transferred from the icon or the hands of Myrna exuding oil or blood, and the healings of sick people, to the message of Soufanieh and a change of heart and lives for those brought into contact with Our Lady of Soufanieh. Jean-Luc Marion frames this transformation as the experience of *signa* (1991[1982]: 8–9; see also Weddle 2010: 141ff.; Ward 2011: 150). The devoted Christians around Myrna use the terms *mu'ajizāt* and *'ajāib* to render miracles,[5] but what is critical here is again their specific status as signs, *rumūz*. Many just come to see the wondrous workings, without taking the message of Soufanieh into account; however, a major concern for the followers is to substantiate the message. As Robert Orsi (2008, 2016) has noted, clerical authorities hastily attempt to tame and direct the uncanny presence and excess of the miraculous.[6] The identification of evidence, what I term "evidentification," is important in that it is this very attempt at taming or directing the excess of the miraculous that points to its quality as a sign. Precisely because of the lack of certainty and the problems in fixing any single meaning on such excessive events, proof and evidence are needed to corroborate indexicalities that mark out what should be seen in the miracles. The indexicalities are created through words, which, in the community of believers, are aimed at moulding characters that do not see everything but focus on the sign in the miracles. This process takes place in sermons and testimonies, in which an attempt is made to fixate the miraculous as a sign of grace.

The Italian historian Carlo Ginzburg addresses the question of evidence, regarded as clues, in several of his works (1980[1976], 1999). Clues mark the work of art or history with traces of its originator, which the attentive eye can detect. A similar feat has been captured by Edwin Ardener as "vestiges of creation" (1989). These traces, as clues, point to those who have been taught to see in them the sign more than the wonder. In this respect, it is significant that, during the Enlightenment, the Catholic Church chose to decree that no one should designate a phenomenon as a miracle until the church had approved of the event as more than just hearsay (de Certeau 1992). During the Enlightenment, a positive regime was established, and not just in terms of scepticism towards religious or transcendental powers, whereby stories or the testimonies of others alone were not enough to establish the credibility of a supernatural occurrence. Not only science in its modern inception in this period but also the Catholic Church demanded evidence before declaring a phenomenon to be a miracle. David Hume famously captured this modern form of scepticism by placing the senses over and above tradition and oral testimony: "Our evidence, then, for the truth of the *Christian* religion is less than the evidence for the truth of our senses" (1975[1777]: 109; emphasis in the original). To Hume, testimony is rendered suspect, since it can only vicariously approximate what has occurred, whereas the senses in his optic have an unprecedented primacy. Testimony as proof, from such a sceptical perspective, is never enough to establish the facts, even if, as a secondary source, it demands attention. If testimonies alone are counted as proof, as the entire proof, then Hume is not willing to accept them as a source at all. Here, Hume asserts that we have proof against proof, since "a miracle is a violation of the laws of nature; and as a firm and unalterable experience has established these laws, the proof against a miracle, from the very nature of the fact, is as entire as any argument from experience possibly can be imagined" (114).

Whereas Hume, like the Enlightenment tendency in general, formed a novel and sceptical assessment of miracles, he and like-minded thinkers were unable to eliminate the uncanny experiences, such as those found in mystics and mysticism, altogether. Hume and the like would relegate these forms of conviction to remnants of superstition and ignorance. But in fact, what has happened is that modern science, as well as testimony, has been used by the church to establish what counts as a miracle, albeit with one major difference: for the church to establish a phenomenon as a proper miracle *ipso facto* is to make it stand for something else, to make it establish the evidentiary force of the divine, whereas modern science typically prefers to gloss over miracles as merely what has not been explained by natural causes *yet* (Woodward 1990: 191ff.; Baldacchino 2011). In Damascus, the miraculous – as we have seen – has not lost its force altogether, although for various Christians, the concrete instantiation is always up for negotiation. Even more so when the modern state – as pointed out by Carl Schmitt (2005[1922]: 42) – is frequently working against the miraculous as an exception to natural order and a divinely ordained realm in order for the state itself to become the miracle, albeit of a modern, secular nature. The Syrian state, with a similar logic to date, only reluctantly or when under pressure uses the religious domain to emphasize its own agenda (Pierret & Selvik 2009).

The quality of the evidence itself has been taken up in recent anthropological writing (Hastrup 2004; Engelke 2008). One of the critical aspects that has emerged is how evidence is made to stand for something else and thereby obtains the status of a sign-value, a process in which the senses are incremental in making evidence seen, felt, or heard (Keane 2008). Maurice Bloch (2008) asserts that a fundamental part of evidence rests on the eyes. Whereas Bloch may be right in attributing this primacy to the eyes generally – it is also the case in Syria and Damascus that people want to see for themselves and not just be told stories of the miraculous – a central feature he overlooks is the cognizant part the ears play in forming *what* to see. The problem with Bloch's obsession with cognition and vision is that he is not attentive to the way in which the human senses work in tandem to give one unified perception, one perception where we, at times, hear with the eyes and see with the ears (Deleuze & Guattari 2004[1980]: 342ff.; Deleuze 2006: 160; Howes 1991; Schmidt 2000; Ingold 2000: 245).

A particularly fertile way to conceive of the process of making and giving evidence is found with the neologism "infinition," which Martin Holbraad (2008) dubs the unfinished character of proof. What has counted as proof at one point in time only necessitates further proof at later stages by craving recounting and narration. A series of instantiations, however, is created whereby what was regarded as evidence is used as such in narration and hence proves something else. Because the human memory is frail, and people may reinterpret past incidents, the individual needs to be retold in order to relive and redirect the focus on the force of the proofness of the proof. Holbraad therefore aptly captures the unfinished nature of much evidence, as well as its infinite status, where divine touch remains so only in a constant reinscription. Rationality, in this sense, is not a property that belongs solely to either anthropologist or interlocutor; rather, it resides in between, as a contested and negotiated space, where different experiences, traditions, and articulations are made. Negotiations over the possibilities of icons exuding oil and apparitions of the Virgin Mary and Jesus are present in Damascus, and as responses vary from person to person, even the same people would have different opinions over time. Evidence therefore pertains to domains of knowledge and thus to a variety of situated epistemologies. Here, the desire to see, to listen, and to touch has different economies within the same society. Where some are convinced, others are not; where some are thrilled at the narration of the miraculous, others are only reluctantly so; and where some aim to come to Soufanieh, others hesitate and even fear to do so. In this regard, the decision of what to regard as fantastic, supernatural, or miraculous is critical (see Todorov 1973), even if – or better yet precisely because – it is not necessarily possible to settle the matter once and for all.

## Suspensions of Belief: Miraculous Cure, Convictions, and Conventions

Another standard reaction towards Myrna and Soufanieh among many Christians was not one of outright enmity but rather of indifference. Typically, I would embark on conversations with a variety of Christians who would all know of Myrna and Soufanieh but would be more hesitant towards deciding on what to infer from the stories. "I don't know," George would say, as we and three other young men sat in Steeds, one of the fancier restaurants in the Christian quarter of Qusour. "I mean, I live only a couple of hundred metres from her home, and I never went there, ha ha ha." George laughs. I know George and the other young men from the Melchite Catholic Church of Our Lady of Damascus, *Kanīsat al-Sayyida Dimashq*, where I met them in the *Legio Mariam*, which I attended on a weekly basis for six months in 2005. George works in computer engineering, and the other two, Ziad and Ilyas, work as a goldsmith and a lawyer, respectively. The three men have all been or still are involved in the activities of the church. George and Ziad participated in the Catholic World Youth Congress in Australia in 2008 and hence must be said to emphasize putting their faith into action. Obviously, however, there is a hesitant stance among all three of them when we touch upon Myrna and Soufanieh. They applaud the fact that I am undertaking this research, but they do not want to go and have a look for themselves. It should appear all the more interesting, because Abuna Elias Zahlawi is one of the three priests in the very same church they attend. In other words, even though they all greatly admire Abuna Elias Zahlawi, he has not yet succeeded in bringing a focus to Our Lady of Soufanieh, or at least not so much as to have these three young men frequent the place.

This conversation points us in the direction of the mixed motivations and forms of indulgence with which saintly figures are met (James 1982[1902]; Bandak & Bille 2013b). Frequently, I would hear people advising me not to believe anything I had not seen with my own eyes. In other words, I would be warned not to be fooled. My local hairdresser and a good friend of Myrna's husband, Nicolas, would laugh and stretch his arms out and look upwards when asked his opinion about the happenings in Soufanieh: "I don't know … only God knows!" he would say and then laugh. This cautious stance was countered by a great many who had actually seen miraculous happenings but still remained reluctant to get drawn into the community of the pious. In this regard, the recent spate of studies on pious Muslims in the Middle East (Mahmood 2005; Hirschkind 2006; Deeb 2006) runs the risk of placing a greater uniformity on the pious subjects than is really the case (Soares & Osella 2009; Schielke 2008, 2009, 2010; Starrett 2010). Even though this book does not delve into Muslim identities but Christian ones, it is quite clear that a great variation exists in how identities are articulated in relation to ideas for or against piety. These are not fixed positions, however; rather, they are fluid, in the sense that they are used in time of need (Bandak 2012).

Nabil, whom we encountered in chapter two where he showed his skills in speed praying, had some interesting stories to tell when one day we started to discuss the miracles of Soufanieh at great length. Nabil was at the time working as a real estate agent. But some years back, before serving his time in the army, Nabil fell very sick with a particularly malignant form of skin disease. He went to several doctors with his mother, but none of them could give him a remedy; quite the opposite, the diagnosis was that it was a severe disease with dire implications. He would not be able to join the army. Although a stint in the army is considered a harsh time by most Syrian men, Nabil considered it preferable to a severe disease. At night in his home, while the family was asleep, his mother Umm Fadi had a dream in which Saint Anthony met her in a church with Nabil lying on the floor of the church in front of them and told her that her son would be cured. When she woke up, an icon of Saint Anthony in the home shed drops of blood, and as Nabil awoke, they learned that he was healed. Nabil added another miraculous event to this one. Now no longer exempt from military service, he joined a unit in the vicinity of Damascus. A presidential decree changed the rules, however, so that everyone had to be posted a greater distance from their home. Nabil was initially annoyed at this rule, but nothing could change the new decree. A week after his transfer, the remaining seven members of his unit rolled the vehicle that they always drove, killing them all. "God must really like me! It was a second miracle … Think of this – God used the president to save me!" Nabil here left out all sorts of bad conscience over being the only one spared.

Nabil saw his life changed by these two miracles. He emphasized the certainty of his faith. At the same time, he would suspend many of his moral choices, as in his sexual relationships with Muslim girls. When asked about Soufanieh, Nabil contended that there was no surprise in the miracles and that he had twice experienced miracles on his own body. He also praised the message of unity, saying that it was greatly needed among the Christians of Syria. A unification of Easter would signal that the Christians were one people and not many. Regarding the consequences for his own life, however, Nabil would rather not go to Soufanieh. He emphasized that he somehow felt prevented from going there, afraid of what would happen to him if he should actually step over the threshold. He thus preferred to leave it to the grace he himself had experienced and not embark on any investigation of the details of Soufanieh, suspending any form of judgment until later.

## Knowledge, Ignorance, and Indifference: Strategies of Intensification

A central feature for the various people I have presented so far in this chapter is the differing attitudes held regarding the status of the miraculous. In a certain sense, the choice not to go into the details of the happenings of Soufanieh is a specific strategy of not getting involved but remaining unaffected through a dual suspension of both belief and disbelief. Ghassan Hage (2002) has termed such a process, by which a person invests in certain realities, "strategies of intensification." By placing or not placing a stake in a given reality, it can become more or less intense. If a person follows Our Lady of Soufanieh as Salwa, Fadi, or Raif do, all the minor details hold the divine seeds of knowledge and must be attended to. It is the opposite for people such as George, Ilyas, Ziad, or Nabil, who deliberately postpone any judgment on Soufanieh. And yet again, for people such as Tony and Hanan's family, the aunt in particular, the reality may be a present one but represent the opposite of what the followers of Soufanieh would want it to.

By focusing on the differing strategies people have for letting or not letting the miraculous seize them, we embark on a classic discussion with social, theological, and existential ramifications of how knowledge affects choices and attitudes held. The choice not to visit Soufanieh, even if the place is known, indicates an uneasiness with and potential fear of the miraculous, as if it were common knowledge that the place could actually affect the life of a George, Hani, Ziad, or Nabil. For these figures, however, personal change is not strived for. Rather, a certain distance, knowing about it but not divesting too much time and energy in it, is found to be a suitable response in an otherwise busy daily life. Here, the choice is not to let this reality affect the person. This stance is a highly significant form of indifference that is formative as the background upon which Our Lady of Soufanieh must be heard and seen. While the motives and situations of the people described may vary, what – from the perspective of the Soufanieh family – is encountered is the dangerous couple of indifference and ignorance. By not taking a stand but remaining in the gap between belief and disbelief, general society proves how difficult it is to listen for the voice of God. This theme would often be underlined by the priests in Soufanieh in novenas and sermons: that, at a particular time, God's specific timing, everything will be revealed, and the whole world shall come to acknowledge who he is. Abuna Zahlawi would emphasize this reality in a sermon by telling of an old friend of his who does not *yet* believe. Here, perhaps, lies a deeper problem as to why the world cannot, or will not, see. It was this more troubling theme that Abuna Zahlawi laboured upon on the anniversary of the first apparition of Our Lady of Soufanieh. The problem, Abuna Zahlawi ventured, is that people will not see.

In this sense, what we encounter is a problem of knowledge. Why is it that not everybody accepts the signs of Soufanieh and, more widely, God? Why is it that the miracles do not once and for all settle the matter?

By making the claim that it is due to ignorance and indifference, the priests and followers can render the choice not to see the workings of God in the mundane and extraordinary life of Myrna and Soufanieh completely irrational. The evidence and evidentification is found in Myrna, in the stories, and in the life and becoming that each individual strives for and that the followers therefore themselves participate in producing. Only ignorant or indifferent people would not accept it. In this respect, even the ignorance of the wider society can be taken as further evidence of the veracity of Christ's sayings on misjudged prophets. This notion points to an interesting coincidence in the evaluation of indifference, as the explanation can be found not only in a sermon, such as the one given by Abuna Elias Zahlawi, but also among people such as Nabil. For some, there is too much to take into account to settle on just one dimension, and hence the dual suspension of both belief and disbelief locates the individual in the gap, where a choice can be taken at a later stage. For the followers of Soufanieh, this delay strategy is a dangerous one, as you never know if you will be able to listen if you postpone the moment. Deaf ears and blind eyes are a dangerous coupling.

What we encounter, then, are problems of knowledge. The problem of knowledge has been addressed both in recent anthropological discussions (see Barth 2002) as well as in older philosophical discussions (see Foucault 1970; Kuhn 1970). A focus on which forms of knowledge people utilize in different times, situations, and contexts offers a more sensitive framing of social stakes across scales and cultural settings. More recently, discussions of epistemology have been broadened by a focus on what people do not know, be it purposely held zones of not-knowing, which Clifford Geertz has phrased "passions of ignorance" (2000: 259) and Michel Foucault as "a will not to know" (1980[1976]: 55), or structural blind spots, which paradigmatically fall outside the zones of attention. In his work, anthropologist Roy Dilley addressed these forms of ignorance, which, as he eloquently puts it, always mark knowledge as its shadow (2007, 2010; see also Chua 2009; High, Kelly, & Mair 2012). Dilley takes his point of departure from the conceptual innovation of James Ferrier (1854), who, besides the typical use of ontology and epistemology, coined and introduced the term "agnoiology." The term, admittedly not too elegant, covers what people are not interested in knowing or cannot know and is a significant contribution to our understanding of the social life of a phenomenon such as Soufanieh. In this sense, there exist two ways of not knowing: one that admits to being unaware of certain features and one that deliberately aims at not knowing. Dilley also crafts parts of his most recent version of the argument around different assessments of ignorance in Christian traditions. On the one hand, ignorance can be considered innocent, as the state before the Fall of Man. On the other, ignorance can be considered a willful and evil condition in which people do not want to know. The different stances held by Christians in Damascus attest to the different perspectives of what counts as knowledge and which forms of evidence corroborate this knowledge as fact. Implicit knowledge is also constitutive in this regard, alongside what people do not want to know or just simply cannot know.

We now turn to a final issue that I wish to address in this chapter, one that is also significant as a specifically Christian topic. As Abuna Zahlawi emphasized in the sermon previously alluded to, a split in humanity is present when regarding miracles as signs or simply marvels. Here, even Jesus voices criticism of the popular demand for signs, since people should believe the scripture, and signs can be understood only insofar as the scripture is believed. If miracles only instigate curiosity and marvel, they lose their pertinence as signs and cannot aid personal transformation. The sign-value of the miracle cannot force people to another conviction, but it always has the capability of destabilizing the normal situation and conventional knowledge and of rupturing how things are understood to be. This destabilization is not something that the followers, Myrna, or the priests can control. What they can control, and what they do control, however, is directing and re-inscribing the importance of the message of Soufanieh as it is manifested in the miracles as signs of grace. But these signs of grace – as this chapter has tried to demonstrate – are always resting upon and even nested by fragility and undecidedness, which leads to further negotiations of what counts as evidence, what a witness is, and what counts as knowledge, ignorance, and indifference.

# Chapter Six

# Prophecies of Unity

The paradigms of the imitation of Christ, and mystical union with Christ, are available for making saints out of "middling good" Christians: that is, they serve as extensions of the salvific, incarnative process, in the continuing life of the Church, the mystical body of Christ.

– Victor and Edith Turner, *Image and Pilgrimage
in Christian Culture*

As will be evident from chapter five, the message of Our Lady of Soufanieh causes different responses. Some people take staunch positions against Soufanieh, whereas others deliberately suspend judgment in a studied form of disregard. For the followers of Our Lady of Soufanieh, such as Salwa, Fadi, and Rima, these reactions only add to the sense of urgency to bring her message to the world. In chapter four, we saw how life stories of specific individuals such as Rima and Fadi, in different ways, mirror and co-exemplify the life of Myrna and Our Lady of Soufanieh. If these life stories are aligned with Myrna's life and the broader divine narrative of the Virgin Mary, the story is not supposed to stay in the private sphere. Talk must be corroborated by action. The individual as well as the collective life of Soufanieh must conform to the message of Our Lady of Soufanieh and, in this way, both evidentialize and attract more people to come forward.

In late 2009, many of the core members of the extended family of Soufanieh believed there to be a decline in popular attention, which explains the sense of urgency whereby they searched for and undertook novel initiatives. As we heard Fadi say, if people will not come to Soufanieh, then Soufanieh will have to go to them. This conclusion was shared by a number of people in the core group around Myrna and resulted in concerted efforts to bring Our Lady of Soufanieh to all of Syria during the annual month of celebrations in the autumn of 2009. While the anniversary has been celebrated each year since the inception of Soufanieh as a centre of Marian devotion, the form of the celebrations has varied over the years. Each year the celebrations have centred on the very days in late November when Myrna had her first apparition, and the historical pattern has been for the festivities to take place in Damascus proper in the home of Myrna and Nicolas, and in the Greek Catholic Patriarchate, *Kanīsat al-Zeitun*.

However, the week of celebrations in 2009 was preceded by four trips to central cathedrals in Syria: the cathedrals in Aleppo, Tartous, Homs, and Khabab. And it was not only the extended family of Soufanieh who journeyed to these four cathedrals; for the first time since the very early days, the original icon of Our Lady of Soufanieh was also taken on the trip to be promoted in the different churches for adoration and worship. As we shall see, however, the four trips had quite different results. Besides this novel strategy for making Our Lady of Soufanieh more broadly known, the week around the date of the first apparition was planned and organized with sermons, concerts featuring the famous Lebanese singer Jawmana Mdawwar, celebrations in the Melchite Catholic Cathedral in Damascus led by Bishop Yusif al-Absi, and, of course, celebrations in Soufanieh itself. The focus of this chapter will not be on these celebrations. Rather, I will use the novelty of the trips to promote Our Lady of Soufanieh in different cathedrals across Syria as the extended case to reflect the notion of unity, which is so central to the followers of Our Lady of Soufanieh in their modelling of sainthood. Unity, as we will see, is related to the tenets of love and faith, and is to be lived out in daily life but also more forcefully during the celebrations honouring the anniversary of Our Lady of Soufanieh. The ideology of unity will be central to my discussion of the anthropological engagement with pilgrimages and will be given as a further elaboration of the work to present Our Lady of Soufanieh as an example, not merely in a local context but also in a national one.

In their classic study of pilgrimage in Christian traditions, Victor Turner and Edith Turner (1978) proposed both the liminoid character of the phenomenon as well as the propensity of pilgrimage to fashion "communitas," a particular feel and form of unity. Pilgrimage in Victor and Edith Turner's conception brings people together and allows for a social unity to flourish between the individual participants. The notion of communitas was developed by Victor Turner across several of his books (1969, 1974) and posited as a root paradigm for understanding more widely the features of religious and specifically Catholic culture. By designating pilgrimage as a root paradigm, Victor Turner deliberately presented pilgrimage as an analytical framework. Pilgrimage, in other words, beyond being a significant trope in religious practice, can also be used as a prism through which to discuss the relationship between social structure and anti-structure. While this idea has been highly popular, it has also been famously contested (Sallnow 1981, 1987; Eade & Sallnow 1991a; Badone 2007). In the literature, we seem to be left with a clear choice between communitas and contestation or, in my terms, unity and discord, which seem more appropriate in relation to my ethnographic case. If we are to understand the viability of both, we need to consider the ways in which unity and discord are nurtured, both in the minutiae of everyday life and in celebrations and pilgrimages, which attract more public attention.

This chapter, then, examines the ideology of unity and the fractures and discord that are often played out alongside this very ideology. I argue that, for the followers of Soufanieh, there exists an intricate relationship between the prophecies of unity and the practices of discord, and not just pertaining to the everyday level: they are also played out during the annual celebrations. The trips are here a collective attempt at modelling sainthood. I shall start by examining the innovation of trips promoting Our Lady of Soufanieh in cathedrals in Syria. Here, the focus will be on the trips to Aleppo and Homs, respectively. We will then follow the evaluation and assessment of the trips, both during their enactment and after, at the novenas in the home of Myrna. Having examined the highly different trips, I shall discuss the relation between unity and discord in a Christian formulation and, in this way, critically engage with the literature on pilgrimage as seen either through the figure of communitas or contestation. The modelling of sainthood for the followers of Our Lady of Soufanieh, I shall argue, is situated in and nurtured by the tension between unity and discord.

## Planning and Travelling with Our Lady of Soufanieh

The program of annual celebrations in 2009 was extensive and had a central and novel focus: not only bringing people to Soufanieh proper but bringing Soufanieh to the people of Syria. The idea was introduced at one of the Tuesday evening novenas, and it was immediately seized upon by the devoted followers. According to Fadi, he was one of the central people proposing the idea. His reasoning, which I heard reflected in many other informal talks and recorded interviews, was that the Virgin herself previously did the job of attracting people, but now this task was allocated to the followers. A radical sense of participation in divine work is hence at play. For Fadi, this work is important, and the origin of the idea, he argues, is not so important. The idea of participation is underscored in novenas and sermons, and is often in marked contrast to what is presented as a Protestant conception of divine work. "Protestants think that Jesus is the general director!" Abuna Elias Saloun expounded with vehemence during one of his sermons. The implication is that there is no room left for Mary, the saints, or the individual believer in the divine economy of service; if God has already saved the person regardless of his or her actions, no incentive is left for service. Accordingly, it is more appropriate to speak about an economy of service than what David Morgan (2009) has termed an "economy of salvation." The point in this broader Catholic devotional landscape is that the quest is not merely for individual salvation but for a collective transformation through service. By implication, every single member of the extended family of Soufanieh participates in making divine history in and through service. The individual is needed as part of the solution. Mary depends on the prayers and supplications of the individual as they move her to plead for Jesus and God himself to work miracles of faith, healing, and forgiveness.

The planned trips were awaited with much anticipation, and plenty of people participated in making them happen. As the most significant recent development that year was the very idea of bringing the original reproduction of Our Lady of Soufanieh on tour, a new frame had to be made and the icon taken from its otherwise fixed position in the triptych in the inner courtyard of Myrna and Nicolas's home. The icon had, in fact, been taken from its stand once before at the very beginning of the history of Soufanieh, when it was taken to the Greek Orthodox Church of the Holy Cross, *Kanīsat al-Salib*, for inspection and veneration. That journey was not a great success, as the icon did not ooze oil and was therefore doubted by the Greek Orthodox clergy. The icon, enclosed in a plastic bag, was brought back in disgrace to Myrna and Nicolas. For the ardent followers of Our Lady of Soufanieh, however, the story corroborated God's particular logic of donation. In their rendition, the icon had been placed in the church, but boxes to collect money had been placed just in front of it. Such commerce was seen as directly opposed to the spirit of the miracle as being free of charge and for everybody. However, the tour with the icon for the twenty-seventh anniversary was expected to be a huge success. Let us now turn to the first tip to Aleppo and how it fared, as it attests to the difficulty in making the grace of God and, by extension Soufanieh, acceptable to all.

## Prophecies of Unity, Practices of Discord: The Trip to Aleppo, 1 November 2009

Just before ten o'clock in the morning on Sunday, 1 November, hymns are sung in the inner courtyard of Myrna and Nicolas as the icon of Our Lady of Soufanieh is removed from its stand and placed in a wooden frame. Myrna wipes the screen with a piece of cloth, and everybody beholds the icon in its new place. Hymns in praise of Mary continue to be sung and led by Rula, Salwa, and Rita. Cameras capture the moment. Different people pose with Myrna and Nicolas and the reframed Our Lady of Soufanieh. More songs and small talk ensue. Abuna Elias Saloun, one of the central priests, exchanges a few words with Myrna before taking the icon from its stand and bringing it outside to the waiting cars. Abuna Elias Saloun and the icon are followed by all the people and cameras present. Outside, Raif's black four-wheel-drive Hyundai Tucson is parked just next to the door. Raif, Myrna, and Abuna Elias Saloun all make sure the icon is placed properly in the car. The door is then closed. Myrna and Nicolas's son Johnny takes the driver's seat behind the wheel.

The rest of the company board a white Mercedes Benz bus and find a seat. We soon start the journey, while Salwa, as one of the central organizers, initiates a prayer following the standard pattern of commencing with Our Father, followed by Hail Mary, and ending with the prayer of Soufanieh, O Beloved Jesus. Everybody stops talking and joins in saying the prayer. After the prayer concludes, Rula and others walk up and down the aisle, and offer people sweets and coffee before leading them in singing hymns and devotional songs, in particular for Mary.

Abuna Elias Saloun is seemingly reluctant to participate in the festivities, and we enter into a long conversation. Abuna Elias Saloun is concerned that Myrna and the icon are not on the bus. He is worried: "I don't think we have learned anything during the last twenty-seven years here in Soufanieh ... What is the central message?" He immediately answers the rhetorically posed question: "Unity! ... Why then are the icon and Myrna not among us?!" Abuna Elias Saloun, with great clarity, addresses what he sees as a contradiction in terms with the whole organization of the trip we are undertaking: "And we have empty seats. There are empty seats here, and then Myrna and the icon are taken in a private car ... Look, there are plenty of seats!" He sighs and then says, as if to assure us he is not working against the grain or Myrna: "I said this to Myrna as well, but they wanted to go in the car because it would be more convenient ... More convenient? ... Is it more convenient to sit in a car, than here in a bus with air conditioning and with all the others from Soufanieh?" I ask if it might be that Myrna needs to travel on her own after her recent trip to Egypt. Abuna Saloun replies instantly:

> Of course, Myrna has just come back, but is it more convenient to go alone? And for the value of the symbol [*ramz*] that we are all travelling together with Myrna and with the icon, this is not right ... We are travelling without the Virgin! She is not here, and she is the main reason for us going ... Of course, she is with us, but again as a symbol, this is not right!

At one point, Abuna Elias Saloun takes his cell phone and calls Myrna's husband Nicolas and explains the problem. He then resumes his exhortation on the meaning of unity: "Unity is always a result [*natīja*], following upon peace [*salām*], love [*maḥabba*], and belief [*imān*] in Christ ... There's much talk about unity, but very little unity in practice. Unfortunately!" Then he sighs and says: "Even in Soufanieh, people have a hard time understanding what real unity is!" Abuna Elias Saloun is not depicting the road to unity in rosy colours.

Not long after, Salwa approaches from the front of the bus to where we are sitting. Somehow, she must have heard about the problem, either by it having spread through the bus or having received a phone call from the car with Myrna, Nicolas, Raif, Johnny, and the icon of Our Lady of Soufanieh. In a reverential manner, Salwa asks: "Father, what is the problem?" Abuna Elias Saloun explains his issue with the lack of unity: "I think the icon and Myrna should be here with us. Look around – there are empty seats ... Are we not passing on the message of Soufanieh, the message of unity?" He emphasizes his last point. "It will work out," Salwa answers. Then, trying to solve the situation by looking to the future, she says: "Next week, we will all go to Tartous in the same bus!" This proposal does not ease Abuna Elias Saloun's worries, and he responds: "I still don't think we have learned anything after twenty-seven years in Soufanieh. That's how I see it."

At a later break, when most of us get off the bus to stretch our legs, Raif comes over to the bus and asks Abuna Elias Saloun if they can talk. The two of them join Myrna and Nicolas in the black Hyundai. Later, Abuna Elias Saloun returns to the bus. He is in a much better temper but still holds his opinion. "We talked on the issue," Abuna Elias Saloun starts. "And Myrna explained that Abuna Elias Zahlawi had originally intended to come with us, and they deemed it wiser to bring him in a separate car for the sake of convenience ... But he was too exhausted to come with us, and then they decided to drive in the car anyway." He pauses after recounting their arguments. "I still think we all should have been driving together in the same bus. Who benefits from Myrna driving in a separate car with the icon? What is the benefit?" He pauses again. "I told Myrna this … They and the icon should have been with us." Abuna Elias Saloun's position has thus not changed, but he seems more at peace with the situation now.

The service in the Greek Catholic Cathedral of Our Virgin Mary in Aleppo turns out to be very different from expectations. Upon arrival in Aleppo, in the quarter of Jdeyde, it is raining. Umbrellas are opened as the group from Soufanieh gather around Myrna and the icon. Abuna Elias Saloun and Hani are assigned the task of carrying the icon from the trunk of the car to the church. Abuna Elias Saloun leads the singing as the icon is taken in a minor procession to the church. The Bishop of Aleppo, Jean-Clément Jeanbart, along with several other clerics, receives the icon in a rather disinterested manner and leads the icon, Myrna, and the group from Soufanieh inside the church. The moment is well captured by many cameras. The mass in the church is rather ordinary. The icon of Our Lady of Soufanieh is placed on a table with candles lit to the left of the altar. A small vase with a sparse number of flowers is placed in front of the icon. Several of the people from Soufanieh have assumed different strategic positions in the church. Rula is on the right-hand side, next to a tray with candles. Hanadi, Rafik, and some of the others are also on the right side of the church. Abuna Elias Saloun sits further up front to the left. On the right side, facing the altar, sits Myrna. Myrna is dressed modestly in a black robe and sits next to her son, Johnny, and husband, Nicolas. Approximately 200 people are present for the mass, and the church is by no means packed. However, apart from the icon and the central seating of Myrna, the service does not highlight the presence of Our Lady of Soufanieh and her followers. The liturgy follows the normal pattern. The same goes for the hymns. The sermon by Bishop Jeanbart centres on the role of Christians in the Middle East, but not a word during the main section of the sermon draws attention to the presence of Our Lady of Soufanieh and her company. Only at the very end does Bishop Jeanbart mention in passing Our Lady of Soufanieh and the presence of the icon here tonight.

Soon after, the Eucharist is initiated, and all present in the church participate. As the mass ends, people line up to kiss the icon and likewise kiss, touch, and/or exchange words with Myrna. A pastor at first holds the icon, as people approach and treat it with veneration, kissing and touching the screen of the framed icon. Later, it is placed on the stand again. People crowd in front of Myrna to greet her or kiss her cheeks, or to have their photograph taken with her. For quite a while, people continue to pour forward to the icon and to Myrna. In the meantime,

Abuna Elias Saloun, Hani, Rula, and Salwa lead the singing of hymns over the microphone. Some are repeated, since this session lasts for half an hour. The singing marks the end of the program. There is no formal reception and no wishes of peace on the part of the bishop.

As we get back to the bus, Hani and I enter into a conversation. Hani starts: "Like I said to Johnny, you know, Myrna's son, perhaps the Virgin was busy somewhere else tonight … ha ha ha … No, I'm joking, of course she was here tonight … She is always with us!" The brief line of words and nervous laughter is significant. Hani reveals his unease with the disparity between his expectations and the mass that has just been concluded. Should Mary not have been met in a different way? Should she not have made herself more visible? Hani negotiates the incident, not just with himself but with Johnny and me. Mary was here, was she not? He reassures himself and me that, of course, she was. Hani's unease attests to the precarious nature of assessing the fruits of such a trip. As a less experienced follower of Our Lady of Soufanieh, Hani has not seen any miracles. He had hoped to see a miracle on the trip to Aleppo and to be reassured of his own conviction. His expectations were not realized, so avenues of questions are opening.

Tea, coffee, and sandwiches are distributed in the bus as we start driving the five hours back towards Damascus. I resume my conversation with Abuna Elias Saloun, asking about the bishop and his position, as heard in the sermon. He ponders the obnoxious character of Bishop Jeanbart: "He was never convinced about Soufanieh, but he never went there … I know him!" Abuna Elias Saloun is highly critical in his assessment: "He spent many years in Damascus before he was appointed bishop in Aleppo, and he never placed his feet in Soufanieh." Some others join in the conversation, commenting on the atmosphere. Two women say interchangeably: "The atmosphere was cold, cold, cold!" Both of them have a look of mixed disdain, sadness, and horror on their faces. Abuna Elias Saloun continues: "That's how it is! Many here don't want unity, and this bishop in particular doesn't want unity; he would rather they all remain the same." The atmosphere seems less enthusiastic now as the bus returns to Damascus.

The talk evolves, and Abuna Elias Saloun starts an exhortation in which he explains the many miracles that Our Lady of Soufanieh has already worked. "Many of you have seen miracles, and some of you haven't," he says. Hani says, "I never saw anything! That's not the reason why I come here." Abuna Elias Saloun continues:

You know that the miracles are important if they lead to God … Many in the beginning come and are so eager to see miracles … I met a young man like this recently; he kept on asking to see miracles ... But we have to learn to wait. The important thing is not the miracles, but faith [*imān*].

Abuna Elias Saloun continues his exposition by drawing on a register of the miraculous. "Many of us have experienced these things, but are they important in our daily life?" Abuna Elias Saloun looks around. "I have experienced many things ... My arm was healed, you know that it was really weak and about to be paralyzed ... God healed it." He shows his arm, simulating how it got weaker and weaker but now is fully functioning and of full strength. "And we have experienced this with Myrna on numerous occasions. But why are we surprised? God can do this!" He adds a telling example:

> As I was at the monastery in Lebanon, Myrna once visited us, she ate with us, and suddenly all started to shout. I wasn't paying attention to what occurred ... Then Myrna's dress was all soaked in oil ... Not just a little, it was soaked in oil. And everyone was really excited about it. But why? For God, everything is possible.

Abuna Elias Saloun thus rebukes the mere fascination and attraction of the miraculous, since it could defer the genuine quest for God's ho-liness and, as we saw in the previous chapter, allow a person to remain in the sense of marvel, which does not lead to a more sanctified life but stays as just simple fascination. Abuna Elias Saloun continues: "It is the same today! See how many photos are taken! Why? Why all these photos? Don't we know that God is capable of this, that we can keep it within us [*fi-l-juwwa*]." Hani does not seem fully convinced and says: "What about doubt [*shakk*]?" Unfortunately, no response is given, since we are gently ordered to find our seats in the bus by the tour leader.

The bus is back on the highway moving towards Damascus again. Several have resumed the singing. Salwa asks me how I have found the trip so far. I say it has been very pleasant joining them. I ask her the same question. "It was really bad in the church ... There was no reception, nothing at all," Salwa says, deeply disappointed. I ask if it will be alright. "Did you hear the sermon?! Nothing was mentioned about Soufanieh or Myrna," Salwa says, visibly affected by the absence of unity in zeal, purpose, and devotion. The strived-for effects never occurred, and disappointment was thus a natural reaction. "Shame, shame, shame!" Rafik exclaims. "It's an icon of Our Lady, so just for that sake, they ought to have received it more properly ... Then add a bus with fifty people coming all the way from Damascus. Shame!" Rafik holds his tongue for a moment before continuing: "I think Myrna was saddened by the lack of reception here ... It's the first time in twenty-seven years that the icon has left her home, and then not many show up." Rafik, then, is totally in agreement with the general feeling on the bus from all those commenting on the service.

Nabil, at one point during the trip home, is addressed by Rula and Jessie, who are sitting behind Rafik and me. "How did you get to know about Soufanieh?" Rula asks Nabil in a pause from one of his songs. "I came here a couple of years ago and immediately felt that this was something very different from all the other churches here ... There is no focus on confessional relations [*'ilāqāt tā'ifiyya*] ... The whole idea of unity between Christians is very beautiful!" Nabil does not get much further before he is interrupted by Jessie in particular. "You know, it's actually not just unity between Christians ... It's unity in the family, in the society; it's unity between human beings!" In this presentation, there are no limits to unity, even though practice today has attested to the difficulties of bringing unity in people's lives. The modelling of sainthood in a broader Syrian landscape was not particularly successful on this first Sunday of the month of the annual celebrations.

Heavy rain falls in Damascus as we end the first trip with Our Lady of Soufanieh. The actual results of the first time the icon had left home for twenty-seven years have not lived up to hopes and expectations.

### Unity and Discord: Spreading the Message of Soufanieh

The first trip led to harsh criticisms similar to those already presented in the words of Abuna Elias Saloun, Salwa, and Rafik: the cold reception was a disgrace, personified in Bishop Jeanbart's lack of a welcome; for the mere sake of the icon of the Virgin Mary, there should have been some form of veneration; and when Myrna and fifty people from Damascus had taken the trip, how much more appropriate would such veneration have been? However, the critical assessment and words uttered did present a dilemma for the very spirit of unity on several levels. On the most obvious level, the pilgrimage to present Our Lady of Soufanieh and attest to the message of unity in Aleppo was not successful when the head of the clergy only allowed the devoted group from Soufanieh to participate alongside the ordinary service. It was a failure in terms of not being able to bring the spirit of unity to truly flourish in the cathedral of Aleppo. Such a failure was not considered to be directly a consequence of the extended family of Soufanieh's lack of piety or devotion; it was seen as a problem among the clergy and most pronounced in the figure of Bishop Jeanbart. When Bishop Jeanbart did not welcome the travelling icon and the followers of Our Lady of Soufanieh, it presented a problem for the message of unity. This lack of recognition attests to the power relations and institutional hierarchy of the Catholic Church, something that at one and the same time is accepted and discussed on the street (see also Badone 1990; Bandak & Boylston 2014). Institutional power is not detested here. What is at play is a negotiation between the forces of popular convictions and the church's institutional authority. On a rather serious level, however, the critical words and assessment that the followers of Soufanieh levelled against the bishop and the atmosphere in the cathedral in Aleppo presented a more severe dilemma. The assessment and criticism could very well be right: The bishop ought to have welcomed Our Lady of Soufanieh. He ought to have welcomed Myrna. And he ought to have welcomed the extended family of Soufanieh. However, for the spirit and ideology of unity, such hard words of evaluation were not aimed at creating unity or mending cleavages but rather, if not creating discord, they were at least keeping it open. If meekness, humility, servitude, forbearance, forgiveness, and love of one's neighbour are core values emphasized in the messages of Our Lady of Soufanieh over the years, then the hard words and criticism of the bishop and the atmosphere in the cathedral in Aleppo were a blot on the individuals uttering them and hence, by extension, on the whole family of Soufanieh. In other words, judgment and evaluation of other people is to be left to God, and suffering in his or Our Lady of Soufanieh's name was to be endured. What we touch upon yet again is the theme of too much talk, or perhaps not the theme of too much talk but rather too much talk of the wrong kind.

The dilemma of how to live unity and not just talk about it related even more directly to Abuna Elias Saloun himself, which was a severe problem, because he, as a priest and senior member of the extended family of Our Lady of Soufanieh, should be able to display a greater sense of maturity in words and deeds. Abuna Elias Saloun had himself been an obstacle to the embodiment of unity. This insight did not take many days to dawn upon Abuna Elias Saloun and the core members of Soufanieh. Abuna Elias Saloun, by his very ingenuity in discussing the lack of unity in the bus, had been conducive not in creating unity but its adversary, discord. His zealous attempt to promote unity in the way the pilgrimage was carried out had also focused on the disunity of driving to Aleppo in two separate vehicles rather than on what was understood and accomplished in unison: two vehicles moving alongside each other on the same mission. Empty seats in the bus or not, the spirit of internal accusations and criticisms was saddening, not only to the community of believers but more importantly to the Virgin Mary herself.

The topic was too important to leave unaddressed, and back in Damascus, the two subsequent novenas dealt with the issue of unity head on. During the first novena following the trip to Aleppo, Abuna Elias Saloun took up the topic of unity for closer inspection. The evening starts with a free prayer said by Rita; it centres on the role of the Virgin Mary and the need for the devotees to pray and work harder. Then follow Our Father and the Hail Mary, which are prayed in full concentration by everybody present. Abuna Elias Saloun reads aloud the message received by Myrna in stigmata in 1990: "My children, you, yourselves, will teach the generations the word of unity, love, and faith. I am with you. But you, My daughter, will not hear My voice until the Feast (of Easter) has been unified." Having read the message aloud, Abuna Elias Saloun invites reflection and dialogue on the theme of a lack of unity:

> This month, November, the thought was given to us by the Virgin that we should participate in the message [nata'ammalu bi-r-risāla] ... But we didn't work this participation [naḥnu mā 'amalnā at-ta'āmul]. Each one of us will have to try and may ask the question about how to learn to do this. We have all seen that the number of people who really want unity is very small, who really want it and who walk the path of unity ... The question is why? Why in your opinion? I'm interested in your opinions.

Abuna Elias Saloun pauses shortly before he emphasizes:

> Indeed, there are very few who search for unity in the right way, because there are a lot who do it in a wrong way – they talk so much in one way or another. There is much talk, but little action. There are so many splits; there is a split in ourselves [inqisām bi dhātinā], and we talk about unity ... Jesus focuses on this point as one of his primary ones. If each one of us isn't one with ourselves, then how do we work towards unity? It is not possible! It will lead to disdain [huz'a] and envy [taḥāsud], which will create splits in the self. Then it will be only words! Each one of you has a response ... So few are walking the walk of unity.

Several responses are given. "We must first and foremost turn our gaze towards the Lord, not to everybody else," someone reflects. "It is the weakness of man," a lady says.

However, soon the talk takes a more problematic turn as Tony brings the denominational differences into play: "The first thing is that every denomination among us creates something like its own society and creates its own churches with its own set of leaders ... Like the Maronites and the Armenian Orthodox." Abuna Elias Saloun cuts him off: "We don't want to go into those details." Tony, however, does not leave it at that but continues: "This is what we feel as people." Abuna Elias

Saloun tries to repeat the question, and Myrna also joins the conversation and tries to defuse the direction of the dialogue. "Some don't think that this is important," Tony says, trying to make a comment. But he is cut off again by Abuna Elias Saloun, who jokingly says: "You will kill him twice." Myrna supports him: "Exactly!" Several smile and laugh at this comment, which points to the suffering inflicted on Christ himself by talking about the lack of unity, the divisions and splits within the church. Abuna Saloun points to the crucifixion of Christ and says that people can add to the suffering of Christ by their misdemeanours, particularly regarding the topic of unity. The topic is then addressed by different people without the unwanted details.

The devil, however, could easily hide in the details, for the problem with bringing about unity, in the sense outlined by Abuna Elias Saloun and the followers of Soufanieh, also rests on the uneasy and troubled relationships, not just in the trip to Aleppo and the immediate aftermath. Rather, the central theme of unity, which we have met throughout this book, needs to be unpacked further. Unity [*waḥda*] is one of the core tenets of the messages of Our Lady of Soufanieh. The understanding of unity, however, is more diverse. One thing is certain: the issue of unity, which is centrally captured in the two different celebrations of Easter, is a prevalent concern among most Christians. On the Christian street, it is difficult to find people arguing against the shame of holding two different celebrations of Easter. A practical solution to that problem, however, is apparently not imminent, and an often-heard criticism is that it is due to the clergy's obsession with positions and chairs. The discourse about unity apart, the topic is a more delicate one in practice. The respective churches still have their histories and reasons for suspicion. In particular, the Orthodox churches are still wounded by the separations caused by the Catholic missions in the seventeenth and eighteenth centuries. Unity is, accordingly, also a theme with which ordinary Syrian Christians – beyond those who are devout – reckon.

Several themes recur in the dialogue during the novena: the role of the clergy, the role of the individual, and the sorrow of Jesus and Mary over the discord in the Christian community. Many are critical of the role of the clergy, and this topic is raised several times during the evening. However, this critique is not endorsed or encouraged by Abuna Elias Saloun. At one point during the dialogue, he says:

It is a problem to cause more splits [*inqisāmāt*]. Pride makes us stupid. We do not walk the walk of unity! Point after point, we must turn to Jesus and search after what he wants us to do ... This means each one of us must begin with oneself [*bi dhātu*] ... And talk well about the clergy!

From this stance, he underlines the same point as may be recalled from the bus trip, namely that unity is a result and not something we can take for granted. By implication of this line of thought, everybody is at fault in not working – enough – for unity, even Abuna Elias Saloun himself, which he readily admits to:

> I know that I also have caused splits, I myself, and this is wrong. I felt from the beginning that what I was doing was wrong, but I am very committed to the need for unity ... I feel that what the Virgin says is very, very important.

From this admission, Abuna Elias Saloun can tie the individual transgression to a lack of understanding: No one present has understood the pain inflicted on Jesus by the transgressions. Jesus is sad! Mary is crying! The whole gospel, according to Abuna Elias Saloun, centres on the message of unity. What no one has yet understood is the message of Jesus according to the gospel of John (17:21): "That all of them may be one, Father, just as You are in me and I am in You. May they also be in us so that the world may believe that You have sent me."

After this quotation, which most of the people present know by heart as it is frequently used in sermons and expositions, Tony once again makes a critical response: "What is the solution besides prayer? We are praying!" The critical point is that, when one feels that one is praying, why is there no unity? After some talk, Abuna Elias Saloun tries to close this discussion by saying: "The danger is that we just talk. That we rely on ourselves. Jesus gave us the greatest example in this [*Yesū ' a 'ṭānā akbar mithāl*]." The greatest example is the unity between the Father and the Son, one that each person should not just talk about but enact in their lives.

At this point, Myrna has something to say: "We need to be one with God to be one with others." She continues addressing what she finds critical here: "What is unity without love?" Unity needs to be in a spirit of faith and love, whereby Myrna underscores the centrality of the three tenets given by Our Lady of Soufanieh. She continues and addresses the issue of the clergy: "We are talking about the chairs of the clergy. When they hear this talk ... we are the reason for this. Believe me, we are the reason for this. God have mercy on us, it is our fault!" Myrna explains her position: If people think and talk badly about the clergy, the clergy will not feel supported, and they need support, as many of them are far away from their families. One should, accordingly, not dwell on the clergy's misdeeds but rather pray for them. The evening draws to a close, but the final words have not yet been said. After a pause, Myrna elaborates on the meaning of the words of the message from Our Lady of Soufanieh: "The meaning is not just that Jesus will be saddened a second time. It is more than that. It is that he will be inflicted by diseases ... It is not just a unification of Easter – it is more than that." Myrna takes this idea further since, to her, it implies unity in the families. Unity must start to build in the family. Myrna presents her interpretation in line with the message of Our Lady of Soufanieh:

> I said this, because the Virgin and Jesus said: "You will teach the genera-
> tions." This means a new generation. When I see the church in its mistakes
> and the lack of peace in the heart of the church, it is the result we are re-
> sponsible for ... Unification of Easter is not sufficient.

She pauses briefly, and then completes her thought: "The home is the foundational school. The focus must be on the family." The problem is the lack of unity in the midst of churches, monasteries, and in the midst of families, not just between different denominations.

Unity was expected to be the outcome, but instead the experience was various forms of discord. The lack of unity, however, does not diminish the pious longings; on the contrary, it makes the extended family of Soufanieh work and pray even more zealously. The dilemma of unity and discord is, in this sense, not just a singular incident pertaining to the specific trip to Aleppo; rather, the question of judgment and assessment of spiritual temperature is an ongoing part of a devoted scrutiny of self and society. Here, moral assessment of both the conduct of the individual, the church, and the wider Syrian society is a way to participate in divine work, By making one's own self and heart available to Mary and Jesus, one could work wonders in ever-widening circles: in the family, in the neighbourhood, in Damascus, in Syria, and in the world. Participation does hold the seeds for bringing about unity and God's plan, but it also contains the seeds for postponing it by not willingly enough attending to and living in concordance with the message in one's own life. People, in this sense, are participating in what Paolo Apolito (1998[1992]) has called "cosmic drama."

## Welcome to Our Lady of Syria: The Trip to Homs, 15 November 2009

Although the first trip to Aleppo resulted in disappointment for most, it did not stall the program as such. The following Sunday, a trip was undertaken to Tartous, and two weeks later a third trip followed, this time to Homs, with a planned extra mass in the village of al-Nabk. The trip to Homs follows the same pattern as the first trip to Aleppo. This time, however, two buses carry the greater number of people on the trip, as there are now more people from Soufanieh and two minor pilgrim groups joining from Germany and France, respectively. A German journalist has also joined the trip to write a story for a popular German magazine.

As we arrive in al-Nabk, Rita and several others observe two policemen escorting the cortège of two buses and four cars. "Ihhh, look, we are being escorted by the police! Wonderful!" Rita exclaims, and several start to clap. We are escorted all the way to the street, from which a narrow alley leads up to the church. The church's orchestra and scouts have been waiting and immediately start playing. A large number of passersby stop to see what the hubbub is all about, many of them clearly not Christians, given the way they are dressed. A procession is organized, with Bishop Isidore Battikha leading the way in front of the icon of Our Lady of Soufanieh, carried by Abuna Elias Saloun, Myrna, and the extended family of Soufanieh. Inside the church, the icon is placed in front of the altar. A short service follows, in which a strong and positively endorsing sermon is delivered by Bishop Isidore Battikha. "This is not just Our Lady of Soufanieh," he says. "This is Our Lady of Syria!" Myrna is given a central role in the mass, also in kneeling and praying at the front of the church, in front of the altar and the icon of Our Lady of Soufanieh. Several of the women from Soufanieh lead the singing of hymns, and many of the scouts have taken up positions all along the central aisle of the church. Many people are using their cell phones or cameras to record the event. At one point, several of the leading figures from Soufanieh assume positions in front and beside the altar, from where they start singing some of the classic hymns from Soufanieh.

A huge reception is held afterwards in the nearby church hall. People want to greet and touch Myrna. Myrna and Abuna Elias Saloun are sitting on couches at one end of the hall, where Myrna's father is also seated. On the wall, photos of Bishop Isidore Battikha, Pope Benedict XVI, and President Bashar al-Assad are hanging.

After some time, the orchestra starts playing again outside. The music is the signal that prompts the company to leave the church hall and walk outside, where the icon is taken in a procession back to the waiting cars and buses. Some of the younger males offer the procession cakes filled with pistachio nuts as a token of respect and as sustenance for the rest of the trip. The people of al-Nabk, by extension, thus also participate in spreading the message of Our Lady of Soufanieh, Our Lady of Syria. Rafik makes a rapid assessment of the service as we walk: "The welcome was beautiful … But there was no prayer in the church." He pauses before continuing: "It's necessary to have a prayer in the church." He therefore appears to be happy, albeit not completely satisfied, with the otherwise exquisite reception. We are soon deafened by the orchestra and the sound of trumpets, cornets, and all sorts of brass instruments accompanied by snare and bass drums.

We get back on the bus and are again escorted to the highway by the same two police officers on their motorbikes. One officer gets off his bike in the inside lane and parks it, preventing anyone but the company of Soufanieh from passing. The other officer waits on our left side. Their help in getting us back on the highway by signalling to some oncoming trucks to slow down is again appreciated vocally by Rita and several others. Before we get onto the highway, Raif opens the car door and walks up to the officers expressing his and our gratitude. Everyone in the bus claps enthusiastically.

With the spirits elevated by both spiritual and popular songs, we arrive in Homs. Here, the program is extensive and incorporates services in two different churches. We start in the Syrian Orthodox Church, where a short, albeit important, service is held. We are again received by an orchestra and scouts, and the icon is carried in a procession to the Church of Our Lady. As more people arrive here in Homs, Bashar and Hani try to fence them off so that they do not crowd Myrna too much. They hold each other's hands and walk in a chain. The service is important in the sense that unity between the different Syrian denominations is clearly attested to with visits to both Orthodox and Catholic churches.

Almost immediately after the service at the Syrian Orthodox Church, the group from Soufanieh starts walking with another orchestra in a procession through Homs to the Greek Catholic cathedral. The procession has, by now, grown in numbers, and it continues to grow as we approach the cathedral. Fadi and several other people capture the moment on cameras, and Myrna's son, Johnny, is filming bits of the procession on his iPhone. We wait in front of the church as the Syrian national anthem is played. People sing along with no hesitation.

This service has it all: A large number of people are present. A strong service and sermon, in which Myrna is allowed to give her testimony, is followed by a lengthy sermon again by Bishop Isidore Battikha on the work of unifying the Easter celebrations. Myrna goes straight to the heart of the matter by saying: "What have you come to see?" She glances over the packed pews as she continues: "Have you come to see a miracle? A special lady?" She pauses again. "I am just an ordinary woman, Myrna Nazzour, but God is able to work great things." People listen attentively. In the sermon, Bishop Battikha points to the coming Easter 2010, which will be joint, and says that, hopefully, it will signal a more permanent unification. After the service, people immediately cue up to kiss and touch the icon of Our Lady of Soufanieh, to film or take photos of it, to be photographed alongside the icon and Myrna. After this success, everybody from Soufanieh is highly charged as we go to the buses. Several continue to talk about the beauty of the services and Myrna's testimony.

## Unity Embodied: Myrna in Focus

While the trip to Aleppo was unsuccessful in several ways in manifesting sainthood to others in and through the message of unity, it did not diminish the efforts and longing to see unity embodied and Myrna well received. However, as a positive reception could not be taken for granted – as the trip to Aleppo had so amply made clear – and as discussions of unity had subsequently taken place in Soufanieh, the trip to Homs came as a token of the agency of Our Lady of Soufanieh to move hearts and, by extension, of the efficacy of the devoted concerns, prayers, and efforts. Such moments where unity actually is or seems to be embodied corroborate the wider sense of importance and participation. In other words, it would be wrong to conceptualize the devotion to Our Lady of Soufanieh as predicated upon absence alone. Rather, there is an intricate interplay between presence and absence, one in which the individual and collective efforts, on the one hand, are the only way to move Mary but where, on the other hand, she is sovereign in her doings.

What the devoted followers of Our Lady of Soufanieh longed for and actively sought was – to circumscribe Jon P. Mitchell (1997) – *moments with Mary*, moments where her grace would become manifest both for the individual and the group. The trip to Homs did indeed bring out unity and was considered a huge success. This success was immediately felt in the bus, where spirits were high and people were even more ready to serve when the buses arrived in front of Soufanieh again that evening. Myrna and the extended family of Soufanieh had been met by Bishop Isidore Battikha, pastors, laity, orchestras, and scouts, and the processions had seen a vibrant welcoming of Our Lady of Soufanieh in all three churches. In terms of numbers and attention, the trip had been a success. However, more important than the numbers and attention was that Myrna had been allowed to give her testimony in the cathedral in Homs. By being allowed to speak in the church, Myrna had been assigned a role of official saint-to-be, a role she had willingly accepted and used. In clear opposition to the organization of the service in Aleppo, Myrna and the followers of Our Lady of Soufanieh were not merely accepted and given a role as a suffix to the service; rather, Myrna and the introduction of Our Lady of Soufanieh had been its centrepiece. Hereby, for the followers of Our Lady of Soufanieh, the central undergirding assumption of Myrna being a living saint was met and corroborated publicly.

Furthermore, Myrna had used this time to emphasize the grace of God in an exemplary manner; she had pointed away from herself and towards God's and the Virgin's work in her and, by extension, in everyone present. "What have you come to see?" was Myrna's opening line. Indeed, what had people come to see? Myrna pointed to the message of Our Lady of Soufanieh – it was not her who was worth beholding but the grace bestowed upon her by God and the Virgin herself. This gesture of pointing away from herself was, in a Christian and saintly sense, the foremost mark of a distinction of sanctity. By pointing away from herself, Myrna only underscored her saintly virtue. The paradox is also pointed out by Jean-Luc Marion (2009): the saint is raised from invisibility, in a gesture of transfer of attention to God, which then gives back the saintly prospect. By pointing away from herself, Myrna becomes the centre of popular attention. This concept is also seen in the desire to touch and talk to her as shown in al-Nabk and Homs. Badges, DVDs, prayer cards, and booklets were all distributed but could not satisfy the demand. Our Lady of Soufanieh, as emphasized by Bishop Isidore Battikha, was not only a local veneration but a national one; she was, in his words, to be seen as "Our Lady of Syria." This statement made the participation of every single member noteworthy. Not only had everybody worked for the sake of Our Lady of Soufanieh, but here, the Virgin, Myrna, and the extended family were treated with due veneration, and each member participating in this journey was likewise responsible for its success.[1] The success could be felt in the elated emotions and expressions of Hani. While the first trip did not yield the expected outcome and had frustrated Hani, the second trip highlighted to him how unity, faith, and love were to be understood. His process of learning, going from a minimal knowledge of Christian tenets of belief to an engrained sense of participation, was formative for a developing and maturing Christian character.

## Moved by Mary: The Intention of Tradition

Our Lady of Soufanieh may very well be primed to meet people where they are. In fact, she has already travelled all over Syria and the world in the form of prayer cards, booklets, DVDs, and internet downloads. The replications by various technological means are a critical feature of popular Catholicism and, even more poignantly, Marian devotion (see Morgan 1998, 2009, 2012; Orsi 2005; Apolito 1998[1992], 2005[2001]).

However, there is still a central impetus for people to pray and meet Our Lady of Soufanieh at her own premises in Damascus. Robert Orsi captured this desire very well: "There is still special merit in journeying to the sites where Mary is said to have visited. But her presence is not exhausted at them. Rather, she is repetitively present, generously and lovingly so, as her devout see it" (2005: 59). Similarly, the movement of Myrna and the original icon of Our Lady of Soufanieh to cathedrals in Syria is an occasion that was seen to hold special merit. The movement of Our Lady of Soufanieh to the world, in other words, is not a substitute for pilgrimages and devotions to the original location as such but, rather, a complementary move that participates in making her known and fulfilling the message of unity.

In anthropological studies of pilgrimage, movement has only recently been taken up as a fertile avenue for research (Coleman & Eade 2004a; Coleman 2022). Pilgrimage entails movement. People and individuals move by foot to shrines and places worthy of veneration (see, for example, Frey 1998) or by other means of transport, for instance trains and buses (see Kozlowski 2008; Naletova 2010; Kormina 2010). But also, and furthermore, people are moved. As eloquently captured recently by Anna-Karina Hermkens, Willy Jansen, and Catrien Notermans (2009), people are *moved by Mary*. People are moved by Mary in the sense that they are made to move physically in space, in pilgrimage, in service, in stretching out for others. And people are moved by Mary in an emotional sense of being touched, moved, and affected. In this sense, there exists a tie between motion and emotion (Coleman & Eade 2004a: 22).

The dual nature of movement was already pointed to by Henri Bergson in his early work (1997[1889], 2004[1896]). This take on time is significant in that it allows us to focus on the intensity of the experience of time. For Bergson, it was the very intensity of the experience of duration in time that was of interest. Time can be measured quantitatively on the scale of mechanical watches; measurement, however, does not say much about the experience of time. The experience of time is connected to both the duration and the qualitative development of mental states and emotions related to anticipation of time past, present, and to come. It is precisely the intensity of time that characterizes the extended family of Soufanieh. Life may be lived in a calendric time, as argued by Benedict Anderson (2006[1983]: 22ff.), but that way of living not only makes way for a modern experience of empty homogeneous time but for a time where Mary is no longer able to span generations. It is, in fact, what Anderson – in line with much secularization theory – contends.

However, for the devotees, Mary is very much capable of moving people, not just in their invocations of her as a past figure but via their direct access in prayers where Mary and the saints populate the calendar with their presence (Bandak & Henkel 2021: 9ff.). Mary is a nexus of affect, as argued by Valentina Napolitano (2009), and the calendar, in this sense, is populated with saints and days honouring her. Anniversaries, fiestas, and liturgical saints days are important markers in that they focus particular attention on the life of the saint and may present particular occasions for the display of genuine affection, the possibility of healings, and the veneration of saints as protectors of the nation or diaspora (Wolf 1958; Boissevain 1965: 74–96; Gudeman 1976; Orsi 1985; Tweed 1997: 125–31; Mitchell 2002; Christian 1989[1972]; de Busser & Niedzwiedz 2009; Peña 2011). Celebrations of central days in the life of Mary likewise epitomize her continuing influence in the life of the devout, which in Syria involves notable celebrations interweaving the everyday and various high points of Marian feasts, such as her nativity on 7 September, celebrated vigorously in Saydnaya, or other more general celebrations such as the Feast of the Exultation of the Holy Cross on 14 September, celebrated in Maaloula (Bandak 2012; see also Poujeau 2010), and of course, Christmas and, most importantly, Easter. The feast days of the churches interweave with ordinary days and days important for the Syrian state (Rabo 2005: 36–46). And what's more, Islamic feast days mark the wider society's proclivities at times coinciding with the same dates. For the followers of Our Lady of Soufanieh, however, the celebrations of the Virgin's first apparition in Soufanieh mark her continual presence and the longing for fulfilment of the prophecies of unity.

Touring with the icon of Our Lady of Soufanieh is not seen as a departure from that tradition, an invention of tradition in terms of Hobsbawm and Ranger (1983); rather, it is seen as the *intention* of tradition (see also Bandak & Boylston 2014). The intention of tradition, as seen by the followers of Our Lady of Soufanieh, is to announce the power and love of Our Lady of Soufanieh and her message given to Myrna. In this intention, her followers can participate and make a case for Myrna's sainthood and, by extension, their own role in this tradition.

## Communitas and Contestation: Root Paradigms and Exemplary Force

In the anthropological literature, pilgrimage has tended to be framed in terms of *either* communitas *or* contestation. Victor Turner famously developed the idea of communitas across several of his books (Turner 1969, 1974; Turner & Turner 1978). Communitas, he asserted, was to be understood in three different, albeit related, forms: existential, normative, and ideological communitas. *Existential communitas* is spontaneous and allows individuals to merge with others unbounded by ordinary identities and positions; *normative communitas* is the structuring of the existential experience into lasting social systems aided by various forms of organization and control; and lastly, *ideological communitas* is the ideals and models that are thought to exemplify and guide existential communitas (Turner 1974: 169). In their joint work, Turner and Turner (1978) extend this idea: "'Ideological communitas' refers to a wide variety of ideal, utopian models for societies which are conceived to exemplify or supply optimal conditions for existential communitas" (135). For Victor Turner (1969, 1974), communitas in sum is the feel of togetherness that a group comes to hold during pilgrimage, but which can be organized with greater or lesser success into an enduring social system. It is a particular feel, Turner argues, that crosses the individual and the group. In this sense, the three aspects are seen to add up. Pilgrimage, to Turner, is what he designates a root paradigm, whereby the practice of pilgrimage is turned into a model for wider social practices. For Turner, pilgrimage is seen as an exemplary form, a paradigm that attests to the process whereby "middling good Christians," in the apt formulation of Turner and Turner (1978: 16), can be made into saints in their imitation of Christ.

In his work, Turner (1974: 29) draws upon the idea of paradigms in relation to Thomas Kuhn (1970) and his famous rendition. Kuhn expanded on his work on scientific thinking and worked with paradigms, or "exemplars," as he later substituted the term (187). Scientific tradition, according to Kuhn, uses its models to direct a common particular interest. Turner (1974), in a related manner, used pilgrimage as a root paradigm that he found more naturally aligned with people's practices. Pilgrimage was used by Turner as a model that allowed him to extend his work on liminality beyond the famous work of van Gennep (1960[1909]), so that not only fixed age groups and initiation rites are captured, but also other forms of collective life (Turner 1974). Pilgrimage, in this sense, is a significant piece of a wider puzzle in that it fosters relations between different individuals outside a normal situation or structure. However, in their work on pilgrimage, the Turners do not present the conflicts contained within pilgrimage. Victor Turner's work may, in many other places, stress social dramas and situations in which differing agendas are at play, but that is not an aspect presented regarding pilgrimages. We are presented with different historical periods of pilgrimages, but the overall contention is that communitas as such is nurtured by pilgrimage.

In one of the first critiques of the notion of communitas, Michael Sallnow argues for taking up contestations, conflicts, and competition as the key elements that are always endemic to pilgrimages in the Andes region and more generally (1981, 1987). It is not communitas that is being sought but rivaling identities and positions. Ideals of egalitarianism that may work to structure the undertaking of pilgrimages are not the same as communitas, Sallnow contends (1981: 176). The ideal of egalitarianism may very well create new forms of alliances, not necessarily ones with a sense of communitas but perhaps with the opposite: contestation. Several scholars have continued work in this vein and argued that the formative work of the Turners may be inhibiting an understanding of what is going on at pilgrimage sites. John Eade and Sallnow (1991a) together edited the highly significant *Contesting the Sacred*, in which they extend the critique of the idea of communitas. Their most salient critique was the lack of contextual and historical accuracy in Turner's work (Eade & Sallnow 1991b: 3). By omitting the competing discourses operative in pilgrimages, Sallnow and Eade argue, Turner relied too much on speculation and too little on actual investigation. Likewise, a point of criticism levelled against Turner has been the inherent idealism or theologically normative view of pilgrimage, which needed to be situated within specific historical and cultural contexts. With the work edited by Eade and Sallnow (1991a), pilgrimage was not so much rendered obsolete as a paradigm as given a new content, that of contestation.

In the extended case presented here, it would be problematic to overstress either side in the discussion. I will argue that it is the very tension between communitas and contestation – or in my terminology, unity and discord – that is socially productive for the followers of Our Lady of Soufanieh. To disregard either side of this discussion will not aid an understanding of the social formation of pilgrimage sites, saints, and their reputation, or their role in local, regional, national, and even transnational settings. Simon Coleman (2002) has, in this vein, aptly proposed that the two perspectives need not be used against each other but must be understood against the background of their initial inception. Coleman argues that Turner's work, as well as that of Eade and Sallnow, must be seen as directed by the specific interests of their respective days:

> Just as communitas was a theoretical construct of its time, so it is possible to see why discrepant discourses and interpretations have appealed to scholars during the 1990s and since, in an era when postmodern fragmentation seems rather more plausible than the search for unmediated experiences of unity. (Coleman 2002: 357)

This insight is central, but more than merely mirroring two different eras, I will argue, these ideas coexist as two viable responses, which, for the followers of Our Lady of Soufanieh, are to be understood as a productive tension that animates further spiritual labour. In this sense, both experiences remain viable responses, but they will be played out differently according to the specific circumstances of a pilgrimage. In the extended case I have presented, it is the tension between the longing for unity and the discord and actual misgivings in seeing it through, both individually and communally, that spur on the followers of Our Lady of Soufanieh.

## Unity and Discord in the Formation of Sainthood

This chapter has shown the inherent role of the prophecies of unity in animating the followers of Our Lady of Soufanieh to promote her message of unity. It has also shown how difficult it is to corroborate a unified reception. As the role of Our Lady of Soufanieh is reduced to a local devotion for some, it is in constant need of further corroboration. At the same time, successes such as the proclamation of Our Lady of Soufanieh as Our Lady of Syria by Bishop Isidore Battikha reassure the followers of Mary's ability to move hearts. Discord and contestation, in various forms, are regarded as pivotal problems when people, as in Soufanieh, have a deliberate ideology of unity. Here, it is not sufficient to explain away discord; it must be worked away. In the anthropological literature on pilgrimage, there has been a tendency to choose between communitas and contestation; this choice, I will argue, is a false one. Communitas, as a particular feeling of unity between otherwise diverse people, is never possible to rule out. Depending on the specific location and place of a given pilgrimage site, communitas may be treasured and staked as central. However, it is just as important to recognize the formative role of contestation and conflict at play in pilgrimage sites or, for that matter, in any social institution. Instead of being two diverse and absolute framings, contestation and communitas must rather be seen as a productive tension that, given historical and social particularities, inform us of the stakes for the devout as well as for wider society. For the followers of Our Lady of Soufanieh, the tension is seen in the relationship between unity and discord. Discord is always a sign of misgivings and failures, and only more whole-hearted surrendering to the Virgin can pave the way for genuine unity. Here, the hope is that drops of her grace will spread like circles in the water. It all starts in the family, but where it ends is not – yet – of our knowing. More work therefore needs to be done.

# Chapter Seven

# Damascus Speaking

History can instruct its contemporaries or their descendants on how to become more prudent or relatively better, but only as long as the given assumptions and conditions are fundamentally the same.

> – Reinhart Koselleck, *Futures Past*

During 2009, the film *Dimashq tatakallam – al-Qadīs Būlos* was distributed all over Syria. *Damascus Speaking – Saint Paul*, as the English title goes, is a significant contribution by several Christian denominations to focus attention on the conversion of Paul on his journey to Damascus.[1] The film signalled a highly interesting joint venture on behalf of the Christians of Damascus; accompanying the film on the DVD for sale in a variety of shops in Damascus are sequences in which various bishops and, in particular, Archbishop Gregorius III Laham of the Greek Catholic Church voice praise both for the production of the film and for the Syrian state and President Bashar al-Assad. The film, in this sense, articulates a representation of Damascus from a Christian perspective and, by doing so, attempts to create a common past on which to build, not just for Christians but for all Syrians.

In this chapter, I will explore the ideas of Damascus as it is – if not lived – then represented by Syrian Christians. Damascus and its role in world history, for Syrian Christians, are encapsulated in the presence of Paul in the very city. I will reflect upon the role of Paul in local reception as articulated in the film but also connect the role of Paul on Damascene soil with the one Myrna is thought to have among her followers. The representation of Paul, as it is invested with meaning critical to the sense of being Christian in Damascus, is used by Myrna and her followers to emphasize the role of Damascus in divine salvation history, which is why this last chapter will examine the function of these two figures. Whereas Paul is held in high regard in Damascus, Myrna, as we have already seen, holds a more ambiguous position, and the emplacement of Myrna on a par with Paul is therefore critical in terms of the followers of Our Lady of Soufanieh gaining credibility beyond their immediate circle of followers. This chapter, accordingly, interrogates the role of examples in relation to precedence: how is it that what has gone before allows later incidents to be read as being of the same kind?

By analysing a recent Syrian film, my aim is to excavate ethnographically some critical themes in local conceptions of Paul. I will then dig into a prominent discussion in continental philosophy on the political theology of Paul instigated by the Jewish philosopher Jacob Taubes (2004) in the late eighties and more recently carried forward by thinkers such as Alain Badiou (2003), Giorgio Agamben (2005[2000]), and Slavoj Žižek (2000, 2001b). If these philosophers, in various ways, read Paul from a Western viewpoint, this last chapter of the book will read Paul from the viewpoint of the East. In so doing, my aim is to open an avenue to an anthropological reflection on the power of the example in its relation to generality and specificity, and universality and particularity. However, reading Paul from the East also attests to the power of ethnography to challenge Western preconceptions and to reflect on what the powerful example may be productive of.

Damascus is like a palimpsest, where different sediments of time easily coexist (Koselleck 2018). The city has been overwritten with stories, incidents, and events throughout several thousand years of habitation (see de Certeau 1984[1980]: 202). Some stories, though, are written and rewritten with greater impact. One of these great impact stories from a Christian perspective is the story of Paul, the foremost Christian Apostle to the Gentiles. The story is significant, as it stands out in a condensed form as a paradigmatic model of conversion (van der Veer 1996: 14–15). It also stands, though, as an exemplar of what God can do to everybody else. The topic of religious conversion, however, is a delicate one in a country such as Syria, given the sensitivities in both Muslim and Christian circles. The narrative of Paul as presented in the film is therefore not a straightforward one of religious conversion but one of inner change.

As pointed out in the introduction and chapter three, an intricate relation exists between representation, example, ideal, model, and resemblance in Arabic, all of which derive from the three root letters *m-th-l*. The chapter at hand is therefore intended to give further credence to the general thinking with and through the example. In this chapter, I aim to analyse a film in order to render various processes of time and place visible in contemporary Damascus. Why use a film to represent the point I want to make here? One reason is that *Damascus Speaking* as a film attests to a particular instantiation of the Pauline story made under the auspices and blessings of both churches and the Syrian state. The film is a particular fabrication of visibility that is suited to local conceptions. Further, the use of film and imagery is not applied as a single entry. Rather, the position I take here is that the film is important because we meet concrete people who have incentives and motivations to use Paul in order to frame a particular relation between locality and universality. This chapter, then, shows how particular understandings of Paul are not just high theory but an actual reminder and example of the place Damascus is believed to hold in the eyes and heart of God. In other words, the drama of mankind is believed to be inscribed on Damascene stones, while Damascus itself is believed to hold an exemplary position in the divine will and foresight.

**If Stones Could Speak: Narration and Event**

*Damascus Speaking* is intriguing in its emphasis on the very place where Christianity became global, Syria, and – to be even more specific – Damascus itself. The film starts with the already briefly mentioned sequences from the first public screening in the Damascus Opera House, *Dār al-Assad*. We see different notables at the heart of finer culture arrive in Damascus and the welcoming committee, consisting of theological supervisor Dr. Gamal Makkar, author Maisaa Salloum, and director Khalid al-Khalid. The sequence is accompanied by Bryan Adams's classic "(Everything I Do) I Do It for You" in a Richard Clayderman-esque version. We see the Opera House first with empty seats and then packed. The music fades, and all stand up as the Syrian national anthem is played. The camera pans over the audience: nuns, veiled and unveiled women, men in suits, clerics, and diplomats. Maisaa Salloum is the first to address the audience. Subsequently, we hear Archbishop Gregorius III Laham, who, along with his praise of the team behind the film, exalts "our president, our beloved Bashar al-Assad [*ra'īsunā Bashar al-Assad al-maḥbūb*]." The archbishop is followed by the mufti of Damascus, Sheikh Ahmed Hassoun, the Greek Orthodox bishop, bishops from the other various Christian confessions, and Dr. Gamal Makkar.

The words from the stage are many, but they all conjure up the image of change in the life of a fundamentalist, Paul, who turned into an apostle, a loving and tender character. The mufti, the appointed Muslim leader, also praises this change in spiritual attitude from the stage. The speeches are edited, so we hear only brief excerpts from the orations. But the message of Damascus and Syria as being in the heart of God is duly emphasized. The ensuing presentation of the authors draws ovations from the audience. Glimpses of the reception following the first screening are shown with hymns and modern rhythms. Interviews are conducted in front of running cameras from different broadcasting channels such as MBC, SAT7, and al-Sūriyā. A cake with sparklers is cut with an Arabic sabre, and Archbishop Gregorius III Laham assumes a prominent role in leading the chanting of "hallilūyā, hallilūyā, hallilūyā." Indeed, he succeeds in having most around him join in the chanting, first a few but later quite a number. The screening of the film is an apparent victory. But what kind of victory is it? To understand this phenomenon, we need to take a closer look at the film.

The opening scenes from the Damascus Opera House give way to the film proper. We are taken from the festivities of the Opera House as a voice-over recasts the time and setting from Damascus today to that of Paul:

> Today we will cross the boundaries of time and space, and travel back to the first century AD to witness one of Damascus's most recounted moments: a zealot whose religious fervor led him not to love but to hatred and persecution of those whose convictions differed from his. While travelling to Damascus, just outside the city – Damascus, today the bustling capital of Syria and the oldest continuously inhabited city in the world – here the great light of truth shone on him to remove the blindness of his hatred. One could say this was the light of truth, the light of Jesus Christ. And this man was forever transformed. He became the greatest ambassador for Christ in all history: Paul the Apostle.

This insertion in divine time and planning is assisted in a second move. Now it is Maisaa Salloum who continues. "It is said stones cannot speak," she reflects as she passes a church. Maisaa Salloum continues walking, now in front of an ancient building:

> Jesus once referred to this as he entered Jerusalem. As the multitude of disciples started to rejoice and praise God loudly, saying: "Blessed is he who comes in the name of the Lord! Peace in Heaven and glory in the highest!" some of the Pharisees from the crowd said to him: "Teacher, rebuke your disciples." But Jesus answered and said to them: "If they should keep quiet, the stones will cry out."[2]

The camera pans over the landscape, with several churches depicted. The voiceover takes the lead: "Today these stones of Damascus will speak in a language the world can understand. We will give these stones their voice. And they will tell tales of love and light. And they will bear witness to many historical and sacred events." Next, we are taken to the centre of Damascus, to Umayyad Square, where we again meet Maisaa Salloum, who says: "This is Damascus ... My heart and my roots are here. My song is in Damascus and my peace. Can we find peace and joy by studying history?"

And indeed, what would the stones of Damascus tell us? What kind of redemption is found in history? These questions are highly pertinent, not just for social theory but for ways of living in the world, as found in the Middle East today. Damascus – along with Aleppo – is designated as one of the oldest continuously inhabited cities in the world, a position pointed out by Christians and Muslims alike in Damascus (see Burns 2005; Rabo 2005). Due to their sheer age, the stones and materiality would probably be able to tell many stories, some bigger than others, of what has befallen Damascus. For the Christians, however, one specific story is carried forward, the story of Paul and the change in his life upon coming to Damascus. A line from the cover of the DVD captures this change: "He [Paul] entered it [Damascus] as a persecutor and left it as an apostle." For Maisaa Salloum, it is important to frame the historical accuracy of the narrated events. Testimony is not just found in the Bible and in personal accounts but also, as it were, in the stones and very materiality of Damascus, which are here brought to bear witness.

The film is placed in the by-now-famous genre of the Syrian *musalsalāt*, TV serials, epitomized for Arab audiences in the immensely popular series *Bāb al-Ḥāra* (Salamandra 1998, 2004: 102–24; see also Armbrust 1996; Abu-Lughod 2005). In a melodramatic fashion, the TV serial for eleven seasons has presented Damascus at a standstill several generations back in time, a time when things were unafflicted by modernity. The film, in this sense, lends itself to a reification of the idea of a better past, when people were somehow better, more authentic, and less depraved. This change in dominating narrative (Bruner 1986) has seen the old city of Damascus revived as a place noteworthy for its past (Salamandra 2004; more generally Gilsenan 1982). The dramatized version of being Syrian and Arab found in this particular TV serial is borrowed and developed in *Damascus Speaking*. The fact that over twenty well-known Syrian actors participated in the making of *Damascus Speaking* embellishes the pride of the currently high standards in Syrian productions.[3]

However, one critical difference exists between most TV serials and *Damascus Speaking*: in *Damascus Speaking*, it is important to make the audience aware of the happenings presented not as fiction but as concrete, historical fact, as events that really took place, and the characters as figures who comported themselves around the very same city of Damascus two millennia earlier. The story, in other words, is framed as history not fiction. The tone is set when Archbishop Gregorius III Laham, in his speech in the Opera House, designates the film as a documentary, *al-film al-wathā'iqī*, while heaping praise upon the film as well as on the current regime. It might be more accurate to describe the film as a docudrama, which is what the theological and general supervisor of the film, Dr. Gamal Makkar, does in interviews given on the Syrian broadcasting channel *al-Sūriyā*.[4] While both designations emphasize the documentation, different emphases are given regarding the dramatization. It could, of course, just be a slippage or approximation due to the scant usage of the English term "docudrama," which is not typically used in Arabic mainstream language. At the same time, the designation "documentary" emphasizes the veracity of the film on an altogether different level. This film in not aimed merely at entertaining the public but also, and more importantly, at educating it.

Film as a medium, anthropologist Birgit Meyer has argued, presents and spreads a particular form, a sensuous form, which incorporates wider and different audiences into particular moral landscapes (2010a; 2010b). While this idea might hold true on the most extracted level, as in the various cases Meyer has presented over the years from Ghana, not much attention is devoted to the ways in which different messages can be carried within the same sensuous forms. When Meyer (2010b) uses the conceptual framing of French philosopher Jacques Rancière, "the distribution of the sensible," she somehow tames the notion too easily. To Meyer, this concept is made to articulate with her own preoccupation with aesthetics, whereas in his broader work beyond aesthetics, Rancière is interested in the distribution of relations between what is sayable and thinkable, and what is visible and invisible, and what is even anti-representational in different regimes of identification (2004[2000]: 19; 2007: 113). In other words, expression bears the marks of what cannot be said or rendered, but furthermore, what can be said and rendered rests on the basis of what cannot be seen (see also Marion 2008[2005]; Henry 2009). The film, then, presents the life and conversion of Paul not just as one random incident in the long and winding history of Damascus; rather, the event is presented as one of the epicentres of world history. It rests on the invisible forces moving history, forces beyond mere human subjectivity and intentionality. The author and presenter of the film, Maisaa Salloum, points out the veracity of the story and identifies the direction of the lesson to be learned as stemming not only from human knowledge, fragile and changing as that may be, but as located in the fact of the event taking place and being witnessed not just by humans but by the city of Damascus itself. The history is inscribed on the stones of the city, and apparently, they do not forget easily. The stones are, nevertheless, given voice in this film; they are made to speak and cast with a particular story to present: Paul's story.

## National Motifs and Christian Narrative

In the film, the story of Paul's conversion is told. Paul, whose name was originally Saul, was born in Tarsus. He had both a Jewish and a Roman identity, since his mother was Jewish, but his father had obtained Roman citizenship. We learn of his animosity, even hatred, towards the Christians of Jerusalem, where the killing of Stephen, the first martyr of Christianity, did little to settle Saul's insatiable desire to either lock up or kill Christians. In the film, we learn about this aspect of Saul's character in the dungeons of Jerusalem, where he emphasizes with mean eyes the haste in this endeavour, while whipping and groaning from Christians being subjugated resounds all around him. We are inserted into an atmosphere in which the Jews of old are represented as wicked and bloodthirsty. The Jews are presented in a demeaning light, to say the least, epitomized in the character of the High Priest. The High Priest embodies the spirit in a particular way, as he is presented as a diabolic figure who rejoices in the spilled blood of Christians. When Stephen is dragged away to be stoned after his famous speech given in front of the Pharisees (Acts 6 and 7), the masses shout: "Stone him, stone him!" The High Priest breaks into a vile smile, which shows not only satisfaction with a just sentence – the death sentence of Stephen – but pleasure, and even desire, to see Stephen stoned to death. Stephen is killed as Saul watches over the robes of the stone-flinging Pharisees. In an exemplary saintly gesture, Stephen, as he dies, forgives his perpetrators their deed and falls to the ground, leaving it soaked with his blood, thus becoming the first Christian martyr to imitate Christ's own gesture of forgiveness even in death (see Kleinberg 2008: 16).

One theme is critically brought to the attention of the audience here: the common enemy of Judaism (see also Bowman 1993). This enemy of times past translates immediately into the modern state of Israel, with which Syria has few, if any, positive experiences (see Perthes 1995, 2004; Sato 2003, 2005). By presenting the Jews as bloodthirsty and evil, the film is able to prepare the main line of Saul's imminent transformation more forcefully. Furthermore, by using the theme of genealogical enmity, the film emphasizes the part of national ideology where the role of the modern Syrian state is to guarantee that the injustices committed by the Israeli state are neither neglected nor forgotten. Narrating the life of Paul in this way allows for a national motif to exist alongside a specifically Christian narrative. This aspect is important, because the film is intended, at least on behalf of the director and author, to vindicate a particular part of the history of Damascus and thereby redeem Syria from the margins of world attention.

## Christian Champions of History: Paul and Ananias

Besides the relatively straightforward presentation of Paul's trip to Damascus, the apparition in which Christ – from the sky – blinds his eyes and announces the radical change in Paul's life, his stay with the Christian family of Judas, his meeting with Ananias, or *Ḥanāniyā* in Arabic, and his escape from the walls near one of the seven gates of Damascus, Bab Kisan, the representation is jotted with intermezzos intriguing with their foci on specific places, not just in Damascus past but in Damascus present. The presenter walks along Straight Street, *ash-shāri ʿatu-l-mustaqīm*, or descends the steps to the Chapel of Ananias, which is today in the custody of the Franciscans. Ananias is presented as a fervent believer who leads the community of Christians in prayer, since they are all aware of the imminent danger of Saul's arrival in Damascus. Ananias is shown as calm and obedient when God tells him in a vision to go to the house of Judas, where Saul will be waiting. By doing as he is told, Ananias becomes an instrument in the hands of God, and the film emphasizes this point. Ananias and Paul are both participating in the divine event, where history is redeemed, first in their own personal lives and subsequently in the lives of others. By the hand of Ananias, scales fall from the eyes of Saul, and Saul is immediately addressed as brother. Saul is changed from the onset. With the baptism and consequent sequences, we meet Paul as a content and even relaxed man. By combining the Damascus of today with the dramatic representation of Damascus past, the standstill can be used to reflect not only past and erased histories – prehistory, as it were, showing how Damascus once shone as the epicentre of Christian history – but also to forecast a particular future (see Bryant & Knight 2019). The past presented with Damascus as a spiritual capital of the world signals the possibility of coexistence in the time to come, a time that many Christians conceive of with increasing anxiety. Problems in neighbouring Lebanon and Iraq have made Syrian Christians wary of their own possibilities. In the film, we are told that numerous Christians settled in Damascus after being persecuted in Jerusalem and that the Christian community of Damascus was incremental to the formation of Christianity. Pointing to the churches interspersed in Damascus today, the film points out that the Christian legacy is not over but still living and binding together times past and present.

The role of Damascus in the film is significant. In a program on the film in which both Maisaa Salloum and Dr. Gamal Makkar took part, the latter said: "Damascus is in God's heart!"[5] The idea of divine providence and election is significant, and is found underpinning the lines and scenes of the film. When the Acts of the Apostles and the various epistles of Paul are read, the mention of Paul's Damascus experience is invariably present whenever reference is made to his conversion. But the emphasis here is not on the locality of Damascus in and of itself. Rather, it is on the transformation and revelation of the divine plan of universal redemption, and not just Jewish redemption, whereby Paul is the chosen vessel. The film accomplishes two complementary moves. On the one hand, it sets the frame on the particularities of Damascus and Syria by presenting the formation of Paul's character as irrevocably tied to this locality. On the other hand, it announces a global and universal message aimed at humanity as a whole, which Paul, after his conversion, was the prime instrument in promoting. In the film, then, there is no neglect of the global turn of Christianity – rather the contrary – but the importance of Damascus is reinscribed in Christian history, not just as a backdrop to a founding story but as part of the very foundation to be built upon. In the latter part of the film, Maisaa Salloum expresses this insight very eloquently: "If Palestine was the cradle of the Lord Jesus, Syria is the cradle of the Christian message." This concept is presented in the film with Paul travelling to different parts of the world giving his testimony, as found in a sequence in which Paul, in front of a crowd, says:

> This is what happened to me. I have come to learn the Way. I had eyes, but did not see, and ears, but did not hear. I had a heart without understanding. But now I can see and hear, and Jesus has enlightened my heart with his love and mercy. You are waiting for the coming of the Messiah, the King of the Jews, but the Messiah you are waiting for has already come. He is the one that you rejected, denied, and crucified.

The movement of the divine message from Damascus to the world is used in the film to present the elevated status of Damascus in salvation history. The particular characters of Paul and Ananias give the locality of Damascus today a richness of historical vestiges present to those who know of them. In this regard, it is not just a construction on the part of the film but a historical presence felt by many Christian Syrians.

In a walk through the old city with two informants, both followers of Our Lady of Soufanieh, we walk from the home of Myrna to the Chapel of Ananias near Bab Sharqi after the afternoon prayer in Soufanieh. George and Abu Rami stop at several of the small altars to pray the rosary, light a candle, or say a personal prayer. As we reach the Chapel of Ananias, both fall silent. We descend the stairs and sit for a while in the little church in the presence of icons depicting scenes from the life of Paul. The proximity to the place where it all happened clearly moves George. As we leave the silence of the chapel and some moments later turn right at Straight Street, George says: "Saint Paul has walked here, just imagine that!" Both Abu Rami and I assent to this statement, since it is written in the Bible and often evoked here in Damascus as a claim to a particular Christian form of history and right to the place. But for these two people here, it is not just felt as a claim to an identity; it is perhaps felt more as an existential proximity to holiness, a knowledge that the divine permeates the city of Damascus. This single remark places the weight of history right here as we walk. Tradition is felt, living and breathing, and the numerous churches in the area comfort both George and Abu Rami. Abu Rami, who is a refugee from Iraq, confides in me during our walk that the two places he finds solace in Damascus are Soufanieh and the Chapel of Ananias. He explains that he goes to services at these two places. As we approach the Armenian Catholic Church in Bab Touma, Abu Rami stretches his geographical imagination, saying: "If I am going to live in a foreign country, I should like to live close to a church … I would go there every day, even if I didn't understand the language." George comments on this topic with the same affection: "Ahhh … wouldn't it be fantastic to live next to a church." Abu Rami continues reiterating: "Even if I didn't understand the language, I would go there and pray."

**Love and Redemption: A Message from Damascus**

The film ends with a sequence in which Paul, in later life, writes one of his most cherished passages, namely chapter thirteen of the first letter to the Corinthians on faith, hope, and love. We see Paul write on parchment with a feather as we hear his voice reciting parts of the passage. We hear the first verse: "Though I speak with tongues of men and of angels, but have not love, I have become sounding brass or a clanging cymbal."[6] Paul continues, and we hear verse twelve:

> For now we see in a mirror, dimly, but then face to face. Now I know in part, but then I shall know just as I also am known. And now abide faith, hope, love, these three: but the greatest of these is love.

These famous words are well chosen. By emphasizing faith, hope, and love, a general message is sent about change from hatred to love, from animosity and separation to friendship and communion. The film, by extension, displays the very possibility of coexistence between Christians and Muslims and of spiritual change, and locates Damascus as the heart of such change. Such a message articulates well with the Syrian regime's underplaying of religious differences in that it underlines the unity of mankind and narrates a particular Syrian prehistory to bring this concept forward. In this sense, the film functions as both an internal marker of a desired present and future, and also as an invitation for others to witness the charms of Syria in general, and Damascus in particular.

The film, accordingly, is aimed at different audiences: an Arab audience, which needs to be enlightened and inserted into the divine trajectory of Damascus; and a foreign audience, which must be made aware of Syria's prominence in Christian and salvation history. The latter, however, featuring the transformation of a zealot into a saint, is situated within and, at the same time, goes beyond the frame of the Syrian state. The Syrian state would love to see the zealots of various denominations dismantled to become loving and tender figures. It would not, however, emphasize a particular Christian message. The message of change in the film, then, is one with different ramifications, which are impossible to understand without taking the political climate into consideration. The regime has done what it can to contain and repress identities that stress sectarian and religious affiliations (van Dam 1996; George 2003; Pierret & Selvik 2009). Politics in Syria, as argued by Lisa Wedeen (1999, 2019), have to a large extent rested on a form of compliance, whereby people have acted *as if* they revered the regime, albeit with less conviction in daily practice. Public displays of loyalty have been seen as a formal necessity, whereas many Syrians in the time before 2011 have been less keen about embracing state ideology in their daily lives (Rabo 2005; Cooke 2007; Sottimano 2009; Bandak 2014b).

For the Christians in Syria, however, the situation in the region in the late 2000s, in countries such as Iraq, Egypt, and Lebanon, already exemplified how things can go wrong for Christian minorities in various ways. The affective display of commotion as a preamble to the film, therefore, does not represent a false image of support for the regime; the regime and president are actually seen as the guarantors of the civil rights of Christians (Bandak 2015b). Christians voice praise for the president, even if the regime is found to be harsh in many practical ways. The praise from the various bishops and church leaders and the participation in the national anthem in the Opera House or, as we saw in the last chapter, during the trip to Homs with the followers of Our Lady of Soufanieh can therefore be seen not merely as a matter of acting *as if* (see also Žižek 2001a: 124). Most Christians, on the brink of the later events that took place in 2011 and beyond, treasured the possibility of living in their country and the basic idea of equal terms, emphasizing Syria as the best place in the Middle East to enjoy these privileges and frequently framing these experiences within an enlightenment discourse (Kassab 2019).

## From Damascus to Rome: Travelling Messages

While the film is addressing an Arab audience first and foremost, it is not solely intended to remain in the Middle East or Syria. The film is available in various copies aimed at different audiences. The version sold in Damascus most frequently during the summer of 2009 was in Arabic with English subtitles, but later versions were available during the winter of 2010, in which the film was dubbed into English, Russian, Italian, French, Hindi, and Urdu. Future plans do not, however, stop there. In interviews given in various media, the team behind the film talks about a further distribution of the film in more than eighty languages![7] The vision of disseminating the film worldwide, however, is not just prevalent among the team in terms of distributing the film in dubbed and subtitled versions. Actual steps to transform this vision into action were being taken with a screening of the film in the Vatican. A ten-minute report on this screening is available on YouTube.[8] The first sequence in this clip is an old map on which Paul's travels to Rome are depicted as a red route. We are then told that the film will now also arrive in Rome, the capital of Christianity for the Catholic world. We are presented with Maisa Salloum, Dr. Gamal Makkar, and Patriarch Gregorius III Laham, along with clerics and lay people from Rome, all of whom attest to the importance and beauty of the film.[9] This preview attempts to emphasize the importance of the making of the film, not just to Syrians but to a global audience. Americans and clerics laud the quality of the film, and some even support the Syrian state for letting the production take place; others display a charming ignorance of Syrian Christianity. To an Arab audience, the film can be felt to have made an impact even in Rome in that the actual screening and public reactions have been evidentially captured and now disseminated on YouTube. Paul and Damascus, in a certain way, remain tied to each other, even if the relative importance of place, as opposed to the conversion and spiritual change, is assessed differently. The message travelling to Rome, therefore, is that Damascus is still a city with a marked relation to salvation history and still a city marked by Christianity. The portability of the Christian message attests to the global diffusion, whereby reversals of centres and peripheries are today commonplace (Csordas 2009a). However, more profoundly, the claim of the film is that the universal message of Christianity is tied to the figure of Paul, who is himself tied to the city of Damascus.

The fact that Rome, that is, the Vatican, has had an interest in promoting Christianity in Eastern and Oriental parts of the world has been clear throughout the last century. Over this period, the Vatican has deliberately focused on the Greek Catholic churches in the formulation of policies to preserve a distinct Oriental character. This focus was made evident in the 1964 decree *Orientalium Ecclesiarum*; later, John Paul II was expedient, after the fall of socialism, in formulating the 1993 *Code of Canons of the Eastern Churches* and the 1995 Apostolic Letter *Orientale Lumen*, where Latinization was to be avoided and churches were to preserve their particular identity (see Mahieu 2008: 209; 2010: 85; Mahieu & Naumescu 2008: 5). In this broader picture, the Middle East was also targeted in the travels of the late Pope John Paul II. Karol Jozef Wojtyla, in the very choice of papal name, had already shown ample proof of his admiration for two prominent Christian apostles, John and Paul, thereby joining these two figures in the figure of *Vicarius Christi*. In 2000, the pope travelled to Jerusalem to celebrate Easter; during the same journey, he also visited Cairo, both places with immediate significance to the life of Christ. The following year, the papal institution gave time to emphasizing the role of Paul in the Mediterranean region. In May 2001, Pope John Paul II made a journey that deliberately aimed to follow in the footsteps of Saint Paul. For the pope, this journey was a "pilgrimage" on which he had already, two years previously, said:

> The visit to the Holy Places of the Redeemer's earthly life leads logically to the places which were important for the infant Church and which saw the missionary outreach of the first Christian community. There are many of them, if we follow the account of Luke in the Acts of the Apostles. But in particular I would also like to be able to pause in meditation in two cities linked especially to the story of Paul, the Apostle of the Gentiles. I am thinking first of all of Damascus, the place which recalls his conversion. The future Apostle was in fact on his way to that city in the role of persecutor, when Christ himself crossed his path: "Saul, Saul, why are you persecuting me?" (Acts 9:4). From there, the zeal of Paul, now conquered by Christ, spread with unstoppable force to affect a large part of the then known world. The cities evangelized by him were many. It would be nice to be able to visit Athens, where Paul gave his magnificent speech in the Areopagus (Acts 17:22–31). If we consider the role played by Greece in shaping the culture of the ancient world, we understand how that speech

of Paul's can in a sense be considered the very symbol of the Gospel's encounter with human culture. (John Paul II, 1999, 29 June: 9)[10]

The trip or pilgrimage took Pope John Paul II from Greece through Syria to Malta and had several important agendas. In Greece, recognition of the wounds inflicted on the Orthodox Church were addressed and steps towards reconciliation taken, whereas in Malta, Paul's shipwrecking was commemorated and the Roman Catholic's patron saint of Malta thereby venerated. In Syria, Pope John Paul II followed in the footsteps of Paul and went to the major sites marking Paul's conversion and escape from Damascus; he was also the first pope ever to visit a mosque, namely the famous Umayyad Mosque, formerly the Church of John the Baptist, and to address both church leaders and laity of the Catholic Church, as well as Christians of various scribes indiscriminately. As always during the reign of Pope John Paul II, the program was loaded with stops to be made at many locations.[11] Syria and Damascus were given three full days during his travels, as opposed to just two days in Greece and an even shorter time in Malta.

By this visit, the importance of Paul's Damascus experience was believed among Syrian Christians to have been recognized fully in wider circles of Christianity. Again, the very locality, in the local conception, was primary. It was not just anywhere that Saul had had his experience. It was on the road to Damascus. Even if emphasis has traditionally been placed on what happened to Paul rather than where it took place, Damascus has always had its mention in the New Testament. During his days in Damascus, however, Pope John Paul II did a great deal of work to both instigate inter-Christian dialogue and rapprochement, and to initiate a dialogue with his Muslim counterparts. In various sermons and masses, Pope John Paul II made great efforts to emphasize the amicable past in Syria between Muslims and Christians, and the splendor of the Umayyad Mosque, where Saint John the Baptist is allegedly buried (Degeorge 2004; Burns 2005). In his address to Muslim audiences, no apologies were given for the wounds inflicted by the crusades, but a call for mutual dialogue and forgiveness was voiced. The visit was welcomed and cherished by most Christians for the attention Syria was concomitantly given in the world's media. Several Muslim and official leaders used the opportunity to once again revile Israeli policies. Bashar al-Assad, at that point only recently elected president, also used the opportunity to voice open criticism of Israel (see also Leverett 2005: 125; Wieland 2006: 27). In an official meeting with the pope, he condemned those "who try to kill the principles of all religions with the same mentality with which they betrayed Jesus Christ."[12] The meeting therefore attested to several agendas, where the personal pilgrimage of John Paul II only made Paul the centre of attention at certain points. This the pope did by visiting several of the locations of historical importance and in sermons and mass by lauding the change in Paul and calling for the same change and for attempts to be made at Christian unity. With the papal presence in Damascus, the role of Christians in Syria was given significant recognition. And with the pope following in the footsteps of Saint Paul, a reinscription of history was made in Damascus, where many, to this day, keep postcards and photos of this elevated moment in their private houses or shops. The moment of papal visitation as *Vicarius Christi*, in this sense, is engraved in private memories, aided by photos and postcards, but is furthermore inscribed in public archives and even on the stones of Damascus, as on the wall of the Greek Catholic Patriarchate of *Kanīsat al-Zeitun*.

## In the Footsteps of Paul: The Miracle of Damascus

The reinscription of Paul was further emphasized in 2008, which was declared by John Paul II's successor, Benedict XVI, as the Year of Saint Paul. On a global scale, the Catholic Church focused on the importance of Paul and, in this regard, mentioned his Damascus experience. This focus made celebrations in local churches in Damascus inevitable. But Ananias was also commemorated, as he is annually on 1 October, in a mass in the chapel bearing his name. Ananias is regarded as the first bishop in Damascus, and he is celebrated for his role in the transformation of Paul. In Damascus, sermons in print, which we shall return to later, in which Archbishop Gregorius III Laham voiced the role of Paul, were made available. The year 2008 also saw more than the production of *Damascus Speaking* come to life around Paul, even if that film is by far the largest representation found to this day.

One other contribution to the representations of Paul was undertaken by the Syrian Ministry of Tourism. It consisted of an Ebla Productions from 2008, named *In the footsteps of Saint Paul*, a low-budget film lasting no more than about eight minutes.[13] Here we have the voice of Abuna Elias Zahlawi presenting the story of Paul as it is inescapably intertwined with Damascus. What is significant is the emphasis on the coexistence for sixty-five years of both Muslims and Christians in the Church of John the Baptist, *Yūḥanā Yaḥya*.[14] Again, the theme of Syria as Christendom's cradle is emphasized, and the story of Paul is turned from a straightforward narration of his life to an appraisal of Syria in the role of the formation of Christian doctrine, hymnology, and the conception of monastic orders. This minor production, although in a more understated fashion, attempts to insert Paul and Damascus in a clearly

Syrian parity. That the film is supported by the Syrian Ministry of Tourism only adds to the conflation of interests in the use and propagation of Paul's life, not just as an example for the past but as an example for today. If change could happen in Paul's life by way of Damascus, it could happen again. This form of cultural heritage articulates well with the Syrian Ministry of Tourism, which has so far never succeeded in bringing large-scale Christian groups to Damascus but has seen Jerusalem bringing this lucrative business within its orbit (see Bowman 1991). To present such a film promotes the idea of Syria as being a very modern state by emphasizing its ancient roots (Mitchell 1992: 212).

The presenter of this short film was Abuna Elias Zahlawi, who, as we have seen throughout this book, is a public figure and one of the most prominent supporters of Myrna. His voice saturates the film, as we see icons from the life of Paul and photos from Damascus. The presentation of Damascus as a blessed city is the inevitable conclusion to the film and ties in neatly with the sermons of Abuna Elias Zahlawi. In the liturgy of his masses delivered in the home of Myrna, he continuously mentions Damascus as a blessed city and, furthermore, the very home of Myrna as blessed. The followers of Our Lady of Soufanieh support this appraisal. One informant had even done a word count in the New Testament and located Damascus as the second most mentioned city, second only to Jerusalem. In this way, several come close to arguing that the role of Damascus supersedes Jerusalem as the new spiritual capital of the world, even more so with the rejection of Christ by the Jews. But that Damascus is blessed is also evidenced in the life of Myrna, of which Abuna Elias Zahlawi – as we have seen thoughout this book – has been an ardent follower. Paul is seen as prefiguring Myrna, and in this sense, the modelling of sainthood that the followers of Our Lady of Soufanieh see in Myrna and aim to corroborate with their own lives is inserted into a logic of a divinely ordained precedent. Paul, as an exemplary example, is made to speak in relation to Myrna, and conversely, Myrna is made to speak in relation to the foundational story of divine change in and through Damascus.

For the followers of Soufanieh, there exists a close tie between what happened to Paul two thousand years ago and what is happening today around the figure of Myrna. As we have already seen, God is believed to have chosen Damascus to play a particular role in salvation history. This role is found in the transformation of Paul's life, whose Damascus experience signals the change of Christianity from merely a Jewish movement to a global mission aimed at everyone, at humanity as such. The famous narrative of Paul's conversion and the concomitant elevation of Damascene soil are used as a key to understanding Myrna's role. In the material both on YouTube and the DVD distributed by the family of Soufanieh, the framing starts with presenting Jesus as the Word of God, quoting the famous beginning of the gospel according to John.[15] It locates the happening firmly in the region, first in Palestine, where Jesus became man, and later in Damascus, where Paul was stopped. As this narrative is presented, panoramas of Damascus, Saydnaya, and the Church of Saint Paul at *Bab Kisan* run over the screen. Then we hear a voice saying: "And after two thousand years, God spoke to Myrna!" The direct nature of the divine intervention in Damascus is doubled. In the mediated versions of *The Miracle of Damascus*, as found on YouTube and in the distributed DVD, the importance of Damascus, in this sense, is inserted thoroughly, and nothing in the tie between Paul and Myrna is left for people to second guess.

However, while the Pauline event is recognized by Christendom generally, this second divine intervention is markedly less known outside certain circles of Catholicism with an interest in Marian devotion. The second version, however, is presented authoritatively with recourse to the first. The logic presented is that, precisely because of the importance Damascus has already had in history through the life of Paul, it should come as no surprise that God is now working for the second time through this very locality to redeem mankind. This notion is the logic of precedent and spatial sanctity. In the YouTube clip, we are told that God spoke again in a home only ten minutes from the Chapel of Ananias. By presenting first the Chapel of Ananias and then the home of Myrna, the short line in actual distance and through time is made evident, as if God had, through the already established precedent, primed Damascus for a later message. Because of the universally recognized story of Paul's dramatic change on the road to Damascus, the story of Myrna and *The Miracle of Damascus*, as it is termed in the YouTube version, is adorned with credibility. For the followers of Soufanieh, the divine impetus to summon Damascus, and more specifically Myrna, is understood as the second time God has addressed a person to influence not just local history but salvation history. The Christian message is understood as consummated in the words received by Myrna. In an interview I conducted in the fall of 2009 with Abuna Boulos Fadel, one of the founding priests of the family of Soufanieh, he made great efforts to insert Myrna in history as a new Paul: not as a literal embodiment of Paul in present day Damascus but, rather, as the choice of God to speak yet again through Damascus, not just to Syrians but to the world writ large. In this regard, Myrna as Paul instantiates divine election and favour amid a world vilifying God's vessel (see also chapter four). In a chiasm with Paul and Myrna at both ends, Damascus stands in the middle as humanity is lifted towards redemption by the grace of the

Virgin Mary and Jesus, who have visited this particular location. In a certain sense, this vision makes Damascus itself a living miracle.

## Paul and Anthropology: Continuity, Discontinuity, and Change

Anthropologically, attention on the importance of Paul has until recently been scant. One exception has been Jon P. Mitchell (2002), who has worked extensively on Malta. In his work, Mitchell emphasizes the importance of Saint Paul, who holds the position of patron saint of Malta and is part of today's local negotiations of Malta's ambivalent relationship with Europe. The story of Paul took him to Malta, where, according to the Acts of the Apostles, he was shipwrecked (Acts 28). Mitchell argues that the annual celebrations of Saint Paul in Malta in a particular way embody the various ways in which people relate to their own history in nostalgic terms and strive for a relationship with Europe. Paul is here a figure who ties Malta to Europe and Christianity, and is therefore used by nationalists to strengthen this part of the identity. The annual celebrations of Saint Paul clearly mark the varied sentiments whereby Paul as a figure incorporates the relationship with Europe into Maltese daily life.

While this concrete use of Paul in Malta can show some parallels on the level of social identity and ideas of connectivity that are also found among Christians in Damascus, a significant difference is found in the relation to history. Paul, as used by the followers of Soufanieh, is deliberately not shown as simply an exemplary figure to attest to a belonging in the Christian world community. For the followers of Soufanieh, this belonging may be important on one level, but the most significant part is the divine circumscription and fulfilment in the messages received by Myrna today. The event of Paul in the past is therefore not conceptualized as mere world heritage to attract more tourists but is conceived of as a scattering event with repercussions in all dimensions of life. It is an event that is not just perceived on the level of social identity but rather as an existential redirection of life. As the life of Paul was changed, so is change possible for each person who is being touched by the light emanating from Damascus once again. It is in this sense that Paul is used as an exemplar, a paradigmatic model, but one still tied to a local tradition and a particular location.

The particularity of this Syrian Christian reading stands out when compared to recent engagements with the figure of Paul in continental philosophy, where there has been a revival of studies and publications on Paul. The reading has been part of a broader theological turn in continental philosophy, which has seen novel assessments of Paul and also issues of existential, political, and theological relevance (see de Vries & Sullivan 2006). The new reading of Paul, therefore, is not just being initiated by Christian thinkers but rather by an interest in the importance of Paul and Christianity for thought. One of the first in the most recent series of readings of Paul was the Jewish-German philosopher Jacob Taubes. Pressed for time while terminally ill with cancer, Taubes gave a series of lectures in Heidelberg in 1987. The theme of the lectures was Paul and his importance for philosophy. In the lectures, Taubes ignites a novel focus on Paul, not from the perspective of theology but from the perspective of a Jewish thinker and philosopher. Taubes's (2004) claim is that Paul has never been seriously dealt with by Jewish thinkers and, beyond this assertion, that philosophy also has a Greek preponderance. What is central to Taubes is the messianic logic found in Paul. This logic, he argues, is the reason why Nietzsche so greatly feared Paul and had only contempt for Jesus. What is profound in Nietzsche, according to Taubes (2004), is the acknowledgement that, in Christianity in the line from Paul through Augustine to Luther, an incongruity between morality and conscious will is unleashed (87). And this incongruity is a profound change in a series of changes of conceptions of time and space in Christian imagination that have radically altered the history of ideas in the West.

Following in the wake of Taubes, a series of reflections on Paul have flourished in continental philosophy. The recent Paul reception has been continued by such prominent thinkers as Alain Badiou (2003), Giorgio Agamben (2005[2000]), and Slavoj Žižek (2000, 2001b). Each has different entries and reasons for rethinking Paul, but none goes into the particularities of Damascus as a location. In these narrations, it is rather the potential for universal thought that is presented. Badiou curiously uses a film by Pier Paolo Passolini, which finally was never made, to locate Paul as a militant harbinger of political truth (2003: 36). In the screenplay, Paul is situated as a fascist, going from Franco's Madrid to Barcelona, who changes his mind on the way and becomes an example of a political revolutionary breaching a true idea of universalism. Paul fits into Badiou's thinking on the figure of the event, and it is for this purpose that Badiou uses Paul. Paul is a figure who thinks and lives the event in a radical way, but – for the atheist Badiou – the most significant contribution of Paul is that this very event is thought of on a universal scale. It is Paul as the founder of universalism that interests Badiou, as well as Žižek, in his examinations of a Christian legacy. Agamben also takes up the story of Paul, but he situates both Paul and the idea of universalism differently. For Agamben, in marked contrast to Badiou, the novelty Paul introduces to Christianity transcends its Jewish confines and borders, where the whole world – irrespective of its tribal, ethnic, and religious affiliations – can become one, even if different (Agamben 2005[2000]: 51). The impetus for these thinkers is to go beyond ideas of classic cultural relativism, even if the universalism strived for by the various authors is not Christian but for humanity.

Building on this recent revisiting of Paul in continental thought, anthropology might reconsider the role of Christianity and Paul as a potential for thought. In a text on his work among Southern Californian Charismatics, Jon Bialecki (2009) uses parts of the discussion in continental philosophy on the political theology of Paul in connection with an anthropological assessment. Bialecki uses Badiou to explore the role of politics among Charismatic Christians. For Bialecki, however, a link is made to recent political addresses in which a Christian disparity is asserted. There may be a fidelity to truth, but this truth, in Bialecki's reading, turns out to be apolitical; politics is not to be of this world but of the one to come. While this argument appears solid for the material Bialecki expounds, it does not seem so in a Syrian setting. Perhaps it would be fair to say that, by using Paul as an example of non-political change, the churches and the film *Damascus Speaking* attest to the generally politicized nature of Syrian affairs. The representation in the film is one in which the particularities of place and location are presented as expedient for world history. Damascus, in local Syrian renderings, pertains today both to local concerns with recognition in the wider world and to existential emplotment in divine history. Hence Damascus is being venerated as a locality, but so is Paul, the figure with whom a thinking of universality became possible.

**Thick and Thin: How to Treat Examples?**

For many ethnographers, the way Paul is treated by a thinker such as Badiou may seem inept (see Coleman 2010). Paul may very well be a perfect exemplar of universalism and radical change, but how are we to understand such an exemplar if we do not go into more specific readings? The basic issue is how much you can strip an example of its context. Is it possible, like Badiou, to use Paul as an exemplar of fidelity to a universal – political – truth, discarding the personal circumstances that brought that very model into play in the first place? Tim Choy (2011), who has done excellent work on what he terms "ecologies of comparison," addresses this issue:

> Even as I read in admiration I find myself wondering, caught by quotidian questions of vocation that the philosopher does not ask. What happened to Paul, I want to know, that he would change his name and his life? What

drew him to persist in witnessing in unfriendly places? I am puzzled, in other words, not by the turn to an example of religious commitment, but how thinly that comparative example is treated. Paul's writings are mined by Badiou and others for their logics; they become a formal model for universalizing new foundations, declaring common cause and reimagining what common cause means. But what are causes and logics, for claims of whatever scale, without those subjects who not only feel that things could be ordered differently, but who act to realize another order? How do such subjects come to be? How do they come to act in fidelity to something other than the world they live in? And what other lives of fidelity might be lived or set up as exemplary, aside from that of the unflinching evangelist? (115)

What are the stakes in the model, and how easily can we transport it to new settings? In the work of Choy, we are led to think that it entails a dual movement towards greater particularity and specificity, on the one hand, and greater universality and generality, on the other. Rather than placing these as antinomies, however, we are here encountering a dual ground whereby both can be captured in the powerful example. The powerful example, however, is not unbounded by social context, but it may very well be productive of new social contexts. Instead of asking for more details on Paul himself, we could also ask for more focus on the context for reception and use. What is it Paul is made to say something about? Here the story of Paul, with its rather clear trajectory of personal change, is invested and infected with a different kind of force in Damascus generally and with yet another and specific force for the followers of Our Lady of Soufanieh. The force rests in the particular act of reading, of reading Paul from the East. What ethnography teaches us here is to push back against a philosophical use of examples devoid of actual life, a use of exemplification that too easily becomes both thin and merely for ostensive purposes.

### Reading Paul from the East

During the Year of Saint Paul, Archbishop Gregorius III Laham made several efforts to inscribe the importance of Damascus for Paul's life. We have already encountered his elated words and sentiments during the first public screening of *Damascus Speaking*, but his efforts in fact went far beyond this event. During the Year of Saint Paul, Gregorius III Laham gave and published several talks and homilies honouring Paul. He gave speeches for the opening and closing of the Year of Saint Paul, and he wrote letters for Christmas, Lenten, and Paschal with meditations on the importance of Paul.[16] Each of these letters placed Paul as an exemplary figure "inseparable" from Damascus. Furthermore, Gregorius III Laham underlined the importance of Paul for his personal life. The Patriarch saw his own life mirrored by a sustained relationship with Paul. He was born in Daraya, the place connected with Paul's conversion, and his mother was from Khabab near Masmiyya, the place where Paul allegedly stayed three years, from 35 to 38 CE, in contemplation after his conversion. The Patriarch spent three years in Rome, from 1956 to 1959, in the monastery of Saint Paul, where he also celebrated his first mass in the Basilica of Saint Paul, and lastly, before assuming the Patriarchal seat, he was, from 1981 to 2000, the titular Archbishop of Tarsus, the birthplace of Paul. Gregorius III Laham's personal life, in the presentation, is connected to the central places in the life of Paul. However, Damascus remains a central location, and one Gregorius III Laham returns to in an assessment of the film and the veracity of the claim of a speaking Damascus.

> This year the Agape Company produced a film entitled *Damascus Speaks: St. Paul.* Yes, that's true! Damascus speaks of the great event of Paul's conversion at its outskirts. Damascus speaks or rather Jesus Christ has spoken in Damascus. In Damascus, Paul saw Jesus risen and alive; in Damascus, Paul was chosen to bear the Message of Jesus to the world through its different languages and cultures.
>
> Paul saw Jesus in Damascus
> Paul listened to Jesus in Damascus
> Paul talked with Jesus in Damascus
> Paul spoke of Jesus in Damascus
>
> It is from Damascus that Paul addressed the world in all languages and cultures. He spoke to them of the Christian Faith, through the Gospel: in Athens, in the civilization and culture of Greeks, and in Rome, in the civilization and culture of Romans, while speaking to Nabateans and Arabs in Hebraic-Aramaic and Syriac languages.[17]

Gregorius III Laham in this vein addresses the film yet again as the closure to one of his talks. Damascus and Paul are tied together, and they reveal a blueprint for religious behaviour and interfaith dialogue. Not just Paul but each individual like Paul should be allowed to see, listen to, talk with, and speak of Jesus in and through Damascus. Read from the East, Paul is a harbinger of peace and coexistence, as he is *made* to point to Christ and the respect for fellow man. In underscoring this line, Gregorius III Laham renders Paul simultaneously a global and a local figure. Damascus is rendered as "the mother to Paul, and Paul its spiritual son." Of the locations important to Paul – Tarsus as his place of birth; Damascus as his place of baptism, that is spiritual birth; and Rome as his place of martyrdom – Gregorius III Laham asserts a universal specificity. Paul is a figure of flesh and blood, and he enables interfaith dialogue. The direction of the argument, then, is that the exemplary force of Paul is the connection to a specific place but also a change from hate to love. The thickness of the example is in the Eastern reading that ties Paul and Damascus to each other as inseparable and instigates a transformed movement of a global Christianity from this particular location. This Eastern reading is tied to a situation where Christians increasingly find themselves vulnerable; at such a time, the story of Paul needs to be a great reminder if Syria is not to turn into a new Iraq or Egypt.

### Secrets and Revelations: Stones and Inscription

It may come as no surprise that anthropologists such as Joel Robbins and Matthew Engelke have captured the sense of change in the broader frame of continental philosophy and tried to instigate a dialogue between anthropological, theological, and philosophical studies of both Paul and global Christianity (Engelke & Robbins 2010). The broader move has been coined by Robbins as "the move from theology as materialist messianic secret to the age of Saint Paul Superstar" (Robbins 2010: 634). By this phrase, Robbins draws attention to Walter Benjamin and his ideas of the messianic moment. And it is precisely Benjamin's idea of messianism and his concept of history that have been inserted into the dialogue in Giorgio Agamben's work on Paul, as it is Agamben's contention that what has been missed in the readings of Walter Benjamin is Benjamin's close relationship to Paul (Agamben 2005[2000]: 138–45). In other words, a secret bond exists between these two thinkers whereby Paul is the dwarf of history that Benjamin builds upon. In his famous text on the concept of history, Walter Benjamin (1999[1968]) captured the spirit of progress in the image of the Angel of the Future, *Angelus Novus*, being forced forward with its eyes turned backwards towards the past, seeing only rubble and ruins (249). And if the past is linked to these ruins (see also Navaro-Yashin 2009) to which the angel is forced only to glance upon with ever-widening distance, we are forced to ask if these ruins, if these stones, can speak. It is precisely this phrase, if stones can speak, that brings us back to Damascus and the film, as the idea of Damascus and its age and prominence is not just a scholarly concern. George, an engineer in his early thirties, used an interesting Arabic line as his signature in his email: "Below each stone in Damascus there is a temple [*taḥta kulli ḥajarin fī Dimashq haykal*]." The questions remain: Can the stones speak? And to whom do they speak? And of what do they speak? Here, we will have to respond that stones can and will speak, but that they will speak only in a social process of signification. The scales will have to be removed from our eyes, as the story of Paul reminds us. This social process of signification, as recently argued by various scholars, is best captured through the lens of learning (Jenkins 1994; Ingold 2000; Berliner & Sarró 2007). In the social process of signification, one learns receptivity to particular circumstances, clues, and facts. And, in this very process, a film like *Damascus Speaking* works to inscribe and reinscribe a certain texture with significance. The age of Damascus, the events that took place here, and the people and generations who lived here, are inscribed in a story of today: a story that, for some, marks the possibilities of coexistence in the modern Syrian nation state; for others, the role of Damascus in divine redemption; and for yet others, God's continual presence on this very soil as attested to in the life of Myrna. Damascus, then, is not regarded as merely an ordinary location among others but one with a proximity to eternity. In this sense, Damascus is a palimpsest, in which a variety of histories and stories are manifest in the material surroundings – but only manifest insofar as they are told and retold. Here, a film such as *Damascus Speaking* functions to expound a secret: the stones do not just tell everybody their story; the listener has to be prepared to receive it. As Roland Barthes remarked in his famous text on semiology and urbanism, the city holds secrets for the person who has learned to attend to them (1994: 199). For such attentive and receptive a person, it is the very materiality in and of Damascus that bears witness to what happened here and prefigures what is to come.

# Towards an Anthropology of the Example

An analysis – a description – of the particular case can only ever be an invitation to look and see, to consider whether, or how far you can use it for your own purposes. But this is where philosophical (theoretical) discussion *begins*, not where it ends.

– Toril Moi, "Thinking Through Examples"

In the pages of this book, we have followed the modelling of sainthood around the figure of Myrna Nazzour, a contemporary Christian stigmatic in Damascus. The central argument I have developed is that such a modelling of sainthood is situated in relation to a structure of exemplarity. Myrna is singled out by her followers as a noteworthy example, chosen by Mary, and they attend to her words and deeds, and aim to model sainthood in their own lives. However, the status of the example is never settled once and for all, as many Christians in Damascus take no notice of Myrna or even reject her. In this way, more than stabilizing a particular way of seeing things, the example sets a local world in motion. It is this very movement that I have traced in this book. The movement has taken us through several fields of relevance to the followers of Our Lady of Soufanieh, each with a distinctive character, albeit all correlated by being located in the same tensioned force field of exemplarity and modelling of sainthood.

The inception of Soufanieh as a place of worship had its beginnings in the critical year 1982, when the Syrian regime was cracking down hard on Islamists. The message of unity, faith, and love that Myrna received from the Virgin Mary later that year, which has been reiterated over the years, underscores the vulnerable situation that Syrian Christians find themselves in. Unity is striven for, and this goal correlates well with the idea of national Syrian unity, even if these two concepts are not synonymous. The modelling of sainthood in and around Myrna's figure is situated in relation to the precarious situation in the region, one in which the Virgin Mary is beseeched for help and guidance on the particular spot in Soufanieh where she revealed herself to Myrna and, by extension, her followers.

Prayer is an exemplary practice for the followers of Our Lady of Soufanieh and for Christians more generally. In and through prayer, the followers of Our Lady of Soufanieh both follow the instruction of the Virgin Mary, given in her messages to Myrna, and plead with her. The daily prayers of the rosary work by repeated mention and by extended meditation on exemplary scenes from the lives of Christ and the Virgin Mary. The prayers need to be understood as inherently social, as a matter of relationships; as such, I argue that they work by re-petition, the constant urge to pray more and place one's burdens in the hands of Mary. The followers of Our Lady of Soufanieh find their response in the gaze met by the image of Our Lady of Soufanieh, which miraculously answers the individual in the form of oil exuded from her icon.

Another way in which the structure of exemplarity is ingrained in the followers is through the weekly services and novenas. In the sermons in the home, a particular structure of exemplarity is set up for the listeners to become a part of. Priests such as Abuna Elias Zahlawi, Abuna Boulos Fadel, and Abuna Elias Saloun place Myrna alongside recognized saints such as John of Damascus, Augustine, Thérèse of Lisieux, and Bernadette Soubirous. In this way, the story of Soufanieh is authorized. Here, we see the exemplification working as an ex-sampling. The priests craft a series by taking certain saints out of the divine stock and meditating on their lives and story. By extension, each of the listeners is invited to become an example him- or herself. The drift of the series needs to be caught and, furthermore, attended to.

For the followers of Our Lady of Soufanieh, the modelling of sainthood has to start in their own lives. Each of the followers has his or her own story, which is fashioned around the happenings in Soufanieh and the relationship with Our Lady of Soufanieh and Myrna. The life of the individual must not simply attend to the message of Our Lady of Soufanieh but must also co-exemplify it in words and, more importantly, deeds. This requirement means that the followers live up to the example in the eyes of their fellow followers to differing degrees. Some are seen to embody the example more fully than others. However, each is hoped to become more and more like the example. Rima is considered a good example in that she has modelled her life upon Myrna's. She is a worthy representative of Soufanieh. Conversely, others such as Fadi are regarded as lesser, if not outright bad examples when their lives are not seen to follow the example.

While the followers aim to model sainthood and the example of Myrna in their own lives, they meet with rather diverse attitudes in Damascus. Even though many Christians accept the general claim of sainthood and miracles, they are less inclined to pay attention to Myrna and her example. Myrna, for many outside the circle of devoted followers of Our Lady of Soufanieh, is not seen as an exemplar, or model, but rather as a *mere* example. For some, she is regarded as pretentious and desirous of publicity; others prefer not to delve into the specificity of Myrna and the alleged miracles surrounding her. The followers of Our Lady of Soufanieh see Myrna and the miracles as evidence and signs of divine intervention. Furthermore, by attesting to the story of Soufanieh, the followers of Soufanieh themselves participate in making the story true by a process I have called "evidentification," an identification of the evidence suited to attesting to Virgin Mary's action and blessing on this particular spot.

The modelling of sainthood, for the followers of Our Lady of Soufanieh, must not remain only in Damascus; rather, it should be spread to all of Syria. The critical message of unity, faith, and love is to be corroborated in public life. However, this task is not a simple one, as the popular attention waxes and wanes, particularly as the clergy of the various churches appear to hold rather diverse opinions about the phenomenon. In 2009, the followers of Our Lady of Soufanieh promoted the message of unity in various churches during the month of annual celebrations. Regarding these journeys, I have argued that the role of the example works in the tension between unity and discord. In classic anthropological discussions on pilgrimage, there has been a tendency to focus on either communitas or contestation. My argument is that both, in the form of unity and discord, animate the followers of Our Lady of Soufanieh – to work harder, when her message is not attended to, and to take even further joy when it is.

Examples are produced in particular contexts. In Christianity, the Apostle Paul has been a paradigmatic example for radical conversion. More recently, Paul has been reintroduced in continental philosophy to reflect the first thinker of universalism. In Damascus, not only among the followers of Our Lady of Soufanieh but also among Christians more widely, the direction is the opposite; there, Paul is read from the East and put forth as an example of God's plan of redemption as going through Damascus, where Paul's conversion took place. The problem we encounter is how thickly or how thinly examples can be used. In Syria, among Christians, Paul is invoked to say something about their situation in the Syrian nation, one the Christians are both happy with but also wary of in a regional climate of growing Islamization. Here,

Damascus is made to speak in and through the figure of Paul. For the followers of Our Lady of Soufanieh, Paul is also seen as a prefiguration of Myrna and thereby attests to the divine love of Damascus, and even more so in troubled times. Damascus is here the example that speaks a message of faith, love, and unity to the world.

In this book, I have worked towards an anthropology of the example. In the next sections of the book's conclusion, I shall lay out perspectives on what is to be gained from thinking with and through the example. My aim is to contribute to a more general questioning by way of the example in three interrelated domains: empirical, methodological, and theoretical. The example, I intend to show, cross-cuts and invites a further rethinking of each of these three distinctive domains.

Empirically, we have seen how particular practices such as prayers, sermons, and life stories are seen as exemplary for the followers of Our Lady of Soufanieh in that they model both the behaviour of the individual followers of Our Lady of Soufanieh and that of Myrna. The exemplarity of Myrna is seen in her own life and in the efforts of the followers to mirror and co-exemplify her. By attending to these practices as exemplary, the empirical stuff of the anthropological analysis is to be situated in relation to the movement of a local world. The exemplification, understood as a singling out, is a significant way in which ethnographical material is used to invite rethinking. In this vein, empirical examples are not merely chosen (see Warnick 2008); rather, they have a force of their own that presses on the anthropologist, necessitating methodological and theoretical labour. It is the empirical stuff itself that forces its way through in the anthropological engagement with examples. The thinking with and through examples is therefore also related to issues of context (Dilley 1999). The example must be placed in context, but further, the powerful example is also itself productive for fashioning contexts.

Probing the role of examples has implications for the methods and ways of working. Methodologically, I have used the example as both a means of following cases, people, and material and as a style of writing. Here, the example is significant, since it neither belongs to a local world nor is a theoretical construct on the part of the scholar. Rather, the example is situated in a space in between, where claims and ideas are seen in and through particular events and incidents that conjure up wider issues of pertinence. In this vein, the thinking with and through examples methodologically invites us to think of the ways in which local worlds and scholarly analysis make parts relate to parts and wholes relate to wholes. I was asked by the followers of Our Lady of Soufanieh to document what happened; I was guided to particular people; and likewise,

I was advised not to interview or talk to specific others. The thinking through examples in methodological terms means that the scholar attends to these local attempts at exemplification, thinking and challenging them from an anthropological perspective. In this book, I have chosen life stories, a sermon, and a film as methodological entries to understanding what the world of the followers of Our Lady of Soufanieh looks like. The entries, in this sense, are also examples exemplary to the anthropologist. Not by mere chance did I pick out random incidents; rather, the most exemplary sermons and life stories were used because they themselves became exemplary for my anthropological understanding of a local world. The sermon by Abuna Elias Zahlawi, for instance, was one in a series of sermons, but in that sermon, he made use of the seriation by ex-sampling in a particularly captivating manner. The life stories of Rima and Fadi both came to stand out as exemplary to me in the way they captured the potential of the good as well as the bad example. But they did not stand out to me alone. I was pointed towards Rima as much as I was pointed away from Fadi. Likewise, the sermon of Abuna Elias Zahlawi was lauded for its exceptional quality in that it moved the listeners. The use of particular parts as exemplary for others is the significant move that I have tried to attend to, as methodologically it gives us the possibility of seeing how things are made to stand for other things. In this process, the examples point us in the direction of the ways in which both ordinary people and scholars craft their worlds, as well as their arguments. The example, in this sense, does not point towards representation alone but towards a thinking along with the worlds we explore. Here, it is possible to work for a coevalness, promoted by Johannes Fabian (1983) and later picked up by Webb Keane (2007: 33–4, 288), in that the worlds of scholars and ordinary people are in a dialogue and, I would add, are where different structures of exemplarity are at play. Methodologically, this idea does not imply that the same aspects are noticed in examples (Elgin 2017) but rather that their force leaves neither ordinary person nor scholar unaffected. Where Paul de Man criticized the example for never arriving at universality and certainty (1984: 276), I will argue that this feature is precisely one of the central values, as we can see here the ways in which local worlds are made to move.

Theoretically, the example works in that it sets things in motion. The example, accordingly, works by moving a field around it; however, this movement happens not by leaving out the details but by attending to them. In this sense, the thinking through examples is a way of becoming more concrete, not more abstract (see also Moi 2015). An anthropology of the example is – to borrow from Lévi-Strauss (1968[1962]) – a science of the concrete. By attending to the concrete details, the ideological structures that guide a given local world become manifest. According to John Lyons (1989), the relation between details and examples is also manifest in the meaning of detail, which, etymologically speaking – like the example – is what is cut out or removed (9). By attending to the details and the crafting of structures of exemplarity, it becomes possible, anthropologically speaking, to locate research in the gap where not just ontological systems, so promoted in some strands of recent anthropology (see Henare, Holbraad, & Wastell 2007), but broader fields can be assessed. Whereas the recent anthropological debate on ontologies asserts a divide between worlds, where "their" things can be thought through, the example poses a different option. Thinking through examples gives the option of seeing that local and scholarly worlds do not necessarily part ways in the thinking and acting by way of examples; that it is not the evidential structure *per se* that differs but rather the specific aims striven for in a given context and by a situated usage. Again, thinking with and through examples is not a departure from the concrete and the details but rather, in the words of Brian Massumi (2002: 18), "the success of the example hinges on the details." Here, the example is not only to be used to sum up already existing wholes but to produce and render other and different wholes by working as a prism to capture and refract the field by its very evocation (see Højer & Bandak 2015). Thinking with examples through prayers, sermons, life stories, and films is a matter of multiple exemplifications that allow the modelling of sainthood to be seen in exemplary fashion. It is in this sense that this book must be read as an exercise in exemplification.

Several critical themes emerge from the anthropological thinking through exemplification that I have explored in this book, and I shall here point only to a few: the role of confession and creed for a formation of the Christian subject; the relation to models *of* and *for* sainthood; and the relations to knowledge, evidence, and proof among both believers and sceptics. The role of confession and creed is critical among the followers of Soufanieh. By saying aloud what you believe in common, faith is made manifest (see Keane 2007: 288; 2008: s116). The messages of Myrna are solidified by being placed on the same footing as those from the Bible and from tradition. The liturgical voice (Ihde 2007: 173ff.) and the saying aloud make public and tangible what would otherwise not be so. By examining the theme of public proclamation, a significant theme of confession can be untied from a one-eyed Foucault-inspired reading, which would have man become "a confessing animal" in his examination of the mechanisms of the confession (Foucault 1980[1976]: 59; see also 1993: 201; 2009). While such a reading renders the workings of modern power through a genealogy over pastoral power with great clarity, it overlooks the dual nature of confession (see Agamben 2005[2000]: 134; 2011). Confession can be both of sins and of faith, the former being private or semi-private, as it is said to a pastoral intercessor, and the latter being public, as it is said in the communal space of others. The analytics of opening this theme from the communal prayers can yield prospects in the way in which Christian subject formation can take place. In this book, I have explored the ramifications of a Catholic vision of such subject formation. This subject formation is seen in and through the modelling of sainthood, both in the primary figure of Myrna and in those of her followers. Where the notion of belief has been heavily criticized in much recent work on religion (see Needham 1973; Pouillon 1982; Ruel 1982; Asad 1993; Rappaport 1999; Orsi 2011), it is important to reflect on the way life is modelled on the example of Christ, Mary, and Myrna, and how prayer, sermons, and devotion instigate a life for further emulation. In the lives of the followers of Our Lady of Soufanieh, the formation of Christian character rests upon both words and deeds, and they interact in a community of others. A central contribution to an anthropology of Christianity is here to situate sainthood and exemplarity in a field of individual and communal confession. It may not be an answer to the critical assessment of the category of belief, but it may be a way to see how a Catholic vision of the subject works through exemplary practices.

Another critical aspect bears on the relation to saints and sainthood. While sainthood in general is not detested by almost any Christians of Damascus, the concrete instantiation is always up for negotiation. In this book, I have explored this gap between models *of* and models *for* sainthood. While the first is to some degree accepted, the latter is suspended by many. Myrna and her public figure are located in the very heart of this gap. While some people acknowledge Myrna as a saint and as a model to emulate – a model *for* sainthood – many would rather suspend judgment altogether. Saints, as pointed out by William James (1982[1902]), are often met with such indulgence and reluctance by their contemporaries, and in the analysis I have here proposed, the different strategies aim at either attempting to overcome this obstacle, as is the case of the followers; contesting it, as some Christian Syrians do; or suspending any judgment until deemed necessary, as yet others do. In exploring the attempts at modelling sainthood in this book, I have tried to allow for productive tensions, where processes of foregrounding or backgrounding become visible (see Bandak & Jørgensen 2012). Here, a focus on the coming into being of a particular pious foreground has been explored, and it is my argument that such a sensibility is needed to avoid rendering social worlds as total, as is a tendency in some of the recent literature on pious worlds. The followers of Our Lady of

Soufanieh are animated by the diverse reactions they, Myrna, and Our Lady of Soufanieh meet. It is productive for the force of the example to meet contestation. Here, my hope is that this book will contribute to an anthropology of the Middle East, since the recent tendency of studying pious worlds appears to take us away from contestations. Ideals and models are abundant in local worlds; however, some gain greater salience than others in people's lives. By attending to these ideals and models, even when they do not succeed, it is possible to see the intersections of a world in which different potentialities coexist for moving people closer or further away from their respective ideals and models.

The last aspect to dwell upon is how knowledge and evidence are used to bridge the gap between extraordinary and mundane in a local world. For the followers of Our Lady of Soufanieh, the miracles are taken as signs, whereas many on the outside stop short of this assessment just to marvel in the wondrous. The nature of evidence and what counts as evidence is therefore a critical theme to reflect upon and has recently been brought to anthropological attention (Engelke 2008). In this literature, however, the example has tended to be explored as a matter of argument in scholarly worlds. Yet, both evidence and examples are operative in particular worlds, and they must be examined with regards to what they bring about in these worlds. The example is often used as evidence or, in Aristotle's terms, "a proof common to all" (2004[1991]: 76–8, 189). However, for the example to count as evidence, it must be framed as such. And even if it were so framed, it would have to be situated in broader structures of knowledge and its opposite, ignorance (see Dilley 2010). The followers of Our Lady of Soufanieh work zealously to become ever more exemplary in the face of adversity. Individual life is to be made into evidence of Our Lady of Soufanieh's constant care. The signs in this endeavour are seen as evidence, but furthermore, the greatest miracle is transposed, to be seen as faith itself. Evidence, examples, and miracles in this sense are about orientation, as argued by Ruth Marshall (2010: 213). For the followers of Our Lady of Soufanieh, miracles are a source of further joy because they point to how the Virgin Mary can move hearts, and the followers see their lives participating in her work. Examples, the book argues, set local worlds in motion. In attending to and thinking through structures of exemplarity, I hope to have presented a promising avenue for future research and, likewise, to have elaborated a conception of what an anthropology of the example can offer. I propose that an anthropology of the example is also an exemplary anthropology that aims at setting the world in motion.

# Of Miracles and the Belatedness of Examples

Why are examples important? A single example is, after all, statistically insignificant. So, it might seem, the ability to provide an example should count for virtually nothing. But often it counts for a lot. The reason, I suggest, is that the example displays an understanding of the topic. It is not just an instance, it is a telling instance.

– Catherine Z. Elgin, *True Enough*

And then it happened. On Easter 2010, on the joint Easter Saturday (*yawm as-sabt an-nūr*), during the service in Myrna's home, her hands started to ooze oil. I saw it, as I was present, sitting just two metres away from her in the packed inner courtyard. Reactions were rather diverse. Hani was shouting in excitement. Rula was crying. Salwa and Rita were smiling. Soon, more and more people gathered in the home: Christians, Muslims, people from all walks of life. Cameras instantly started to record the moment. And as for me? To be honest, it was a lost moment, as I had never been so closed off from my own feelings; instead, as a trained anthropologist, I observed and recorded what was unfolding in front of me. This moment had been longed for by Hani, Rula, Rita, Rima, and all the followers of Our Lady of Soufanieh. This moment was Mary's, and she seemed to speak to the longings and hopes of those present. For me, however, it was a moment in which I did not quite know how to react personally. Instead, I recorded in as much detail as possible the reactions of others, suspending my own judgment.

The priests present soon brought some order to the event. They said there would be oil enough for everyone and people should wait until the Eucharist had been consummated; Myrna would then bless them all with the exuding holy oil. In this way, everybody was first incorporated into the greatest miracle of the church and secondarily into the special blessing of the holy oil. Everyone queued up, first to receive the bread and wine from the hands of the pastors and then for an anoint-ment from Myrna. Several of the followers made sure everything went smoothly with no pushing and shoving. Some called or texted friends and families about the miracle, and many used their cell phones to take photos of Myrna. Everyone, myself included, received the sign of the cross on the forehead from Myrna's fingers. The oil continued to ooze from Myrna's hands for half an hour, as hymns were sung to the Virgin Mary and people kept pouring in.

When the oil stopped oozing, Myrna took a seat in the living room next to the inner courtyard, visibly in pain. No message was given to Myrna this year, only the miraculous sign of holy oil. People were still coming, and the followers made sure to distribute booklets, DVDs, and rosaries for those who were not regulars. Several of the followers spoke to me: Hanadi, Rita, Salwa, and Hani, all praising what had happened. For Hani, it was the first time he had seen the oil being exuded. It hap-pened for my sake, he asserted. He explained how he was about to go to a different place, but then was finally able to come, and now the Virgin Mary had given him this sign. Hanadi, Rita, and Salwa were all happy, albeit in a more controlled way. "Now you have seen it, An-dreas! You have to write about this!" Salwa said, her eyes brimming with joy, envisaging what my book would now look like.

The following evening, the most devoted of the followers were as-sembled in the home of Myrna yet again. Abuna Elias Saloun exhorted the meaning of the evening. What was the significance of the oil exuded from Myrna's hands? There was no message this time. Why? Because Our Lady of Soufanieh wanted us to be the message today, Abuna Elias Saloun asserted. The action of Our Lady of Soufanieh, in this sense, now rested upon the followers to follow her example, to carry the weight of the example, to be and become more and more like her. In this process and structure of exemplarity, every single person must find his or her own way, not alone but rather in the company of Our Lady of Soufa-nieh and the unity of hearts gathered around her. Here a slot is left open for every single person to live the unity, so promoted by the messages.

What is my own stance? With this book, I have explored the role of the example in the lives of the pious followers of Our Lady of Sou-fanieh. I have made every effort to try to cover and present what they take to be the most important aspects of the message and phenomenon of Our Lady of Soufanieh. Whether I have become an example myself or not is for others to judge – or rather, to judge precisely what I have become an example of. For the followers of Our Lady of Soufanieh, I may not quite yet have moved close enough to Mary. However, this book still carries the imprint of Our Lady of Soufanieh, Myrna, and her followers, and in this regard, her example will be for you to judge.

Today Syria looks rather different from the country this book has conveyed. For the last eleven years, civil war has ravaged the country, and Christians find themselves in a novel situation, where for most, their sense of vulnerability has become pronounced in ways unimagined in what I have portrayed in the book. What I should like to ponder here, then, is a set of reflections about what the book in itself could be seen as an example of.

The people who appear in this book today are located in rather different places. Myrna and Nicolas have remained in Damascus, even if they have also lived in Lebanon for parts of this period. When I visited Myrna and her family in Lebanon during the spring of 2014, they firmly presented themselves as living temporarily in Lebanon for the sake of their grandchildren, not as refugees. Actual fighting was taking place near their home. Moments later, during our conversation, Nicolas asked their grandchildren where Mary was, and the whole family applauded when they fetched an icon of Our Lady of Soufanieh. "This is Our Lady. She is always with us!" Nicolas said, while Myrna nodded. Following this affirmation, Myrna and Nicolas explained how the daily prayers are still said in Damascus in front of the countenance of Our Lady of Soufanieh. Fewer attend, though, as the city now is not only difficult to travel in but at times outright dangerous. That Mary is seeing to her flock is hence a constant comfort as well as a concern. Such concern has also been underscored when bishops of the various Orthodox and Catholic churches have issued joint declarations on the Christian duty (*wajībe*) to stay in the region. Such declarations bespeak the severity of the situation, where Syrian Christians, and not only those seeking the protection of Our Lady of Soufanieh, are feeling increasingly vulnerable.

The general climate of bloodshed and hostility has moved the question of the existence of Christianity in the Middle East to the centre of attention for many local Christians. Many of the people we met in this book are no longer in Syria. Abouna Boulos Fadel is now leading one of the famous monasteries in Harissa, Lebanon, dedicated to Saint Paul. Others like Salwa and her family and Rima and her family no longer reside in Syria but live in the United States and France, respectively. Similarly, many others from the extended family of Our Lady of Soufanieh have left the country. Others have remained, though. Myrna's parents and others with fewer direct connections abroad are still living in Damascus. Abuna Elias Zahlawi and Abuna Elias Saloun, likewise, have stayed in Syria. Zahlawi, in particular, has openly supported the regime in interviews and writings across various media. That said, Christians can by no means be seen as one single group, even if many may eventually have sided with the Syrian regime after the initial promise of the uprising darkened. Accordingly, the message of faith, love, and unity that the extended family of Our Lady of Soufanieh still tries to corroborate harks back to Damascus and the knowledge that the Virgin herself appeared on this spot, but in times that now seem so distant.

The fact that the ethnographic presence of this book today seems so distant merits further thought. In his important work *Futures Past: On the Semantics of Historical Time*, Reinhart Koselleck (2004) considers the theme of the example and historical knowledge. In his highly modernist reading of Western history, Koselleck shows how historical thinking up until the French revolution revolved around exemplarity best known in Cicero's formulae *historia magistra vitae* (26ff.; see also Hartog 2015[2003]). In this scheme, history was thought of as the great teacher of life, a collection of examples to be deployed for later generation's edification and instruction. Koselleck (2004) argues that, even if this scheme had its origin in both Greek and Roman thinking, it was overtaken and persisted with the coming of age of the church and Christian tradition. With the Enlightenment, however, in Koselleck's exposition, exemplary account made way for a new experiential space, where history was thought of as a unique series of events and hence lacking the same directing force that history as exemplary account had had. History ceased to have the same role in edification, as no primacy was given to past examples for future orientation; all past examples lost their power (37). What we could call the belatedness of the example is poignantly formulated by Koselleck: "No matter how scholarly, every past example is always too late" (42).

In this book, I have argued that the powerful example, more than stabilizing a local world, sets it in motion. What the Syrian tragedy has shown us is that some examples hold the potential to become global examples. Syria, in these years, has become an exemplary example for the world as such, but for competing and often mutually conflicting purposes. In the Syrian tragedy, Syria has become an example of a failed state, of endemic incompatibility between Christianity and Islam, of Western indifference, of cold Russian speculation on how to corroborate its sphere of interests, and of a world order on the brink of destruction, with the ensuing refugee situation in neighbouring countries in the Middle East and many parts of Europe. Syria, as an example, is hence open to multiple interpretations.

While Syria lends itself as an example for rethinking diverse themes such as those just mentioned, it may be worthwhile reflecting on what it means to say that every past example always comes too late. Ethnography may show us that the inherent belatedness of a book like this one is critical in that it allows us to rethink and resituate what was, what is, and what will be. Exactly by having captured the time before the Syrian tragedy, we may be allowed to reflect on the different stakes and potentialities, which were also present before the current situation started to unfold. To think over again and to resituate, I hope, will never be too late – neither for today nor for the time to come.

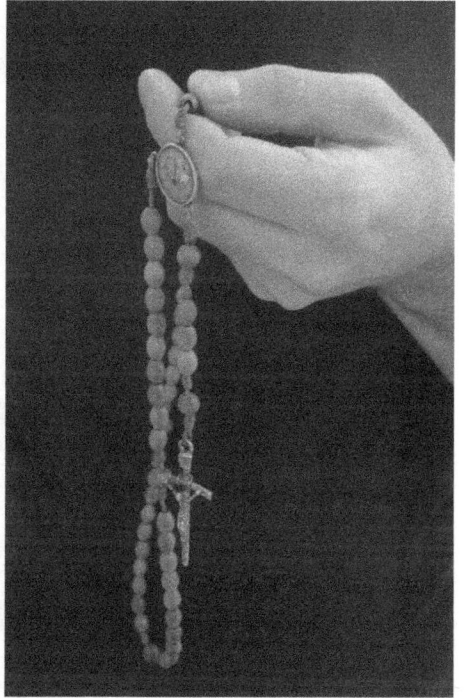

Prayers and icons in front of Our Lady of Soufanieh. No donations are accepted, but petitions and prayers are. Photos courtesy of the author.

Abouna Elias Zahlawi lectures on the day of the twenty-seventh anniversary of the first apparition of the Virgin Mary in Soufanieh. The messages given by the Virgin Mary and Christ to Myrna Nazzour on this spot are retold, and people are invited to listen and themselves live the message of faith, love, and unity. Photo courtesy of the author.

During the twenty-seventh anniversary, the icon of Our Lady of Soufanieh was, for the first time since the inception of Soufanieh as a shrine, taken to different cathedrals all over Syria. The icon was placed in a frame and carried by the followers, first, in an ornamented frame and, later, in a simpler one: the virtue of simplicity on display. Photos courtesy of the author.

In al-Nabk and Homs, Bishop Isidore Battikha welcomed the icon of Our Lady of Soufanieh as Our Lady of Syria. Myrna and her family were received with great commotion, with scouts and orchestras celebrating the presence of Our Lady of Soufanieh. And the moment was captured meticulously. Photos courtesy of the author.

Inscription of the papal visit on the stones of Damascus. Photo courtesy of the author.

Then it happened. During Easter 2010, Myrna's hands started to ooze oil, and she blessed all who wanted to be so blessed. Photos courtesy of the author.

# Notes

## Introduction: Modelling Sainthood in Christian Syria

1 Canon law posits three steps in publications under the auspices of the Roman Catholic Church. The first step is a *nihil obstat*, determining that nothing in terms of faith and morals hinders a proposed publication. The second step is the allowance for a book to be printed, called *imprimi potest*. The third step is the *imprimatur*, which is the formal acceptance of a publication by the local bishop.

2 For an overview of the Syrian demography, see the data made available by The World Bank at https://data.worldbank.org/indicator/SP.POP.TOTL ?end=2017&locations=SY&start=1960.

## 1. Closer to Mary

1 In English, it is more commonly worded in this way: "As it was in the beginning, is now, and ever shall be, world without end." Here, I have kept the shorter translated version from the Arabic to keep to the tone of Soufanieh.

## 2. Repeated Prayers

1 In the anthropological literature on Islam, there are excellent engagements with the theme of worship and prayer; however, these have rarely been brought into conversation with those of Christianity (see Lambek 1993; Henkel 2005; Haeri 2013; Henig 2020).

2 See the website of the Congregation of Rosary Sisters at http://www .rosary-cong.com/.

3 Paul Anderson (2011) presents an exquisite engagement with selfhood and sociality as central features in the Eqyptian Mosque movement, features

that tend to be overlooked in the works by Saba Mahmood. Anderson argues that analysis needs to move beyond a Foucauldian framework of self-cultivation towards a focus on ritual exchange and social interaction. This insight corroborates the ethnography presented here: the devout Syrian Christians see themselves as part of a much wider devotional landscape encompassing family members, neighbours, saints, Mary, Jesus, and God (see Bandak 2017b; Haynes 2017; Webster 2017).

4 Previously, this final scene was the Last Judgment or the Joys of Paradise, but it has since been exchanged for the Coronation of the Virgin Mary (see Winston-Allen 1997: 3, 54–64).

5 Obviously, this vernacular understanding of praying as opposed to playing is a way to construct a particular relationship between self and imagined others, be they other Christians or Muslims. Furthermore, similar constructions of prayer as opposed to play exist in certain Muslim traditions, even if the debate here is constructed as an internal one (see van der Veer 1992).

6 Traditionally, there is a difference in Catholic and Orthodox theology as to which artefacts are seen to be animated. Orthodox Christianity and, for that matter, Eastern Catholicism have traditionally not used statues as part of pious interaction (Mahieu 2010: 79). In Jordan, Marian imagery among Catholics has also been influenced by global trends stemming from, for example, Lourdes (Jansen 2009: 38). However, in Damascus, the use of statues of Our Lady of Lourdes as well as the grotto is commonplace in many families both Orthodox and Eastern Catholic, even if many churches have icons in a style distinct for the area (see Athanasiou 2005).

7 John 20:24–9.

### 3. Exemplary Series

1 You could also mirror this three-time rejection with that of Peter and Christ, even if this analogy is not drawn upon in an overt fashion in the sermon.

2 See Matthew 13:57; Mark 6:4; Luke 4:24; and John 4:44.

3 The regime has done much to underscore the stature of Abuna Elias Zahlawi, and he likewise has done much to emphasize Syria as a place for all. The ceremony for Abuna Elias Zahlawi and his famous Choir of Joy (*Jawqatu-l-Farah*) on 6 July 2009 at the People's Palace in Damascus was turned into a scene to be remembered in line with the regime's ideology and propaganda, here with the First Lady's presence gracing the event – see the video of the ceremony at https://www.youtube.com/watch?v=e_8hF_r7JDk. See also Bandak (2015b).

4 See Revelations 3:15–16, where the topic is addressed in relation to the church in Laodicea. The address here is grave, and the response even more so.

## 4. Life and Story

1  As underscored in previous chapters, hagiography, in various Christian traditions, has been a prevalent lense through which to understand and see life. As argued in the work of historian Catherine Sanok (2007), saints' lives were paramount for establishing a historical consciousness and a comparandum. The formation of a social hermeneutic populated by exemplars worth imitating is hence important also for further cross-cultural comparison beyond the scope of this chapter. Recent anthropological work engages facets of exemplarity in Orthodox tradition (Rogers 2009; Naumescu 2016; Pop 2017) and also that of Charismatic Christianity (Daswani 2016).

2  This preference for the location of the interview was the case with many of the interviews I conducted; my interlocutors preferred to be interviewed in the proximity of Soufanieh – if not on the very premises, then in a nearby garden or café.

3  In this sense, Rima's life story presents her life as being lived in a straight line, whereas it is always also a matter of how the narration constructs that life. In Kierkegaard's (1997[1843]) sense, life is being lived forwards but understood backwards (see also Jackson 2002; Bruner 2004; Khater 2011: 23; Naumescu 2016).

4  In this narrative, the dream is also exemplary, as it is a genre of experience known from the Bible as well as from Christian tradition (Goodich 2007; Jansen 2005; Hourihane 2010; Morgan 2012; Christian 2012; Stewart 2012; Heo 2018). Likewise, more broadly in the region, Mary frequently features in dreams and visions (Jansen 2005; Jansen & Kühl 2008). However, Muslim traditions of visions and dreams also exist (see Gilsenan 2000; Mittermaier 2011).

5  Again, Robbins (2015) would emphasize not merely qualities but values strived for. Here, however, I point to a process of co-exemplification, which addresses a different trajectory than the quest for values as Robbins elucidates in his work. In Robbins work (here and elsewhere; see 2004), we learn about the individualizing forces of Christianity among the Urapmin. In my material, by contrast, co-exemplification rests on collective efforts.

6  Smoking is very common in Syria. Among the followers of Our Lady of Soufanieh, smoking is considered a bad habit, something generally not approved of as a Christian virtue but rather something to unlearn. However, this view was stated more in terms of people being asked not to smoke inside the house of Myrna.

7  Whether Fadi assumes the position of the unworthy consciously or not, this humility is the same gesture that John the Baptist and Saint Paul made in their respective meetings and lives with Christ.

8  Elsewhere, I develop the whole notion of simplicity, or in Arabic *basāṭa*, as this notion holds a particular salience in a Syrian context, where lavish display of wealth generally has been looked down upon. Furthermore, this value is not merely a Syrian simplicity; a Christian inflection hereof is also prevalent, not just among the ardent followers of Our Lady of Soufanieh but as a much wider disposition (but see Bandak 2017a). For an ordinary ethics perspective on Syrian traders in Aleppo, I refer to Paul Anderson's (2019) work.

9  In line with much anthropological theorizing on mimesis and imitation, the point here is that what is being produced is alterity, not identity (see Taussig 1993; Sanok 2007; Mitchell 2015).

## 5. Signs and Evidence

1  There exists a corpus of scholarly work on stigmatics including, for instance, Catherine of Siena, Christina of Stommeln, Francis of Assisi, Lukardis of Oberweimar (see Kleinberg 1992, 2008: 206–24); Gemma Galgani (see Orsi 2005: 110–45); and St. Francis of Assisi (see Davidson 2009; Belting 2010).

2  Gérard Challet gave his testimony upon a visit to Soufanieh for one of the Tuesday evening novenas, which I recorded, and I afterwards had a lengthy conversation with him. He also has a written testimony translated into several languages that he distributes for free, which is recorded in Zahlawi's (2008) magnum opus referred to earlier in the chapter.

3  See Matthew 13:57; Mark 6:4; Luke 4:24.

4  For similar discussions and negotiations among Christians, albeit in Italy, see Apolito (1998[1992]); see Gilsenan (2000) for similar problems among Muslims in Egypt.

5  Significantly, Muslims do not generally use the same terms for miracles; the term *karamāt* is used instead (see Pinto 2004: 197; Mittermaier 2011: 156). However, in some places, it seems that Muslims may also use the terms interchangeably (see Gilsenan 1982: 79ff.).

6  On a broader level, the Catholic Church is upholding a particular form of undecidedness in relation to many visionaries and apparition sites, as the church needs to show in the long run that they are not fraudulent. Silence, or the suspension of an official assessment, can mean a positive stance, which is what Myrna has seen from the Catholic churches in Damascus, even if various bishops and priests may differ in their personal opinions.

## 6. Prophecies of Unity

1  The trip was duly displayed on the official website alongside the parts of that month's more successful events; see https://www.soufanieh.com /ANNIV/27/20091126.syr.ara.prieres.maison.slideshow.pdf.

## 7. Damascus Speaking

1  *Dimashq tatakallam – al-Qadīs Būlos [Damascus Speaking – Saint Paul]*, directed by Khalid al-Khalid, screen play by Maisaa Salloum (2009; Agape 4 Media), DVD.

2  Here Saloum is quoting Luke 19:39–40.

3  This point is remarked on in interviews given on Arab channels. See *al-Sūriyā* (2009, 2 June), *Special Evening on "Damascus Is Speaking – The Apostle Paul."* The program is available on YouTube at https://www.youtube .com/watch?v=Nfu-bSfuuLI.

4  The 2 June 2009 interview on *al-Sūriyā* with Dr. Gamal Makkar is part of the same program mentioned in note 3 above, available on YouTube at https://www.youtube.com/watch?v=Nfu-bSfuuLI.

5  See the interview in the ten minute video aired under the title *The Premier of "Damascus" in the Vatican* (2009, 17 June). The video was made available on YouTube by Lifeagabe Syria, which was also behind the film, at https://www.youtube.com/watch?v=5AMJ5rXbWSI.

6  The translation of Paul's words is from The Holy Bible, New International Version/New Arabic Version English/Arabic (1988: Zondervan).

7  The author, Maisaa Salloum, revealed this plan in an interview given on *al-Sūriyā*. Likewise, it was mentioned in the ten-minute report also mentioned in note 5 above, which is available on YouTube at https://www .youtube.com/watch?v=5AMJ5rXbWSI.

8  I here refer to the same ten-minute report as mentioned in note 5 above, available on YouTube at https://www.youtube.com/watch?v =5AMJ5rXbWSI.

9  The Melkite Greek Catholic Church also officially announced the trip and screening of the film in the diaspora. Among other information, it announced the details of the premiere in the Vatican City. See https:// melkite.org/patriarchate/premiere-of-damascus-and-celebrate-at -saint-maria-in-cosmedin.

10  The words are delivered in a rather lengthy 1999 letter by Pope John Paul II under the title "Letter of the Supreme Pontiff, *John Paul II*, Concerning Pilgrimage to the Places Linked to the History of Salvation." The letter is available on the website of the Vatican at https://www.vatican.va /content/john-paul-ii/en/letters/1999/documents/hf_jp-ii_let_30061999 _pilgrimage.html.

11  The program on the 2001 papal visit to Greece, Malta, and Syria is still available on the Vatican's formal website at https://www.vatican.va /content/john-paul-ii/en/travels/2001/travels/documents/trav_greece -syria-malta-2001.html.

12  This quote went viral and was debated hotly, for example, in the *New York Times* (13 May 2001) under the title "The World: Assad Greets the Pope;

Welcome, Man of Peace. Let's Go Hate My Enemy," by Clyde Haberman, https://www.nytimes.com/2001/05/13/weekinreview/the-world -assad-greets-the-pope-welcome-man-of-peace-let-s-go-hate-my-enemy .html; and in the *Washington Post* (8 May 2011) under the title "The Pope's Silence," by Richard Cohen, https://www.washingtonpost.com /archive/opinions/2001/05/08/the-popes-silence/734947eb-1af0-470c -af56-87a36a21497b/.

13  *In the Footsteps of Saint Paul* was released in 2008 by the Syrian Ministry of Tourism as an Ebla Productions. The script was written by Amr Sawwah. The film is available on Youtube at http://www.youtube.com/watch?v =3RodJ10LUgU.

14  Here, John the Baptist is given the name by which he is more commonly known among Muslims. Among Christians, he is typically referred to as *Yūḥanā Mu'ammadān*. This usage signals the film's intention to appeal to a broader frame than just a Christian one.

15  The first of the thirty-one official parts, *The Miracle of Damascus, Part One*, is placed on YouTube by the Catholic Digital Studio with permission from Rick Salbato. See https://www.youtube.com/watch?v=uOx_xBSn1Rk. The thirty-one parts are based on a five-and-a-half-hour film but edited for YouTube. For a full playlist with all parts, see https://www.youtube.com /playlist?list=PLEF7D832AC95D0515].

16  The Greek Melchite Catholic Church has over the years been active in re-leasing sermons and public declarations also in English on the website of the Eparchy of Newton. Currently, several of their links are no longer func-tioning. However, the Byzantine Catholic Church in America also hosts a website, where these sermons and declarations can be found: "Letter of His Beatitude Gregorios III on the Occasion of the Opening of the Year of Saint Paul," https://www.byzcath.org/index.php/news-mainmenu-49/2513 -letter-of-his-beatitude-gregorios-iii-on-the-occasion-of-the-opening-of-the -year-of-saint-paul; "Patriarch Gregorios III's Sermon for the Closing of the Year of Saint Paul," https://www.byzcath.org/index.php/news-mainmenu -49/2729-patriarch-gregorios-iiis-sermon-for-the-closure-of-the-year-of -st-paul; "Letter for Christmas 2008," https://www.byzcath.org/index .php/news-mainmenu-49/2600-qfor-to-me-to-live-is-christq-patriarch -gregorios-letter-for-christmas-2008; and the "Letter for Great and Holy Lent 2009," https://www.byzcath.org/index.php/news-maimenu-49/2658 -letter-for-great-and-holy-lent-2009-from-patriarch-gregorios.

17  As above, the website of the Byzantine Catholic Church in America has an English translation of the Patriarch's address under the heading: "Paul and the Dialogue of Cultures in the Middle East." See https://www .byzcath.org/index.php/news-mainmenu-49/2675-paul-and-the -dialogue-of-cultures-in-the-middle-east.

# References

Abdu, S. 2003. *al-ṭawā'if al-masīḥiyya fī sūriyyā* [The Christian Denominations in Syria]. Dār ḥasan malaṣ lil-nushir.

Abu-Lughod, J.L. 1987. The Islamic City – Historic Myth, Islamic Essence, and Contemporary Relevance. *International Journal of Middle East Studies, 19*(2): 155–76. https://doi.org/10.1017/S0020743800031822

Abu-Lughod, J.L. 2005. *Dramas of Nationhood: The Politics of Television in Egypt.* University of Chicago Press.

Adorno, T.W. 2005[1951]. *Minima Moralia: Reflections on a Damaged Life* (E.F.N Jephcott, Trans.). Verso.

Agamben, G. 1993[1990]. *The Coming Community* (M. Hardt, Trans.). University of Minnesota Press.

Agamben, G. 2005[2000]. *The Time That Remains: A Commentary on the Letter to the Romans* (P. Dailey, Trans.). Stanford University Press.

Agamben, G. 2009[2008]. What Is a Paradigm? (L. di Santo & K. Attell, Trans.). In *The Signature of All Things: On Method* (pp. 9–32). Zone Books.

Agamben, G. 2011. *The Sacrament of Language: An Archeology of the Oath* (A. Kotsko, Trans.). Stanford University Press.

Al-Haj Saleh, Y. 2017. *The Impossible Revolution: Making Sense of the Syrian Tragedy* (I. Mahmood, Trans.). Hurst.

Anderson, B. 2006[1983]. *Imagined Communities: Reflections on the Origin and Spread of Nationalism.* Verso.

Anderson, P. 2011. "The Piety of the Gift": Selfhood and Sociality in the Egyptian Mosque Movement. *Anthropological Theory, 11*(1): 3–21. https://doi.org/10.1177/1463499610395441

Anderson, P. 2013. The Politics of Scorn in Syria and the Agency of Narrated Involvement. *Journal of the Royal Anthropological Institute, 19*(3): 463–81. https://doi.org/10.1111/1467-9655.12045

Anderson, P. 2019. Games of Civility: Ordinary Ethics in Aleppo's Bazaar. *Ethnos, 84*(3): 380–97. https://doi.org/10.1080/00141844.2018.1551238

Apolito, P. 1998[1992]. *Apparitions of the Madonna at Oliveto Citra: Local Visions and Drama* (W.A Christian, Jr., Trans.). Pennsylvania State University Press.

Apolito, P. 2005[2001]. *The Internet and the Madonna: Religious Visionary Experience on the Web* (A. Shugaar, Trans.). University of Chicago Press.

Ardener, E. 1989. The Construction of History: "Vestiges of Creation." In E. Tonkin, M.K. Chapman, & M. McDonald (Eds.), *History and Ethnicity* (pp. 22–33). Routledge.

Arendt, H. 1982. *Lectures on Kant's Political Philosophy*. University of Chicago Press.

Arendt, H. 1994[1930]. Augustine and Protestantism. In *Essays in Human Understanding, 1930–1954* (pp. 24–7). Schocken Books.

Arendt, H. 1996[1929]. *Love and Saint Augustine*. University of Chicago Press.

Arendt, H. 1998[1958]. *The Human Condition*. University of Chicago Press.

Aristotle. 2004[1991]. *The Art of Rhetoric* (H.L. Tancreed, Trans.). Penguin Books.

Arjakovsky, A. 2010. *Myrna Nazour, messagère de l'unité: Entretiens sur les événements de Soufanieh*. Francois-Xavier de Guibert.

Armbrust, W. 1996. *Mass Culture and Modernism in Egypt*. Cambridge University Press.

Asad, T. 1993. *Genealogies of Religion: Discipline and Reasons of Power in Christianity and Islam*. Johns Hopkins University Press.

Athanasiou, M.H. 2005. *Iqūnāt Dimasq. Mawsū'tu-l-iqūnāti-l-sūriyyati* [Icons of Damascus: Encyclopedia of Syrian Icons]. Markaz Ṭāriq li-l-taḥdīri-l-ṭabāʿī.

Aubin-Boltanski, E. 2014. Uncertainty at the Heart of a Ritual in Lebanon 2011. *Social Compass, 61*(4): 511–23. https://doi.org/10.1177/0037768614547000

Auerbach, E. 1984[1959]. Figura (R. Manheim, Trans.). In *Scenes from the Drama of European Literature* (pp. 11–76). University of Minnesota Press.

Auerbach, E. 2003[1953]. *Mimesis: The Representation of Reality in Western Literature* (W.R Trask, Trans.). Princeton University Press.

Badiou, A. 2003. *Saint Paul: The Foundation of Universalism* (R. Brassier, Trans.). Stanford University Press.

Badone, E. (Ed.). 1990. *Religious Orthodoxy & Popular Faith in European Society*. Princeton University Press.

Badone, E. 2007. Echoes from Kerizinen: Pilgrimage, Narrative, and the Construction of a Sacred History at a Marian Shrine in Northwestern France. *Journal of the Royal Anthropological Institute, 13*(2): 453–70. https://doi.org/10.1111/j.1467-9655.2007.00436.x

Baldacchino, J.-P. 2011. Miracles in the Waiting Room of Modernity: The Canonization of Don Gorg. *The Australian Journal of Anthropology, 22*(1): 104–24. https://doi.org/10.1111/j.1757-6547.2011.00109.x

Bandak, A. 2012. Problems of Belief: Tonalities of Immediacy among Christians of Damascus. *Ethnos, 77*(4): 535–55. https://doi.org/10.1080/00141844.2012.728024

Bandak, A. 2013. States of Exception: Effects and Affects of Authoritarianism among Christian Arabs in Damascus. In E. Fihl & J. Dahl (Eds.), *A Comparative Ethnography of Alternative Spaces* (pp. 197–218). Palgave Macmillan.

Bandak, A. 2014a. Making "Sound" Analysis: From Raw Moments to Attuned Perspectives. In D. Kuzmanovic & A. Bandak (Eds.), *Qualitative Analysis in the Making* (pp. 176–91). Routledge.

Bandak, A. 2014b. Of Rhythms and Refrains in Contemporary Damascus: Urban Space and Christian-Muslim Coexistence. *Current Anthropology*, 55(S10): S248–61. https://doi.org/10.1086/678409

Bandak, A. 2015a. Exemplary Series and Christian Typology: Modelling on Sainthood in Damascus. *The Journal for the Royal Anthropological Institute*, 21(S1): 47–63. https://doi.org/10.1111/1467-9655.12165

Bandak, A. 2015b. Performing the Nation: Syrian Christians on the National Stage. In C. Salamandra & L. Stenberg (Eds.), *Syria from Reform to Revolt: Vol. 2. Culture, Society, and Religion* (pp. 195–229). Syracuse University Press.

Bandak, A. 2017a. Opulence and Simplicity: The Question of Tension in Syrian Catholicism. In V. Napolitano, K. Norget, & M. Mayblin (Eds.), *The Anthropology of Catholicism: A Reader* (pp. 155–69). University of California Press.

Bandak, A. 2017b. The Social Life of Prayers – Introduction. *Religion*, 47(1): 1–18. https://doi.org/10.1080/0048721X.2016.1225904

Bandak, A., & M. Bille. 2013a. Introduction: Sainthood in Fragile States. In A. Bandak & M. Bille (Eds.), *Politics of Worship in the Contemporary Middle East: Sainthood in Fragile States* (pp. 1–29). Brill.

Bandak, A., & M. Bille (Eds.). 2013b. *Politics of Worship in the Contemporary Middle East: Sainthood in Fragile States*. Brill.

Bandak, A., & T. Boylston. 2014. The "Orthodoxy" of Orthodoxy: On Moral Imperfection, Correctness, and Deferral in Religious Worlds. *Religion and Society: Advances in Research*, 5(1): 25–46. https://doi.org/10.3167/arrs.2014.050103

Bandak, A., & S. Coleman. 2019. Different Repetitions: Anthropological Engagements with Figures of Return, Recurrence and Redundancy. *History and Anthropology* 30(2): 119–32. https://doi.org/10.1080/02757206.2018.1547900

Bandak, A., & H. Henkel. 2021. BØN: Antropologiske åbninger i arbejdet med religiøs praksis. *Tidsskriftet Antropologi* BØN nr.84: 3–32. https://tidsskrift.dk/tidsskriftetantropologi/article/view/129925/175695

Bandak, A., & L. Højer (Eds.). 2015. *The Power of Example: Anthropological Explorations in Persuasion, Evocation and Imitation*. Wiley-Blackwell.

Bandak, A., & J.A. Jørgensen. 2012. Foregrounds and Backgrounds: Ventures in the Anthropology of Christianity Introduced. *Ethnos*, 77(4): 447–58. https://doi.org/10.1080/00141844.2011.619662

Barth, F. 2002. An Anthropology of Knowledge. *Current Anthropology*, 43(1): 1–18. https://doi.org/10.1086/324131

Barthes, R. 1977. From Work to Text (S. Heath, Trans.). In *Image, Music, Text* (pp. 155–64). Farrar, Straus and Giroux.

Barthes, R. 1994. Semiology and Urbanism (R. Howard, Trans.) In *The Semiotic Challenge* (pp. 191–201). University of California Press.

Bautista, J. 2017. Hesukristo Superstar: Entrusted Agency and Passion Rituals in the Roman Catholic Philippines. *The Australian Journal of Anthropology*, 28(2): 152–64. https://doi.org/10.1111/taja.12231

Belting, H. 1994. *Likeness and Presence: History of the Image before the Era of Art* (E. Jephcott, Trans.). Chicago University Press.

Belting, H. 2010. Saint Francis and the Body as Image: An Archeological Approach. In C. Hourihane (Ed.), *Looking Beyond: Visions, Dreams, and Insights in Medieval Art & History* (pp. 3–14). Penn State University Press.

Benjamin, W. 1999[1968]. *Illuminations* (H. Zorn, Trans.). Pimlico.

Bergson, H. 1997[1889]. *Time and Free Will: An Essay on the Immediate Data of Consciousness* (F.L. Pogson, Trans.). Kessinger Publishing.

Bergson, H. 2004[1896]. *Matter and Memory* (N.M. Paul & W.S. Palmer, Trans.). Dover Philosophical Classics.

Berliner, D., & R. Sarró (Eds.). 2007. *Learning Religion: Anthropological Approaches.* Berghahn.

Bialecki, J. 2009. Disjuncture, Continental Philosophy's New "Political Paul," and the Question of Progressive Christianity in a Southern Californian Third Wave Church. *American Ethnologist*, 36(1): 110–23. https://doi.org/10.1111/j.1548-1425.2008.01102.x

Bialecki, J., N. Haynes, & J. Robbins. 2008. The Anthropology of Christianity. *Religion Compass*, 2(6): 1139–58. https://doi.org/10.1111/j.1749-8171.2008.00116.x

Bielo, J. (Ed.). 2009. *The Social Life of Scriptures: Cross-Cultural Perspectives on Biblicism.* Rutgers University Press.

Bloch, M. 2008. Truth and Sight: Generalizing without Universalizing. *Journal of the Royal Anthropological Institute*, 14(S1): S22–32. https://doi.org/10.1111/j.1467-9655.2008.00490.x

Boissevain, J. 1965. *Saints and Firework: Religion and Politics in Rural Malta.* Athlone Press.

Borneman, J. 2009. Fieldwork Experience, Collaboration, and Interlocution: The "Metaphysics of Presence" in Encounters with the Syrian Mukhabarat. In J. Borneman & A. Hammoudi (Eds.), *Being There: The Fieldwork Encounter and the Making of Truth* (pp. 237–58). University of California Press.

Bowman, G. 1991. Christian Ideology and the Image of the Holy Land: The Place of Jerusalem in the Various Christianities. In J. Eade & M. Sallnow (Eds.), *Contesting the Sacred: The Anthropology of Christian Pilgrimage* (pp. 98–121). Routledge.

Bowman, G. 1993. Nationalizing the Sacred: Shrines and Shifting Identities in the Israeli-Occupied Territories. *MAN*, *28*(3): 431–60. https://doi.org/10.2307/2804234

Bowman, G. 2012. Nationalizing and Denationalizing the Sacred: Shrines and Shifting Identities in the Israeli-Occupied Territories. In M.J. Breger, Y. Reiter, & L. Hammer (Eds.), *Sacred Space in Israel and Palestine: Religion and Politics* (pp. 195–227). Routledge.

Boyarin, D. 1995. Take the Bible for Example: Midrash as Literary Theory. In A. Gelley (Ed.), *Unruly Examples: On the Rhetoric of Exemplarity* (pp. 27–47). Stanford University Press.

Boyarin, J. 1993. *The Ethnography of Reading*. University of California Press.

Boylston, T. 2018. *Stranger at the Feast: Prohibition and Mediation in an Ethiopian Orthodox Christian Community*. University of California Press.

Braude, B., & B. Lewis (Eds.). 1982. *Christians and Jews in the Ottoman Empire: The Functioning of a Plural Society*. 2 vols. Holmes & Meier Publishers.

Brown, P. 1981. *The Cult of the Saints: Its Rise and Function in Latin Christianity*. University of Chicago Press.

Brown, P. 1983. The Saint as Exemplar in Late Antiquity. In *Representations*, *1*(2): 1–25. https://doi.org/10.2307/2928382

Bruner, E. 1986. Ethnography as Narrative. In V. Turner & E. Bruner (Eds.), *The Anthropology of Experience* (pp. 139–56). University of Illinois Press.

Bruner, J. 2004. Life as Narrative. *Social Research*, *71*(3): 691–710. https://muse.jhu.edu/article/527352

Bryant, R., & D.M. Knight. 2019. *The Anthropology of the Future*. Cambridge University Press.

Burns, R. 2005. *Damascus: A History*. Routledge.

Candea, M. 2019. *Comparison in Anthropology: The Impossible Method*. Cambridge University Press.

Cannell, F. 1995. The Imitation of Christ in Bicol, Philippines. *Journal of the Royal Anthropoligical Institute*, *1*(2): 277–94. https://doi.org/10.2307/3034694

Cannell, F. 1999. *Power and Intimacy in the Christian Philippines*. Cambridge University Press.

Cannell, F. 2005. The Christianity of Anthropology. *Journal of the Royal Anthropological Institute*, *11*(2): 335–56. https://doi.org/10.1111/j.1467-9655.2005.00239.x

Cannell, F. 2006. Introduction: The Anthropology of Christianity. In F. Cannell (Ed.), *The Anthropology of Christianity* (pp. 1–50). Duke University Press.

Carrithers, M. 1985. An Alternative History of the Self. In M. Carrithers, S. Collins, & S. Lukes (Eds.), *The Category of the Person: Anthropology, Philosophy, History* (pp. 234–56). Cambridge University Press.

Carrithers, M. 1994. Stories in the Social and Mental Life of People. In E.N. Goody (Ed.), *Social Intelligence and Interaction: Expressions and Implications of the Social Bias in Human Intelligence* (pp. 261–76). Cambridge University Press.

Carroll, M. 1992. *The Cult of the Virgin Mary: Psychological Origins*. Princeton University Press.

Chatty, D. 2017. *Syria: The Making and the Unmaking of a Refugee State*. C. Hurst.

Choy, T. 2011. *Ecologies of Comparison: An Ethnography of Endangerment in Hong Kong*. Duke University Press.

Christian, Jr., W.A. 1981. *Apparitions in Late Medieval and Renaissance Spain*. Princeton University Press.

Christian, Jr., W.A. 1989[1972]. *Person and God in a Spanish Valley*. Princeton University Press.

Christian, Jr., W.A. 1996. *Visionaries: The Spanish Republic and the Reign of Christ*. University of California Press.

Christian, Jr., W.A. 2012. *Divine Presence in Spain and Western Europe, 1500–1960*. Central European University Press.

Chua, L. 2009. To Know or Not to Know? Practices of Knowledge and Ignorance among Bidayuhs in an "Impurely" Christian World. *Journal of the Royal Anthropological Institute, 15*(2): 332–48. https://doi.org/10.1111/j.1467-9655.2009.01556.x

Clarke, P., & T. Claydon (Eds.). 2011. *Studies in Church History: Vol. 47. Saints and Sanctity*. Boydel Press.

Coleman, S. 2000. *The Globalization of Charismatic Christianity: Spreading the Gospel of Prosperity*. Cambridge University Press.

Coleman, S. 2002. Do You Believe in Pilgrimage? Communitas, Contestation and Beyond. *Anthropological Theory, 2*(3): 355–68. https://doi.org/10.1177/1463499602002003805

Coleman, S. 2009. Transgressing the Self: Making Charismatic Saints. *Critical Inquiry, 35*(3): 417–39. https://doi.org/10.1086/598817

Coleman, S. 2010. An Anthropological Apologetics. *The South Atlantic Quarterly, 109*(4): 791–810. https://doi.org/10.1215/00382876-2010-017

Coleman, S. 2022. *The Power of Pilgrimage: Religion in a World of Movement*. New York University Press.

Coleman, S., & J. Eade. 2004a. Introduction: Reframing Pilgrimage. In S. Coleman & J. Eade (Eds.), *Reframing Pilgrimage: Cultures in Motion* (pp. 1–25). Routledge.

Coleman, S., & J. Eade (Eds.). 2004b. *Reframing Pilgrimage: Cultures in Motion*. Routledge.

Cooke, M. 2007. *Dissident Syria: Making Oppositional Arts Official*. Duke University Press.

Cornell, V. 1998. *Realm of the Saint: Power and Authority in Moroccan Sufism*. University of Texas Press.

Courbage, Y., & P. Fargues. 1998[1997]. *Christians and Jews under Islam*. I.B. Tauris.

Crapanzano, V. 1973. *The Hamadsha: An Essay in Moroccan Ethnopsychiatry.* University of California Press.

Crapanzano, V. 2000. *Serving the Word: Literalism in America from the Pulpit to the Bench.* New Press.

Csordas, T. 2009a. Introduction: Modalities of Transnational Transcendence. In T. Csordas (Ed.), *Transnational Transcendence: Essays on Religion and Globalization* (pp. 1–30). University of California Press.

Csordas, T. (Ed.). 2009b. *Transnational Transcendence: Essays on Religion and Globalization.* University of California Press.

Daswani, G. 2016. A Prophet But Not for Profit: Ethical Value and Character in Ghanaian Pentecostalism. *Journal of the Royal Anthropological Institute, 22*(1): 108–26. https://doi.org/10.1111/1467-9655.12336

Davidson, A.I. 2009. Miracles of Bodily Transformation, or How St. Francis Received the Stigmata. *Critical Inquiry, 35*(3): 451–80. https://doi.org/10.1086/600094

Davis, P.W., & J. Boles. 2003. Pilgrim Apparition Work: Symbolization and Crowd Interaction When the Virgin Mary Appeared in Georgia. *Journal of Contemporary Ethnography, 32*(4): 371–402. https://doi.org/10.1177/0891241603253492

de Busser, C., & A. Niedzwiedz. 2009. Mary in Poland: A Polish Master Symbol. In A.-K. Hermkens, W. Jansen, & C. Notermans (Eds.), *Moved by Mary: The Power of Pilgrimage in the Modern World* (pp. 87–100). Ashgate.

de Certeau, M. 1984[1980]. *The Practice of Everyday Life* (S. Rendall, Trans.). University of California Press.

de Certeau, M. 1992. Mysticism. *Diacritics, 22*(2): 11–25. https://doi.org/10.2307/465276

Deeb, L. 2006. *An Enchanted Modern: Gender and Public Piety in Shi'i Lebanon.* Princeton University Press.

Degeorge, G. 2004. *Damascus* (D. Radzinowicz, Trans.). Flammarion.

de la Cruz, D. 2015. *Mother Figured: Marian Apparitions & the Making of a Filipino Universal.* University of Chicago Press.

Deleuze, G. 2006. *Two Regimes of Madness: Texts and Interviews, 1975–1995* (A. Hodges & M. Taormina, Trans.). Semiotext(e).

Deleuze, G., & F. Guattari. 2004[1980]. *A Thousand Plateaus* (B. Massumi, Trans.). Continuum.

de Looze, L. 2010. Analogy, Exemplum, and the First Tale of Juan Manuel's *El Conde Lucanor. Hispanic Review, 78*(3): 301–22. https://doi.org/10.1353/hir.0.0115

de Man, P. 1984. *The Rhetoric of Romanticism.* Columbia University Press.

Demoen, K. 1997. A Paradigm for the Analysis of Paradigms: The Rhetorical Exemplum in Ancient and Imperial Greek Theory. *Rhetorica: A Journal of the History of Rhetoric, 15*(2): 125–58. https://doi.org/10.1525/rh.1997.15.2.125

Derrida, J. 1994. *Specters of Marx: The State of Debt, the Work of Mourning and the New International* (P. Kamuf, Trans.). Routledge.

Derrida, J. 2001[1978]. *Writing and Difference* (A. Bass, Trans.). Routledge.

de Vries, H., & L.E. Sullivan (Eds.). 2006. *Political Theologies: Public Religions in a Post-Secular World.* Fordham University Press.

de Vries, H., & S. Weber (Eds.). 2001. *Religion and Media.* Stanford University Press.

Dilley, R. 1999. Introduction: The Problem of Context. In R. Dilley (Ed.), *The Problem of Context* (pp. 1–46). Berghahn.

Dilley, R. 2007. The Construction of Ethnographic Knowledge in a Colonial Context: The Case of Henri Gaden (1867–1939). In M. Harris (Ed.), *Ways of Knowing: New Approaches in the Anthropology of Experience and Learning* (pp. 139–57). Berghahn.

Dilley, R. 2010. Reflections on Knowledge Practices and the Problem of Ignorance. *Journal of the Royal Anthropological Institute,* 16(S1): 176–92. https://doi.org/10.1111/j.1467-9655.2010.01616.x

Ditchfield, S. 2009. Thinking with Saints: Sanctity and Society in the Early Modern World. *Critical Inquiry,* 35(3): 552–84. https://doi.org/10.1086/598809

Douglas, M. 1970. *Natural Symbols.* Barrie & Rockliff.

Douglas, M. 2002[1966]. *Purity and Danger: An Analysis of Concept of Pollution and Taboo.* Routledge.

Dubisch, J. 1995. *In a Different Place: Pilgrimage, Gender, and Politics at a Greek Island Shrine.* Princeton University Press.

du Boulay, J. 2009. *Cosmos, Life and Liturgy in a Greek Orthodox Village.* Denise Harvey.

Eade, J., & M. Sallnow (Eds.). 1991a. *Contesting the Sacred: The Anthropology of Christian Pilgrimage.* Routledge.

Eade, J., & M. Sallnow. 1991b. Introduction. In J. Eade & M. Sallnow (Eds.), *Contesting the Sacred: The Anthropology of Christian Pilgrimage* (pp. 1–29). Routledge.

Eickelman, D. 1976. *Moroccan Islam: Tradition and Society in a Pilgrimage Center.* University of Texas Press.

Elgin, C.Z. 1983. *With Reference to Reference.* Hackett Publishing Company.

Elgin, C.Z. 1996. *Considered Judgment.* Princeton University Press.

Elgin, C.Z. 2017. *True Enough.* MIT Press.

Elsner, J. 2009. Beyond Compare: Pagan Saint and Christian God in Late Antiquity. *Critical Inquiry,* 35(3): 655–83. https://doi.org/10.1086/598818

Engelke, M. 2007. *A Problem of Presence: Beyond Scripture in an African Church.* California University Press.

Engelke, M. 2008. The Objects of Evidence. *Journal of the Royal Anthropological Institute,* 14(S1): 1–21. https://doi.org/10.1111/j.1467-9655.2008.00499.x

Engelke, M. 2009. Reading and Time: Two Approaches to the Materiality of Scripture. *Ethnos, 74*(2): 151–74. https://doi.org/10.1080/00141840902940450

Engelke, M. 2012. Angels in Swindon: Public Religion and Ambient Faith in England. *American Ethnologist, 39*(1): 155–70. https://doi.org/10.1111/j.1548-1425.2011.01355.x

Engelke, M., & J. Robbins (Eds.). 2010. Global Christianity, Global Critique [Special Issue]. *The South Atlantic Quarterly, 109*(4).

Evans-Pritchard, E.E. 1937. *Witchcraft, Oracles, and Magic among the Azande.* Clarendon Press.

Ewing, K. 1997. *Arguing Sainthood. Modernity, Psychoanalysis and Islam.* Duke University Press.

Fabian, J. 1983. *Time and the Other: How Anthropology Makes Its Object.* Columbia University Press.

Faubion, J.D. 2011. *An Anthropology of Ethics.* Cambridge University Press.

Fawaz, L.T. 1994. *An Occasion for War: Lebanon and Damascus in 1860.* I.B. Tauris.

Ferrara, A. 2008. *The Force of the Example: Explorations in the Paradigm of Judgment.* Columbia University Press.

Ferrier, J.F. 1854. *Institutes of Metaphysics: The Theory of Knowing and Being.* Blackwell.

Forbess, A. 2010. The Spirit and the Letter: Monastic Education in a Romanian Orthodox Convent. In C. Hann & H. Goltz (Eds.), *Eastern Christians in Anthropological Perspective* (pp. 131–54). University of California Press.

Foucault, M. 1970. *The Order of Things* (A.M.S. Smith, Trans.). Pantheon Books.

Foucault, M. 1980[1976]. *History of Sexuality: Vol. 1. An Introduction* (R. Hurley, Trans.). Vintage Books.

Foucault, M. 1988. Technologies of the Self. In L.H. Martin (Ed.), *Technologies of the Self: A Seminar with Michel Foucault* (pp. 16–49). Tavistock.

Foucault, M. 1993. About the Beginning of the Hermeneutics of the Self: Two Lectures at Dartmouth. *Political Theory, 21*(2): 198–227. https://doi.org/10.1177/0090591793021002004

Foucault, M. 2009. *Security, Territory, Population: Lectures at the Collége de France 1977–1978* (M. Senellart, Ed.). Palgrave Macmillan.

Freedberg, D. 1989. *The Power of Images: Studies in the History and Theory of Response.* Columbia University Press.

Frey, N. 1998. *Pilgrim Stories: On and Off the Road to Santiago, Journeys Along an Ancient Way in Modern Spain.* University of California Press.

Gadamer, H.-G. 2004[1960]. *Truth and Method* (J. Weinsheimer & D.G. Marshall, Trans.). Continuum.

Gallagher, S.K. 2012. *Making Do in Damascus: Navigating a Generation of Change in Family and Work.* Syracuse University Press.

Garriott, W., & K.L. O'Neill. 2008. Who Is a Christian? Toward a Dialogic Approach in the Anthropology of Christianity. *Anthropological Theory, 8*(4): 381–98. https://doi.org/10.1177/1463499608096645

Geertz, C. 1966. Religion as a Cultural System. In M. Banton (Ed.), *Anthropological Approaches to the Study of Religion* (pp. 1–46). Tavistock Publications.

Geertz, C. 1968. *Islam Observed: Religious Developments in Morocco and Indonesia.* Chicago University Press.

Geertz, C. 2000. The World in Pieces: Cultures and Politics at the End of the Century. In *Available Light: Anthropological Reflections on Philosophical Topics* (pp. 218–63). Princeton University Press.

Gelley, A. 1995. Introduction. In A. Gelley (Ed.), *Unruly Examples: On the Rhetoric of Exemplarity* (pp. 1–24). Stanford University Press.

Gellner, E. 1969. *Saints of the Atlas.* University of Chicago Press.

George, A. 2003. *Syria: Neither Bread nor Freedom.* Zed Books.

Gilsenan, M. 1973. *Saint and Sufi: An Essay in the Sociology of Religion.* Clarendon Press.

Gilsenan, M. 1982. *Recognizing Islam: Religion and Society in the Modern Middle East.* I.B. Tauris.

Gilsenan, M. 2000. Signs of Truth: Enchantment, Modernity and the Dreams of Peasant Women. *Journal of the Royal Anthropological Institute, 6*(4): 597–615. https://doi.org/10.1111/1467-9655.00035

Ginzburg, C. 1980[1976]. *The Cheese and the Worms: The Cosmos of a Sixteenth Century Miller* (J. Tedeschi & A. Tedeschi, Trans.). Johns Hopkins University Press.

Ginzburg, C. 1999. *History, Rhetoric and Proof: The Menachem Stern Jerusalem Lectures.* Brandeis University Press.

Goddard, H. 2000a. Christian-Muslim Relations: A Look Backwards and a Look Forwards. *Islam and Christian-Muslim Relations, 11*(2): 200–12. https://doi.org/10.1080/09596410050024168

Goddard, H. 2000b. *A History of Christian-Muslim Relations.* New Amsterdam Books.

Goodich, M. 2007. *Miracles and Wonders: The Development of the Concept of the Miracle, 1150–1350.* Ashgate.

Goodman, N. 1976. *Languages of Art.* Hackett Publishing Company.

Goodman, N. 1981. Routes of Reference. *Critical Inquiry, 8*(1): 121–32. https://doi.org/10.1086/448143

Greeley, A. 2000. *The Catholic Imagination.* University of California Press.

Gudeman, S. 1976. Saints, Symbols, and Ceremonies. *American Ethnologist, 3*(4): 709–29. https://doi.org/10.1525/ae.1976.3.4.02a00090

Haeri, N. 2013. The Private Performance of Salat Prayers: Repetition, Time, and Meaning. *Anthropological Quarterly, 86*(1): 5–34. https://doi.org/10.1353/anq.2013.0005

Hage, G. 2002. The Differential Intensities of Social Reality: Migration, Participation and Guilt. In G. Hage (Ed.), *Arab-Australians: Citizenship and Belonging Today* (pp. 192–205). Melbourne University Press.

Hage, G. 2005. A Not So Multi-Sited Ethnography of a Not So Imagined Community. *Anthropological Theory*, 5(4): 463–75. https://doi.org/10.1177/1463499605059232

Hammoudi, A. 2006. *A Season in Mecca: Narrative of a Pilgrimage*. Polity Press.

Hanganu, G. 2010. Eastern Christians and Religious Objects: Personal and Material Biographies Entangled. In C. Hann & H. Goltz (Eds.), *Eastern Christians in Anthropological Perspective* (pp. 33–55). California University Press.

Hann, C. 2007. The Anthropology of Christianity *per se*. *European Journal of Sociology*, 48(3): 383–410. https://doi.org/10.1017/S0003975607000410

Hann, C., & H. Goltz (Eds.). 2010. *Eastern Christians in Anthropological Perspective*. California University Press.

Harding, S.F. 2000. *The Book of Jerry Falwell: Fundamentalist Language and Politics*. Princeton University Press.

Harris, R. 1999. *Lourdes: Body and Spirit in the Secular Age*. Penguin Compass.

Hartog, F. 2011. Time's Authority. In A. Lianeri (Ed.), *The Western Time of Ancient History: Historiographical Encounters with the Greek and Roman Pasts* (pp. 33–47). Cambridge University Press.

Hartog, F. 2015[2003]. *Regimes of Historicity: Presentism and Experiences of Time*. Columbia University Press.

Harvey, I.E. 2002. *Labyrinths of Exemplarity: At the Limits of Deconstruction*. State University of New York Press.

Hastrup, K. 2004. Getting It Right: Knowledge and Evidence in Anthropology. *Anthropological Theory*, 4(4): 455–72. https://doi.org/10.1177/1463499604047921

Haynes, N. 2017. Learning to Pray the Pentecostal Way: Language and Personhood on the Zambian Copperbelt. *Religion*, 47(1): 35–50. https://doi.org/10.1080/0048721X.2016.1225906

Henare, A., M. Holbraad, & S. Wastell. 2007. Introduction: Thinking Through Things. In A. Henare, M. Holbraad, & S. Wastell (Eds.), *Thinking Through Things: Theorising Artefacts Ethnographically* (pp. 1–31). Routledge.

Henig, D. 2020. *Remaking Muslim Lives: Everyday Islam in Postwar Bosnia and Hercegovina*. University of Illinois Press.

Henkel, H. 2005. "Between Belief and Unbelief Lies the Performance of Salaat": Meaning and Efficacy in Muslim Ritual. *Journal of the Royal Anthropological Institute*, 11(3): 487–507. https://doi.org/10.1111/j.1467-9655.2005.00247.x

Henry, M. 2009. *Seeing the Invisible: On Kandinsky*. Continuum.

Heo, A. 2013. Saints, Media and Minority Cultures: On Coptic Cults of Egyptian Revolution from Alexandria to Maspero. In A. Bandak & M. Bille (Eds.), *Politics of Worship in the Contemporary Middle East: Sainthood in Fragile States* (pp. 53–71). Brill.

Heo, A. 2018. *The Political Lives of Saints: Christian-Muslim Mediation in Egypt*. University of California Press.

Hermkens, A.-K., W. Jansen, & C. Notermans (Eds.). 2009. *Moved by Mary: The Power of Pilgrimage in the Modern World*. Ashgate.

Hertz, R. 1983. Saint Besse: A Study of an Alpine Cult. In S. Wilson (Ed.), *Saints and Their Cults: Studies in Religious Sociology, Folklore and History* (pp. 55–100). Cambridge University Press.

Herzfeld, M. 1990. Icons and Identity: Religious Orthodoxy and Social Practice in Rural Crete. *Anthropological Quarterly, 63*(3): 109–21. https://doi.org /10.2307/3317403

Heyberger, B. 1994. *Les chrétiens du Proche-Orient au temps de la Réforme catholique (Syrie, Liban, Palestine, XVIIe-XVIIe siècles)*. École francaise de Rome.

High, C., A.H. Kelly, & J. Mair. 2012. *The Anthropology of Ignorance: An Ethnographic Approach*. Palgrave Macmillan.

Hirschkind, C. 2006. *The Ethical Soundscape: Cassette Sermons and Islamic Counterpublics*. Columbia University Press.

Hirschkind, C., & B. Larkin (Eds.). 2008. *Media and the Political Forms of Religion* [Special Issue]. *Social Text, 26*(3). https://read.dukeupress.edu/social-text /issue/26/3/%20(96)

Hobsbawm, E., & T. Ranger (Eds.). 1983. *The Invention of Tradition*. Cambridge University Press.

Hoenes del Piñal, E. 2009. How Qéqchi-Maya Catholics Become Legitimate Interpreters of the Bible: Two Models of Religious Authority in Sermons. In J. Bielo (Ed.), *The Social Life of Scriptures: Cross-Cultural Perspectives on Biblicism* (pp. 80–99). Rutgers University Press.

Højer, L., & A. Bandak. 2015. Introduction: The Power of Example. *Journal of the Royal Anthropological Institute, 21*(S1): 1–17. https://doi.org/10.1111 /1467-9655.12173

Holbraad, M. 2008. Definitive Evidence, from Cuban Gods. *Journal of the Royal Anthropological Institute, 14*(S1): S93–109. https://doi.org/10.1111/j.1467 -9655.2008.00495.x

Hollander, D. 2008. *Exemplarity and Chosenness: Rosenzweig and Derrida on the Nation of Philosophy*. Stanford University Press.

Hopgood, J.F. (Ed.). 2005. *The Making of Saints: Contesting Sacred Ground*. University of Alabama Press.

Hourihane, C. (Ed.). 2010. *Looking Beyond: Visions, Dreams, and Insights in Medieval Art & History*. Penn State University Press.

Howes, D. 1991. *The Varieties of Sensory Experience: A Sourcebook in the Anthropology of the Senses*. University of Toronto Press.

Hume, D. 1975[1777]. *Enquiries Concerning Human Understanding and Concerning the Principles of Morals*. Clarendon Press.

Humphrey, C. 1997. Exemplars and Rules: Aspects of the Discourse of Moralities in Mongolia. In S. Howell (Ed.), *The Ethnography of Moralities* (pp. 25–47). Routledge.

Hvidt, N.C. 2001. Myrna fra Soufanieh. In *Mirakler: Møder mellem Himmel og Jord* (pp. 121–37). Gyldendal.

Ihde, D. 2007. *Listening and Voice: Phenomenologies of Sound* (2nd ed.). State University of New York Press.

Ingold, T. 2000. *The Perception of the Environment: Essays on Livelihood, Dwelling and Skill*. Routledge.

Ismail, S. 2018. *The Rule of Violence: Subjectivity, Memory and Government in Syria*. Cambridge University Press.

Jackson, M. 2002. *The Politics of Storytelling: Violence, Transgression and Intersubjectivity*. Museum Tusculanum Press.

James, W. 1982[1902]. *The Varieties of Religious Experience: A Study in Human Nature*. Penguin Books.

Jansen, W. 2005. Visions of Mary in the Middle East: Gender and the Power of a Symbol. In I.M. Okkenhaug & I. Flaskerud (Eds.), *Gender, Religion, and Change in the Middle East: Two Hundred Years of History* (pp. 137–54). Berg.

Jansen, W. 2009. Marian Images and Religious Identities in the Middle East. In A-K. Hermkens, W. Jansen, & C. Notermans (Eds.), *Moved by Mary: The Power of Pilgrimage in the Modern World* (pp. 33–48). Ashgate.

Jansen, W. 2011. Demanding a Religious Place: Three Female Christian Visionaries in the Middle East. *Journal of Eastern Christian Studies, 63*(3–4): 311–32. https://doi.org/10.2143/JECS.63.3.2149624

Jansen, W., & M. Kühl. 2008. Shared Symbols: Muslims, Marian Pilgrimages and Gender. *European Journal of Women's Studies, 15*(3): 295–311. https://doi.org/10.1177/1350506808091509

Jenkins, T. 1994. Fieldwork and the Perception of Everyday Life. *MAN, 29*(2): 433–55. https://doi.org/10.2307/2804481

Jenkins, T. 2008. Marcel Mauss's Essay On Prayer: An Important Contribution on the Nature of Sociological Understanding. *Revue du MAUSS permanente*, 6 novembre 2008. http://www.journaldumauss.net/spip.php?article418

Jenkins, T. 2012. Anthropology of Christianity: Situation and Critique. *Ethnos, 77*(4): 459–76. https://doi.org/10.1080/00141844.2012.669775

John of Damascus. 2003[726–30]. *Three Treatises on Divine Images* (A. Louth, Trans.). St Vladimir's Seminary Press.

Kaell, H. 2017. Seeing the Invisible: Ambient Catholicism on the Side of the Road. *Journal of the American Academy of Religion, 85*(1): 136–67. https://doi.org/10.1093/jaarel/lfw041

Kassab, E. 2019. *Enlightenment on the Eve of Revolution: The Egyptian and Syrian Debates*. Columbia University Press.

Kastrinou, A.M.A. 2016. *Power, Sect, and State in Syria: The Politics of Marriage and Identity amongst the Druze*. I.B. Tauris.

Kaufmann, W.O. 1996. *The Anthropology of Wisdom Literature*. Bergin & Garvey.

Keane, W. 2007. *Christian Moderns: Freedom and Fetish in the Mission Encounter*. University of California Press.

Keane, W. 2008. The Evidence of the Senses and Materiality of Religion. *Journal of the Royal Anthropological Institute, 14*(S1): S110–27. https://doi.org/10.1111/j.1467-9655.2008.00496.x

Keane, W. 2016. *Ethical Life: Its Natural and Social Histories*. Princeton University Press.

Keenan, B. 2000. *Damascus: Hidden Treasures of the Old City*. Thames & Hudson.

Kemmler, F. 1984. *"Exempla" in Context: A Historical and Critical Study of Robert Mannyng of Brunne's "Handlyng Synne."* Gunter Narr Verlag.

Kempis, T. 1953[c. 1420]. *The Imitation of Christ* (R. Whitford, Trans.). Pocket Books.

Khater, F.K. 2011. *Embracing the Divine: Passion & Politics in the Christian Middle East*. Syracuse University Press.

Khoury, T. 2005. *Sufanieh: Eine Botschaft für die Christen in der Welt*. Oros.

Kieckhefer, R. 1988. Imitators of Christ: Sainthood in the Christian Tradition. In R. Kieckhefer & G.D. Bond (Eds.), *Sainthood: Its Manifestations in World Religions* (pp. 1–42). University of California Press.

Kierkegaard, S. 1940. *Christian Discourses etc.: The Lilies of the Field and the Birds of the Air and Three Discourses at Communion on Fridays*. Oxford University Press.

Kierkegaard, S. 1997[1843]. *Journalen JJ:167, Søren Kierkegaards Skrifter*. Søren Kierkegaard Research Centre.

Kleinberg, A. 1992. *Prophets in Their Own Country: Living Saints and the Making of Sainthood in the Later Middle Ages*. University of Chicago Press.

Kleinberg, A. 2008. *Flesh Made Word: Saints' Stories and the Western Imagination*. Harvard University Press.

Kopytoff, I. 1986. The Cultural Biography of Things: Commoditization as Process. In A. Appadurai (Ed.), *The Social Life of Things: Commodities in Cultural Perspective* (pp. 64–91). Cambridge University Press.

Kormina, J. 2010. Avtobusniki: Russian Orthodox Pilgrim's Longing for Authenticity. In C. Hann & H. Goltz (Eds.), *Eastern Christians in Anthropological Perspective* (pp. 267–86). California University Press.

Koselleck, R. 2004. *Futures Past: On the Semantics of Historical Time*. Colombia University Press.

Koselleck, R. 2018. *Sediments of Time: On Possible Histories*. Stanford University Press.

Kozlowski, V. 2008. The Land of the Virgin Mary: A Greek Catholic Ukrainian Pilgrimage to Lourdes. In S. Mahieu & V. Naumescu (Eds.), *Churches In-Between: Greek Catholic Churches in Postsocialist Europe* (pp. 319–32). LIT Verlag.

Krueger, D. 2004. *Writing and Holiness: The Practice of Authorship in the Early Christian East*. University of Pennsylvania Press.

Kuhn, T. 1970. *The Structure of Scientific Revolution*. Chicago University Press.

Laidlaw, J. 2014. *The Subject of Virtue: An Anthropology of Ethics and Freedom*. Cambridge University Press.

Lambek, M. 1993. *Knowledge and Practice in Mayotte: Local Discourses of Islam, Sorcery and Spirit Possession*. University of Toronto Press.

Lambek, M. 2010a. Introduction. In M. Lambek (Ed.), *Ordinary Ethics: Anthropology, Language, and Action* (pp. 1–36). Fordham University Press.

Lambek, M. 2010b. Towards an Ethics of the Act. In M. Lambek (Ed.), *Ordinary Ethics: Anthropology, Language, and Action* (pp. 39–63). Fordham University Press.

Lambek, M. 2014. The Interpretation of Lives or Life as Interpretation: Cohabiting with Spirits in the Malagasy World. *American Ethnologist, 41*(3): 491–503. https://doi.org/10.1111/amet.12089

Le Goff, J. 1988[1985]. *The Medieval Imagination* (A. Goldhammer, Trans.). University of Chicago Press.

Lesch, D.W. 2005. *The New Lion of Damascus: Bashar al-Asad and Modern Syria*. Yale University Press.

Leverett, F. 2005. *Inheriting Syria: Bashar's Trial by Fire*. Brookings Institution.

Lévi-Strauss, C. 1968[1962]. *The Savage Mind* (G. Weidenfeld, Trans.). University of Chicago Press.

Lianeri, A. (Ed.). 2011. *The Western Time of Ancient History: Historiographical Encounters with the Greek and Roman Pasts*. Cambridge University Press.

Lowrie, M., & S. Lüdemann (Eds.). 2015. *Exemplarity and Singularity: Thinking Through Particulars, in Philosophy, Law, and Literature*. Routledge.

Luehrmann, S. 2010. A Dual Quarrel of Images on the Middle Volga: Icon Veneration in the Face of Protestant and Pagan Critique. In C. Hann & H. Goltz (Eds.), *Eastern Christians in Anthropological Perspective* (pp. 56–78). California University Press.

Luehrmann, S. 2011. *Secularism Soviet Style: Teaching Atheism and Religion in a Volga Republic*. Indiana University Press.

Luehrmann, S. 2018. *Praying with the Senses: Contemporary Orthodox Christian Spirituality in Practice*. Indiana University Press.

Lyons, J.D. 1989. *Exemplum: The Rhetoric of Example in Early Modern France and Italy*. Princeton University Press.

Maalouf, A. 2004[1983]. *The Crusades through Arab Eyes* (J. Rothschild, Trans.). Saqi Books.

Macklin, J. 2005. Saints and Near-Saints in Transition: The Sacred, the Secular, and the Popular. In J.F. Hopgood (Ed.), *The Making of Saints: Contesting Sacred Ground* (pp. 1–22). University of Alabama Press.

Mafra, C.C.J. 2011. Saintliness and Sincerity in the Formation of the Christian Person. *Ethnos, 76*(4): 448–68. https://doi.org/10.1080/00141844.2011.610513

Mahieu, S. 2008. (Re-)Orientalizing the Church: Reformism and Traditionalism within the Hungarian Greek Catholic Church. In S. Mahieu & V. Naumescu

(Eds.), *Churches In-Between: Greek Catholic Churches in Postsocialist Europe* (pp. 207–30). LIT Verlag.

Mahieu, S. 2010. Icons and/or Statues? The Greek Catholic Divine Liturgy in Hungary and Romania, between Renewal and Purification. In C. Hann & H. Goltz (Eds.), *Eastern Christians in Anthropological Perspective* (pp. 79–100). California University Press.

Mahieu, S., & V. Naumescu (Eds.). 2008. *Churches In-Between: Greek Catholic Churches in Postsocialist Europe.* LIT Verlag.

Mahmood, S. 2005. *Politics of Piety: The Islamic Revival and the Feminist Subject.* Princeton University Press.

Mahmood, S. 2016. *Religious Difference in a Secular Age: A Minority Report.* Princeton University Press.

Makdisi, U. 2007. *Artillery of Heaven: American Missionaries and the Failed Conversion of the Middle East.* Cornell University Press.

Makdisi, U. 2019. *The Age of Coexistence: The Ecumenical Frame and the Making of the Modern Arab World.* California University Press.

Maniura, R., & R. Shepherd (Eds.). 2006. *The Inherence of the Prototype within Images and Other Objects.* Ashgate.

Marcus, G.E. 1995. Ethnography in/of the World: The Emergence of Multi-Sited Ethnography. *Annual Review of Anthropology, 24*(1): 95–117. https://doi.org/10.1146/annurev.an.24.100195.000523

Marcus, M. 1985. "The Saint Has Been Stolen": Sanctity and Social Change in Eastern Morocco. *American Ethnologist, 12*(3): 455–67. https://doi.org/10.1525/ae.1985.12.3.02a00040

Margry, P.J. 2009. Marian Interventions in the Wars of Ideology: The Elastic Politics of the Roman Catholic Church on Modern Apparitions. *History and Anthropology, 20*(3): 243–63. https://doi.org/10.1080/02757200903112628

Marion, J.-L. 1991[1982]. *God without Being* (T.A. Carlson, Trans.). University of Chicago Press.

Marion, J.-L. 2001[1997]. *Being Given: Toward a Phenomenology of Givenness* (J.F. Kosky, Trans.). Stanford University Press.

Marion, J.-L. 2004[1996]. *Crossing the Visible* (J.K.A. Smith, Trans.). University of Stanford Press.

Marion, J.-L. 2008 [2005]. *The Visible and the Revealed* (C. Geschwandter, Trans.). Fordham University Press.

Marion, J.-L. 2009. The Invisibility of the Saint. *Critical Inquiry, 35*(3): 703–10. https://doi.org/10.1086/598808

Marshall, R. 2010. The Sovereignty of Miracles: Pentecostal Political Theology in Nigeria. *Constellations, 17*(2): 197–223. https://doi.org/10.1111/j.1467-8675.2010.00585.x

Massumi, B. 2002. *Parables for the Virtual: Movement, Affect, Sensation.* Duke University Press.

Masters, B. 2001. *Christians and Jews in the Ottoman Arab World: The Roots of Sectarianism.* Cambridge University Press.

Matter, E.A. 2001. Apparitions of the Virgin Mary in the Late Twentieth Century: Apocapyptic, Representation, Politics. *Religion, 31*(2): 125–53. https://doi.org/10.1006/reli.2000.0296

Maunder, C. 2012. Marian Visionaries in Roman Catholicism as Popular Theologians: "The Lady of All Nations" of Amsterdam. *Journal of Contemporary Religion, 27*(2): 291–304. https://doi.org/10.1080/13537903.2012.675742

Maunder, C. 2016. *Our Lady of the Nations: Apparitions of Mary in 20th Century Catholic Europe.* Oxford University Press.

Mauss, M. 2003. *On Prayer* (W.S.F. Pickering, Ed., S. Leslie, Trans.). Berghahn.

Mayblin, M. 2010. *Gender, Catholicism, and Morality in Brazil: Virtous Husbands, Powerful Wives.* Palgrave Macmillan.

Mayblin, M. 2014. People Like Us: Intimacy, Distance, and the Gender of Saints. *Current Anthropology, 55*(S10): S271–80. https://doi.org/10.1086/678265

Mayblin, M. 2017. The Lapsed and the Laity: Discipline and Lenience in the Study of Religion. *Journal of the Royal Anthropological Institute, 23*(3): 503–22. https://doi.org/10.1111/1467-9655.12650

McBrien, R.P. 2001. Lives of Saints: From Mary and St. Francis to John XXIII and Mother Teresa. HarperSanFrancisco.

Meltzer, F., & J. Elsner. 2009. Introduction: Holy by Special Application. *Critical Inquiry, 35*(3): 375–82. https://doi.org/10.1086/598807

Meyer, B. 1999. *Translating the Devil: Religion and Modernity among the Ewe in Ghana.* Edinburgh University Press.

Meyer, B. 2010a. Aesthetics of Persuasion: Global Christianity and Pentecostalism's Sensational Forms. *The South Atlantic Quarterly, 109*(4): 741–63. https://doi.org/10.1215/00382876-2010-015

Meyer, B. 2010b. "There Is a Spirit in That Image": Mass-Produced Jesus Pictures and Protestant-Pentecostal Animation in Ghana. *Comparative Studies in Society and History, 52*(1): 100–30. https://doi.org/10.1017/S001041750999034X

Mitchell, J.P. 1997. A Moment with Christ: The Importance of Feelings in the Analysis of Belief. *Journal of the Royal Anthropological Institute, 3*(1): 79–94. https://doi.org/10.2307/3034366

Mitchell, J.P. 2002. *Ambivalent Europeans: Ritual, Memory and the Public Sphere in Malta.* Routledge

Mitchell, J.P. 2015. Ontology, Mimesis, and Divine Intervention: Understanding Catholic Visionaries. In M. Bull & J.P. Mitchell (Eds.), *Ritual, Performance and the Senses* (pp. 11–30). Bloomsbury.

Mitchell, J.P., & H. Mitchell. 2008. For Belief: Embodiment and Immanence in Catholicism and Mormonism. *Social Analysis, 52*(1): 79–94. https://doi.org/10.3167/sa.2008.520105

Mitchell, N.D. 2009. *The Mystery of the Rosary: Marian Devotion and the Reinvention of Catholicism*. New York University Press.

Mitchell, T. 1992. *Colonizing Egypt*. University of California Press.

Mitchell, W.J.T. 1986. *Iconology: Image, Text, Ideology*. University of Chicago Press.

Mittermaier, A. 2011. *Dreams that Matter: Egyptian Landscapes of the Imagination*. University of California Press.

Mittermaier, A. 2015. How to Do Things with Examples: Sufies, Dreams, and Anthropology. *Journal of the Royal Anthropological Institute*, 21(S1): 129–43. https://doi.org/10.1111/1467-9655.12170

Moi, T. 2015. Thinking Through Examples: What Ordinary Language Philosophy Can Do for Feminist Theory. *New Literary History*, 46(2): 191–216. https://doi.org/10.1353/nlh.2015.0014

Morgan, D. 1998. *Visual Piety: A History and Theory of Popular Religious Images*. University of California Press.

Morgan, D. 2009. Aura and the Inversion of Marian Pilgrimage: Fatima and Her Statues. In A.-K. Hermkens, W. Jansen, & C. Notermans (Eds.), *Moved by Mary: The Power of Pilgrimage in the Modern World* (pp. 49–65). Ashgate.

Morgan, D. 2010. Image, Art, and Inspiration in Modern Apparitions. In C. Hourihane (Ed.), *Looking Beyond: Visions, Dreams, and Insights in Medieval Art & History* (pp. 265–82). Penn State University Press.

Morgan, D. 2012. *The Embodied Eye: Religious Visual Culture and the Social Life of Feeling*. University of California Press.

Mosher, J.A. 1911. *The Exemplum in the Early Religious and Didactic Literature of England*. Columbia University Press.

Naletova, I. 2010. Pilgrimages as Kenotic Communities beyond the Walls of the Church. In C. Hann & H. Goltz (Eds.), *Eastern Christians in Anthropological Perspective* (pp. 240–66). California University Press.

Napolitano, V. 2009. The Virgin of Guadalupe: A Nexus of Affect. *Journal of the Royal Anthropological Institute*, 15(1): 96–112. https://doi.org/10.1111/j.1467-9655.2008.01532.x

Napolitano, V., K. Norget, & M. Mayblin (Eds.). 2017. *The Anthropology of Catholicism: A Reader*. University of California Press.

Naumescu, V. 2016. The End Times and the Near Future: The Ethical Engagements of Russian Old Believers in Romania. *Journal of the Royal Anthropological Institute*, 22(2): 314–31. https://doi.org/10.1111/1467-9655.12379

Navaro-Yashin, Y. 2009. Affective Spaces, Melancholic Objects: Ruination and the Production of Anthropological Knowledge. *Journal of the Royal Anthropological Institute*, 15(1): 1–18. https://doi.org/10.1111/j.1467-9655.2008.01527.x

Needham, R. 1973. *Belief, Language, and Experience*. University of Chicago Press.

Needham, R. 1985. *Exemplars*. University of California Press.

Nelson, C. 1973. The Virgin of Zeitoun: An Apparition that Provoked Large
    Religious, Political and Social Debates among All Classes. *Worldview, 16*(9):
    5–11. https://doi.org/10.1017/S0084255900019951
O'Mahony, A., & E. Loosley. 2010. *Eastern Christianity in the Modern Middle
    East*. Routledge.
O'Neill, O. 1986. The Power of Example. *Philosophy, 61*(235): 5–29. https://
    doi.org/10.1017/S0031819100019537
Orsi, R. 1985. *The Madonna of 115th Street: Faith and Community in Italian Harlem,
    1880–1950*. Yale University Press.
Orsi, R. 1996. *Thank You, St. Jude: Women's Devotion to the Patron Saint of Hopeless
    Causes*. Yale University Press.
Orsi, R. 2005. *Between Heaven and Earth: The Religious Worlds People Make and
    the Scholars Who Study Them*. Princeton University Press.
Orsi, R. 2008. Abundant History: Marian Apparitions as Alternative Modernity.
    *Historically Speaking, 9*(7): 12–16. https://doi.org/10.1353/hsp.2008.0033
Orsi, R. 2011. Belief. *Material Religion, 7*(1): 10–17. https://doi.org/10.2752
    /175183411X12968355481773
Orsi, R. 2016. *History and Presence*. Belknap Press.
Pacini, A. 1998. *Christian Communities in the Arab Middle East: The Challenge of
    the Future*. Clarendon Press.
Peña, E. 2011. *Performing Piety: Making Space Sacred with the Virgin of Guadelupe*.
    University of California Press.
Perthes, V. 1995. *The Political Economy of Syria under Asad*. I.B. Tauris.
Perthes, V. 2004. *Syria under Bashar al-Asad: Modernisation and the Limits of Change*.
    Oxford University Press.
Pickering, W.S.F. 2003. Introduction to an Unfinished Work. In W.S.F. Pickering
    (Ed.), *On Prayer* (pp. 1–16). Berghahn.
Pierret, T. 2013. *Religion and State in Syria: The Sunni Ulama from Coup to Revolution*.
    Cambridge University Press.
Pierret, T., & K. Selvik. 2009. Limits of "Authoritarian Upgrading" in Syria:
    Private Welfare, Islamic Charities, and the Rise of the Zayd Movement.
    *International Journal for Middle Eastern Studies, 41*(4): 595–614. https://doi
    .org/10.1017/S0020743809990080
Piñas-Cabral, E.H. 1986. *Sons of Adam, Daughters of Eve: Peasant Worldview of
    the Alto Minho*. Clarendon Press.
Pinto, P. 2004. Performing Baraka: Sainthood and Power in Syrian Sufism.
    In G. Stauth (Ed.), *Yearbook of the Sociology of Islam: Vol. 5. On Archaeology of
    Sainthood and Local Spirituality in Islam: Past and Present Crossroads of Events
    and Ideas* (pp. 195–211). Transcript Verlag.
Pitt-Rivers, J. 1991. Postscript: The Place of Grace in Anthropology. In J.G.
    Peristiany & J. Pitt-Rivers (Eds.), *Honor and Grace in Anthropology* (pp. 215–46).
    Cambridge University Press.

Pop, S. 2017. "I've Tempted the Saint with My Prayer": Prayer, Charisma, and Ethics in Romanian Eastern Orthodox Christianity. *Religion, 47*(1): 73–91. https://doi.org/10.1080/0048721X.2016.1225908

Pouillon, J. 1982. Remarks on the Verb "To Believe." In M. Izard & P. Smith (Eds.), *Between Belief and Transgression* (pp. 1–8). University of Chicago Press.

Poujeau, A. 2010. Monasteries, Politics, and Social Memory: The Revival of the Greek Orthodox Church of Antioch in Syria during the Twentieth Century. In C. Hann & H. Goltz (Eds.), *Eastern Christians in Anthropological Perspective* (pp. 177–92). California University Press.

Provence, M. 2005. *The Great Syrian Revolt and the Rise of Arab Nationalism.* University of Texas.

Rabo, A. 2005. *A Shop of One's Own: Independence and Reputation among Traders in Aleppo.* I.B. Tauris.

Rabo, A. 2012. "We Are Christians and We Are Equal Citizens": Perspectives on Particularity and Pluralism in Contemporary Syria. *Islam and Christian–Muslim Relations, 23*(1): 79–93. https://doi.org/10.1080/09596410.2011.634598

Rancière, J. 2004[2000]. *The Politics of Aesthetics* (G. Rockhill, Trans.). Continuum.

Rancière, J. 2007. *The Future of the Image* (G. Elliott, Trans.). Verso.

Rappaport, R. 1999. *Ritual and Religion in the Making of Humanity.* Cambridge University Press.

Ravaz, C. 2009. *Soufanieh: Les apparitions de Damas.* SARL JMG editions.

Reed, A. 2011. *Literature and Agency in English Fiction Reading: A Study of the Henry Williamson Society.* Manchester University Press.

Reeves, E. 1995. Power, Resistance, and the Cult of Muslim Saints in a Northern Egyptian Town. *American Ethnologist, 22*(2): 306–23. https://doi.org/10.1525/ae.1995.22.2.02a00050

Ricoeur, P. 1981. The Hermeneutic Function of Distanciation. In J.B. Thompson (Ed. and Trans.), *Hermeneutics and the Human Sciences: Essays on Language, Action, and Interpretation* (pp. 131–44). Cambridge University Press.

Ricoeur, P. 1984. *Time and Narrative* (Vol. 1; K. McLaughlin & D. Pellauer, Trans.). Chicago University Press.

Rihbani, A.M. 2003[1922]. *The Syrian Christ.* Apamea.

Robbins, J. 2003. What Is a Christian? Notes toward an Anthropology of Christianity. *Religion, 33*(3): 91–9. https://doi.org/10.1016/S0048-721X(03)00060-5

Robbins, J. 2004. *Becoming Sinners: Christianity + Moral Torment in a Papua New Guinea Society.* University of California Press.

Robbins, J. 2007. Continuity Thinking and the Problem of Christian Culture. *Current Anthropology, 48*(1): 5–38. https://doi.org/10.1086/508690

Robbins, J. 2010. Anthropology, Pentecostalism, and the New Paul: Conversion, Event, and Social Transformation. *The South Atlantic Quarterly*, *109*(4): 633–52. https://doi.org/10.1215/00382876-2010-010

Robbins, J. 2015. Ritual, Value, and Example: On the Perfection of Cultural Representations. *Journal of the Royal Anthropological Institute*, *21*(S1): 18–29. https://doi.org/10.1111/1467-9655.12163

Robson, L. 2011. Recent Perspectives on Christianity in the Modern Arab World. *History Compass*, *9*(4): 312–25. https://doi.org/10.1111/j.1478 -0542.2011.00767.x

Rogers, D. 2009. *The Old Faith and the Russian Land: A Historical Ethnography of Ethics in the Urals*. Cornell University Press.

Ruel, M. 1982. Christians as Believers. In J. Davis (Ed.), *Religious Organization and Religious Experience* (pp. 9–31). Academic Press.

Rugh, A. 1997. *Within the Circle: Parents and Children in an Arab Village*. Columbia University Press.

Salamandra, C. 1998. Moustache Hairs Lost: Ramadan Television Serials and the Construction of Identity in Damascus, Syria. *Visual Anthropology*, *10*(2–4): 227–46. https://doi.org/10.1080/08949468.1998.9966732

Salamandra, C. 2004. *A New Old Damascus: Authenticity and Distinction in Urban Syria*. Indiana University Press.

Salamandra, C., & L. Stenberg (Eds.). 2015. *Syria from Reform to Revolt: Volume 2. Culture, Society, and Religion*. Syracuse University Press.

Salbato, R. 1992. *The Miracle of Damascus*. JMJ Publishing.

Salibi, K. 1988. *A House with Many Mansions: The History of Lebanon Reconsidered*. I.B. Tauris.

Sallnow, M. 1981. Communitas Reconsidered: The Sociology of Andean Pilgrimage. *MAN 16*(2): 163–82. https://doi.org/10.2307/2801393

Sallnow, M. 1987. *Pilgrims of the Andes: Regional Cults in Cusco*. Smithsonian Institution Press.

Sanok, C. 2007. *Her Life Historical: Exemplarity and Female Saints' Lives in Late Medieval England*. University of Pennsylvania Press.

Sato, N. 2003. On the Horns of the Terrorist Dilemma: Syrian Christians' Response to Israeli "Terrorism." *History and Anthropology*, *14*(2): 141–55. https://doi.org/10.1080/027572003200102919

Sato, N. 2005. Selective Amnesia: Memory and History of the *Urfalli* Syrian Orthodox Christians. *Identities: Global Studies in Culture and Power*, *12*(3): 315–33. https://doi.org/10.1080/10702890500202803

Scanlon, L. 1994. *Narrative, Authority, and Power: The Medieval Exemplum and the Chaucerian Tradition*. Cambridge University Press.

Scheer, M. 2013. What She Looks Like: On the Recognition and Iconization of the Virgin Mary at Apparition Sites in the Twentieth Century. *Material Religion*, *9*(4): 442–67. https://doi.org/10.2752/175183413X13823695747444

Scheper-Hughes, N. 1993[1992]. Our Lady of Sorrows: A Political Economy of the Emotions. In *Death without Weeping: The Violence of Everyday Life in Brazil* (pp. 400–45). University of California Press.

Schielke, S. 2008. Policing Ambiguity: Muslim Saints-Day Festivals and the Moral Geography of Public Space in Egypt. *American Ethnologist*, 35(4): 539–52. https://doi.org/10.1111/j.1548-1425.2008.00097.x

Schielke, S. 2009. Being Good in Ramadan: Ambivalence, Fragmentation and the Moral Self in the Lives of Young Egyptians. *Journal of the Royal Anthropological Institute*, 15(S1): S24–40. https://doi.org/10.1111/j.1467-9655.2009.01540.x

Schielke, S. 2010. Second Thoughts about the Anthropology of Islam, or How to Make Sense of Grand Schemes in Everyday Life. Zentrum Moderner Orient Working Papers, 2. https://www.ssoar.info/ssoar/handle/document/32233

Schmidt, L.E. 2000. *Hearing Things: Religion, Illusion, and the American Enlightenment.* Harvard University Press.

Schmitt, C. 1996[1923]. *Roman Catholicism and Political Form* (G.L. Ulmen, Trans.). Greenwood Press.

Schmitt, C. 2005[1922]. *Political Theology: Four Chapters on the Concept of Sovereignty* (G. Scwab, Trans.). University of Chicago Press.

Seale, P. 1988. *Asad of Syria: The Struggle for the Middle East*. University of California Press.

Shanafelt, R. 2006. Magic, Miracle, and Marvels in Anthropology. *Ethnos*, 69(3): 317–40. https://doi.org/10.1080/0014184042000260017

Shenoda, A. 2012. The Politics of Faith: On Faith, Skepticism, and Miracles among Coptic Christians in Egypt. *Ethnos*, 77(4): 477–95. https://doi.org/10.1080/00141844.2011.609941

Simon, G. 2009. The Soul Freed of Cares? Islamic Prayer, Subjectivity, and the Contradictions of Moral Selfhood in Minangkabau, Indonesia. *American Ethnologist*, 36(2): 258–75. https://doi.org/10.1111/j.1548-1425.2009.01134.x

Soares, B., & F. Osella. 2009. Islam, Politics, Anthropology. *Journal of the Royal Anthropological Institute*, 15(S1): 1–23. https://doi.org/10.1111/j.1467-9655.2009.01539.x

Sottimano, A. 2009. Ideology and Discourse in the Era of Ba'thist Reforms: Towards an Analysis of Authoritarian Governmentality. In A. Sottimano & K. Selvik (Eds.), *Changing Regime Discourse and Reform in Syria* (pp. 3–40). Lynne Rienner Publishers.

Starrett, G. 2010. The Varieties of Secular Experience. *Comparative Studies in Society and History*, 52(3): 626–51. https://doi.org/10.1017/S0010417510000332

Stauth, G. (Ed.). 2004. *Yearbook of the Sociology of Islam: Vol. 5. On Archaeology of Sainthood and Local Spirituality in Islam: Past and Present Crossroads of Events and Ideas*. Transcript Verlag.

Stauth, G., & S. Schielke (Eds.). 2008. *Yearbook of the Sociology of Islam: Vol. 8. Dimensions of Locality: Muslim Saints, Their Place and Space*. Transcript Verlag.

Stewart, C. 2012. *Dreaming and Historical Consciousness*. Harvard University Press.

Szanto, E. 2012. Sayyida Zaynab in the State of Exception: Shiʿi Sainthood as "Qualified Life" in Contemporary Syria. *International Journal of Middle Eastern Studies*, 44(2): 285–99. https://doi.org/10.1017/S0020743812000050

Taubes, J. 2004. *The Political Theology of Paul* (D. Hollander, Trans.). Stanford University Press.

Taussig, M. 1993. *Mimesis and Alterity: A Particular History of the Senses*. Routledge.

Taussig, M. 2006. *Walter Benjamin's Grave*. University of Chicago Press.

Taves, A. 2012. Special Things as Building Blocks of Religions. In R.A. Orsi (Ed.), *The Cambridge Companion to Religious Studies* (pp. 58–83). Cambridge University Press.

Theodore the Studite. 1981[816–19]. *On The Holy Icons*. St Vladimir's Seminary Press.

Todorov, T. 1973. *The Fantastic: A Structural Approach to a Literary Genre* (R. Howard, Trans.). Case Western Reserve University Press.

Tomlinson, M. 2014. *Ritual Textuality: Pattern and Motion in Performance*. Oxford University Press.

Tracy, D. 2011. On Naming Saints. In F. Meltzer & J. Elsner (Eds.), *Saints: Faith without Borders* (pp. 97–126). University of Chicago Press.

Turner, V. 1969. *The Ritual Process: Structure and Anti-Structure*. Aldine Transaction.

Turner, V. 1974. *Dramas, Fields, and Metaphors: Symbolic Action in Human Society*. Cornell University Press.

Turner, V., & E. Turner. 1978. *Image & Pilgrimage in Christian Culture*. Columbia University Press.

Tweed, T. 1997. *Our Lady of the Exile: Diasporic Religion at a Cuban Catholic Shrine in Miami*. Oxford University Press.

van Dam, N. 1996. *The Struggle for Power in Syria: Politics and Society and the Baʿth Party*. I.B. Tauris.

van der Veer, P. 1992. Playing and Praying: A Sufi Saint's Day in Surat. *Journal of Asian Studies*, 51(3): 545–64. https://doi.org/10.2307/2057949

van der Veer, P. 1996. Introduction. In P. van der Veer (Ed.), *Conversion to Modernities: The Globalization of Christianity* (pp. 1–22). Routledge.

van Gennep, A. 1960[1909]. *Rites of Passage* (M.B. Vizedom & G.L. Caffee, Trans.). Routledge and Paul Kegan.

Ward, B. 2011. Miracles in the Middle Ages. In G.H. Twelftree (Ed.), *The Cambridge Companion to Miracles* (pp. 149–64). Cambridge University Press.

Warnick, B. 2008. *Imitation and Education: A Philosophical Inquiry into Learning by Example*. State University of New York Press.

Weber, M. 2003[1905]. *The Protestant Ethic and the Spirit of Capitalism* (T. Parsons, Trans.). Dover Publications.

Weber, S. 2009. *Damascus: Ottoman Modernity and Urban Transformation*. Aarhus University Press.

Webster, J. 2017. Praying for Salvation: A Map of Relatedness. *Religion*, 47(1): 19–34. https://doi.org/10.1080/0048721X.2016.1225905

Weddle, D.L. 2010. Christianity: Signs of Divine Presence. In *Wonder and Meaning in World Religions* (pp. 141–76). New York University Press.

Wedeen, L. 1999. *Ambiguities of Domination: Politics, Rhetoric, and Symbols in Contemporary Syria*. University of Chicago Press.

Wedeen, L. 2019. *Authoritarian Apprehensions: Ideology, Judgment, and Mourning in Syria*. University of Chicago Press.

Wehr, H. 1961. *A Dictionary of Modern Written Arabic*. Cornell University Press.

Weinstein, D., & R.M. Bell. 1982. *Saints and Society: The Two Worlds of Western Christianity, 1000–1700*. University of Chicago Press.

Westermarck, E. 1926. *Ritual and Belief in Morocco* (Vols. 1 and 2). Macmillan.

Wieland, C. 2006. *Syria: Ballots or Bullets? Democracy, Islamism, and Secularism in the Levant*. Cune Press.

Wills, G. 2005. *The Rosary*. Viking.

Wilson, S. (Ed.). 1983. *Saints and Their Cults: Studies in Religious Sociology, Folklore and History*. Cambridge University Press.

Winston-Allen, A. 1997. *Stories of the Rose: The Making of the Rosary in the Middle Ages*. Pennsylvania State University Press.

Wittgenstein, L. 1998[1977]. *Culture and Value: A Selection from the Posthumous Remains* (G.H. von Wright & H. Nyman, Eds.). Blackwell Publishing.

Wittgenstein, L. 2009[1953]. *Philosophical Investigations*. Wiley-Blackwell.

Wojcyk, D. 1996. "Polaroids from Heaven": Photography, Folk Religion, and the Miraculous Image Tradition at a Marian Apparition Site. *Journal of American Folklore*, 109(432): 129–48. https://doi.org/10.2307/541832

Wolf, E. 1958. The Virgin of Guadelupe: A Mexican National Symbol. *Journal of American Folklore*, 71(279): 34–9. https://doi.org/10.2307/537957

Woodward, K. 1990. *Making Saints: How the Catholic Church Determines Who Becomes a Saint, Who Doesn't, and Why*. Simon & Schuster.

Zagzebski, L. 2017. *Exemplarist Moral Theory*. Oxford University Press.

Zahlawi, E. 2008. *aṣ-Ṣūfāniyya khilāl khamsatin wa 'ashrīn 'āmān, 1982–2007* [Soufanieh through Twenty-five Years, 1982–2007]. Dār al-Majid lil-tabā'a wal-nushir wal-khadimāt al-tabā'aiyya Muhammad Insaf Tarabulsi.

Zeghal, M. 2009. On the Politics of Sainthood: Resistance and Mimicry in Post-Colonial Morocco. *Critical Inquiry*, 35(3): 587–610. https://doi.org/10.1086/600093

Ziadeh, R. 2012. *Power and Policy in Syria: Intelligence Services, Foreign Relations and Democracy in the Modern Middle East*. I.B. Tauris.

Zigon, J. 2008. *Morality: An Anthropological Perspective*. Bloomsbury.

Zimdars-Swartz, S.L. 1991. *Encountering Mary: From La Salette to Medjugorje*. Princeton University Press.

Žižek, S. 2000. *The Fragile Absolute: Or, Why Is the Christian Legacy Worth Fighting For?* Verso.

Žižek, S. 2001a. *Did Somebody Say Totalitarianism: Five Interventions in the (Mis) Use of a Notion*. Verso.

Žižek, S. 2001b. *On Belief*. Routledge.

# Index

imitation vs. recognition, 65, 69; and
original, backward effect on, 67, 84;
technologies of, and spreading of
story, 66
reproductions of Our Lady of Soufanieh,
26, 27, 63; and fracturing of distinction
between copy and original, 63; and
healing, 122; in Myrna's house, 26,
27, 28; oil exuding from, 36, 38, 46–7,
63, 69
Ricoeur, Paul, 20, 115
Rihbani, Abraham Mitrie, 80
Rima (pseudonym), 97; change
experienced by, 97, 103, 105, 113;
divine grace in home of, 104; dream
of, 98–9, 101; emigration of, 194; as
exemplar, 101, 104, 105, 107, 114,
116, 185; learning process for, 102–5,
112; learning to pray, 113; life story
of, 97–105, 188; and message of
Soufanieh, corroboration of, 104,
106–7; miracle experienced by, 103–4;
as "Mother Teresa of Damascus," 97,
113, 114; and Myrna, relationship of,
102–3, 113, 114
Rita (pseudonym): and author's
interviews, 105; miracle witnessed by,
192, 193; on trip to Aleppo, 140; on trip
to Homs, 151, 152; at Tuesday evening
novena, 33, 62, 147
Riyadh (pseudonym), 35
Robbins, Joel, 56, 92, 105, 182, 205n5
Roman Catholic Church. See Catholic
Church
Roman Catholic Order of the
Congregation of Rosary Sisters, 50
Romania, creation of, 18
rosary, 50, 197; addition of Creed to,
55–6; daily performance of, 29–31,
49, 54, 62, 113, 185; in dream, 99;
as exemplary practice, 48, 51, 70;
history of, 51–2; Islamic, 61; in Marian
apparitions, 51; as mechanical prayer,
Mauss on, 48; as meditation, 51,
52, 53, 70; as medium of presence,
56–7, 61; as prototypical prayer, 52;
before Saturday mass, 31–2; social
experience of, 57; standard, 49; at
Tuesday evening novena, 33; and
visualization, 56

Rula (pseudonym): miracle witnessed
by, 192; on trip to Aleppo, 140, 142,
143, 145; at Tuesday evening
novena, 35
rumūz. See signs
Russo-Ottoman War of 1877–78, 18

Saddam Hussein, 43
Said (pseudonym), 35
saint(s): Christian, preconceived
notions regarding, 123; days
of, 156; as exemplars, 14, 84;
ignorance/indifference regarding,
14–15, 190; imitation/emulation
of, 93, 94, 104; in Islam, 12; lives
of, as exempla in sermons, 85;
living, Myrna as, 5, 11–12, 153–4;
petitioning, in prayer, 57;
range of responses to, 14–15;
relationships between ordinary
people and, 12; in series of
exemplars, 88–9, 185; transfer
of attention to, 154; visibility of,
paradox regarding, 118, 120, 123. See
also sainthood; specific saints
sainthood: from anthropological
perspective, 12, 13; claims to,
inherent fragility of, 118, 123; in field
of confession, 190; models of vs.
models for, 14, 126, 190; protocols of
establishing, 11–12. See also modelling
of sainthood
Salbato, Richard, 21
Sallnow, Michael, 157–8
Salloum, Maisaa, 162, 163, 164, 165,
168, 171
Saloun, Abuna Elias: civil war and,
194; on example not to be imitated,
83; interviews with, 20; on miracles,
143–4; novena on unity, 147–9; on oil
exuded from Myrna's hands, 193;
on Protestant conception of divine
work, 139; sermons at Our Lady of
Soufanieh, 32, 185; on trip to Aleppo,
140–6; on trip to Homs, 151; and
Tuesday evening novena, 33, 34;
zealous attempt to promote unity,
140–2, 146
salvation, economy of, vs. economy of
service, 139

# Anthropological Horizons

Editor: Michael Lambek, University of Toronto

*People of Substance: An Ethnography of Morality in the Colombian Amazon* / Carlos David Londoño Sulkin (2012)

*"We Are Still Didene": Stories of Hunting and History from Northern British Columbia* / Thomas McIlwraith (2012)

*Being Māori in the City: Indigenous Everyday Life in Auckland* / Natacha Gagné (2013)

*The Hakkas of Sarawak: Sacrificial Gifts in Cold War Era Malaysia* / Kee Howe Yong (2013)

*Remembering Nayeche and the Gray Bull Engiro: African Storytellers of the Karamoja Plateau and the Plains of Turkana* / Mustafa Kemal Mirzeler (2014)

*In Light of Africa: Globalizing Blackness in Northeast Brazil* / Allan Charles Dawson (2014)

*The Land of Weddings and Rain: Nation and Modernity in Post-Socialist Lithuania* / Gediminas Lankauskas (2015)

*Milanese Encounters: Public Space and Vision in Contemporary Urban Italy* / Cristina Moretti (2015)

*Legacies of Violence: History, Society, and the State in Sardinia* / Antonio Sorge (2015)

*Looking Back, Moving Forward: Transformation and Ethical Practice in the Ghanaian Church of Pentecost* / Girish Daswani (2015)

*Why the Porcupine Is Not a Bird: Explorations in the Folk Zoology of an Eastern Indonesian People* / Gregory Forth (2016)

*The Heart of Helambu: Ethnography and Entanglement in Nepal* / Tom O'Neill (2016)

*Tournaments of Value: Sociability and Hierarchy in a Yemeni Town, 20th Anniversary Edition* / Ann Meneley (2016)

*Europe Un-Imagined: Nation and Culture at a French-German Television Channel* / Damien Stankiewicz (2017)

*Transforming Indigeneity: Urbanization and Language Revitalization in the Brazilian Amazon* / Sarah Shulist (2018)

*Wrapping Authority: Women Islamic Leaders in a Sufi Movement in Dakar, Senegal* / Joseph Hill (2018)

*Island in the Stream: An Ethnographic History of Mayotte* / Michael Lambek (2018)

*Materializing Difference: Consumer Culture, Politics, and Ethnicity among Romanian Roma* / Péter Berta (2019)

*Virtual Activism: Sexuality, the Internet, and a Social Movement in Singapore* / Robert Phillips (2020)

*Shadow Play: Information Politics in Urban Indonesia* / Sheri Lynn Gibbings (2021)

*Suspect Others: Spirit Mediums, Self-Knowledge, and Race in Multiethnic Suriname* / Stuart Earle Strange (2021)

*Exemplary Life: Modelling Sainthood in Christian Syria* / Andreas Bandak (2022)

www.ingramcontent.com/pod-product-compliance
Lightning Source LLC
Chambersburg PA
CBHW020249030426
42336CB00010B/688